ASSESSING THE EFFECTIVENESS OF ADVERTISING

Assessing the Effectiveness of Advertising

by

MARK LOVELL

Lovell and Oakes

and

JACK POTTER

Managing Director, Alpha (UK) Research Ltd

BUSINESS BOOKS

London

© Mark Lovell and Jack Potter, 1975

ISBN 0 220 69730 2

This book has been set in 11 on 12 pt Times by
Inforum Limited of Portsmouth and printed in
Britain by W & J Mackay Limited, Chatham
by photo-litho for the publisher:
Business Books Limited
24 Highbury Crescent, London N5 1RX

Contents

Illustrations

*Illustrations marked * are reproduced by permission of Leo Burnett*

viii

Foreword

Advertising is notoriously difficult to study and assess. It is suspected by some of exerting sinister powers, and to be capable of persuading otherwise rational people to lose all perspective in their rush to buy. In fact it is extremely rare that marketing evidence points to this. But some others regard it as a waste of time, money and effort, by contrast with other marketing techniques that can be deployed. This is not the case either—except when advertising is poorly conceived and executed.

The business world can do with a book that speaks with authority about advertising research. Experience of the many different kinds of advertising is important before anyone can aspire to such authority. Sensitivity and a thorough understanding of research methodology are also required.

This is why Mark Lovell and Jack Potter have written a significant book. They bring a great deal of experience to bear on the subject. They analyse case histories sensitively and with an eye to giving practical advice. They are conscientiously thorough in presenting arguments for and against the relevance of various research techniques at successive stages of campaign development. Finally, they offer clear, intelligible guidelines, attractively presented.

Although this can well be used as a reference book, I recommend studying the first three chapters in detail before attempting to apply the specific advice in the later chapters. The early section provides an important perspective, within which to get down to the business of assessment.

I believe this book will be extremely helpful to marketing men everywhere, and to anyone who intends to measure advertising or to commission advertising research.

John Treasure, Ph D

Preface

There are two types of book that we *could* have written. The first is a straightforward textbook that limits itself to methodology, to help people faced with the command "Test this ad!" to do just that. It would not concern itself with questions about whether the order should be given in the first instance, because this might be distracting or depressing. The second kind that we avoided is a discussion at an academic level about all the reasons why advertising researchers should have been strangled at birth. This would never have got to the point of helping anybody who, rightly or wrongly, has to get on with the job of devising, or looking over recommendations for research on a campaign.

We want this book to be useful, so there is plenty of "how to do it" in the chapters that follow, as well as case histories and specimen questionnaires. Please note that if you wish to adapt the questionnaires for your own use, much more room should be allowed for respondents' answers than space permits in this book.

There is no point in ducking serious issues—for example, why, we believe, so much of current advertising research is misconceived and sterile, and what people should do about it. There are, therefore, sections that examine the broader context, and the assumptions behind the pre-testing and the post-testing, as well.

Introduction

The last person to write with authority and confidence on the subject of advertising research did so in 1923. His name was Claude Hopkins and he made more money out of advertising than any other agency man in his day. Presumably he knew what he was talking about. Listen to him:

> The time has come when advertising has, in some hands, reached the status of a science. It is based on fixed principles and is reasonably exact. The causes and effects have been analysed until they are well understood. The correct methods of procedure have been proved and established. We know what is most effective and we act on basic laws. Advertising, once a gamble, has thus become under able direction, one of the safest of business ventures. Certainly no other enterprise with comparable possibilities need involve so little risk.

Such words are unlikely to strike a responsive chord among advertisers today, as they sit down to plan a campaign for a new product. The high risk of mediocrity or failure, and the deadly corporate and personal consequences of this, are seldom far from the thoughts of client and agency alike. Any advertising research expert brought in, if he has any sense, will not claim that his expertise can guarantee the success of the advertising. If pressed, his reply will probably echo the words of Charles Ramond in the first issue of the *Journal of Advertising Reasearch*:

> A problem is not attacked, but painfully translated into a set of answerable questions. There are no breakthroughs, only small decreases in the unexplained variance. Instead of final conquest, there will simply be better advertising decisions, measurably better.

There are few less-stirring offers than that of a small reduction in the unexplained variance, painfully achieved. Yet the modesty of Ramond's view is essentially correct, we believe.

The achievements of advertising research, though real, are

not always tangible and rarely, by themselves, spectacular. It is probably more controversial and a more frequent arouser of misgivings than any other type of marketing research.

There are all kinds of reasons for this that we could discuss at length. But one of them deserves to be nailed to the wall and made the central issue of the book. First, then, we will parade some of the key sources of problems in advertising research, and finish up with the *Big One*—the public enemy that has to be destroyed before sound practical work can be discussed.

1   UNDERSTANDING AND PREDICTING CHANGES IN HUMAN BEHAVIOUR—This is more difficult than any other branch of science; and advertising research is an applied branch of this science. The work of psychology in constructing, testing and applying models of human behaviour is still at a rudimentary state of development; it is simply not up to the task of explaining satisfactorily the effects of relatively mild stimuli, such as advertisements, on relatively casual behaviour, such as is involved in buying most products.

If we could completely understand how advertising produced its effects, the progress represented by this understanding would be frightening: this would imply a grotesque degree of precision in advertisement creation, to the point of manipulation.

However, to say that advertising research is imprecise is not, of course, to say that it is useless. The parallel with economic theory is close. Economists are often wrong and have to change their theories to fit new facts. Governments run the economies of countries on an experimental basis, although they do not major on this fact. Nevertheless, the efforts of the Government's economists mean that there are less rational guidelines for policies, while mistakes can be identified and recognised. Advertising research, although unable to take the risk out of the business entirely, can make learning by experience less painful and more fruitful.

2   OVERCLAIMS—Advertising research has attracted some of the slickest once-off single-purchase self-publicists in the business. These have made amazing overclaims to seize their target's attention and try to corner the market. When their offerings are deflated, the enthusiasm they have aroused turns sour and infects attitudes to all advertising research and even to market research as a whole.

3   WHAT IS ADVERTISING, ANYWAY?   Terminology is another problem. At the risk of stating the obvious, the word "advertising" itself covers a whole range of very different activities. Generalisations about advertising research are therefore even more suspect. At one end of the scale a housewife, putting a card in the window of her local newsagent, to get rid of an unwanted pushchair, is advertising. At the other end, advertising describes the activity of a group with £500 000 to spend, not selling anything, but creating a better image for a nationalised industry. The housewife knows *exactly* what she wants and how her advertising will work. The group will be far less certain, and possibly divided, about what their advertising will achieve and how it can do so. There are countless shades of difference between these extremes.

4   MARKETING MIX—Another very important factor that complicates advertising research is the interdependence of a single advertisement with others in the same campaign, with others in different media, with promotional effort and even with salesman's enthusiasm and the quality of the product in use. *Part* of a single advertisement's effectiveness may be a question of its individual impact, appeal and communication—but only part.

Advertising research has to be realistic about this interdependence. It must examine each new context, to interpret how one component is likely to affect another, given evidence of different kinds.

5   TIME MATTERS, TOO—In 1923, when Claude Hopkins wrote his masterpiece on advertising, the word was used to mean mainly press advertising, with a very strong product orientation. Probably he did have much of this subject sewn up. Nowadays, apart from having many additional functions, advertising includes the use of television, radio and posters designed to catch TV cameras at sports meetings.

Time also affects individual campaigns. An advertisement of one kind needs to deliver its main point immediately, at first sight—for example, "The Rudkins and Balrog Sale Opens on

Saturday at 9am." Another may depend on several exposures, or on having part of its message being transmitted
already—for example, advertisements showing the juxta-posi-
tion of a cigarette with expensive objects of high quality, need
more time and exposures to make the implicit communication
about the brand clear-cut in the consumer's mind. Pre-testing
can in most cases indicate the effects of only *one* showing, and
it is often difficult to check the influence of past work on those
effects. Post-testing has the problem of determining the optimum time for conducting research to evaluate a campaign.
Some post-testing is, arguably, not going to tell the *whole*
story about a campaign even if it is conducted after the campaign has been running for six months.

6 COUNTER-PRODUCTIVE EMOTIONS—One other
problem experienced by anyone who has been within a mile of
an advertising research project is the fog of emotion that can
get in the way of an objective inquiry. Everyone knows that
large amounts of money, as well as reputations, and ultimately
jobs, may be at risk when some advertising research is being
undertaken. Advertising and marketing men can be great wor-
riers, and this knowledge sometimes turns to outright fear.
Fear is counter-productive, because it engenders resentment
and obscurantism, and prevents people getting the best out of
advertising research.

Towering over all the unpleasant truths that have preceded, is
a bleak insistence on pursuing advertising research in a way
that separates it from all other researching, thinking, and planning that is, or should be, done for the brand. Advertising
research is not a tap, to be turned on at need. Nor, for that matter, is advertising. Both require investigation, as part of a total
logical scheme, if they are to make much sense.

But surely—everybody *does* this nowadays. . . .

No! Not in our experience. Some very sophisticated companies are still painting by numbers, and complaining when the
results fall short of Royal Academy standards.
What goes wrong is a failure to work out exactly what it is
that advertising should be doing—what it should be doing

long term, and short term, alone and in combination. Of course there are all sorts of disguises to which people resort to conceal this state of affairs—there are strategy statements which sound wonderful and could mean anything. Our favourite at the moment reads as follows (one small change has been made, for obvious reasons):

> The target, consisting of all housewives, must be informed that ———— is a convenient snack product for all the family, with the unique taste and texture that makes it most acceptable on all occasions when either a sweet or a savoury snack is required.

The refusal to set any kind of priority is a wretched indictment of the fact that fear of failure is the primary motivation behind most sophisticated marketing and advertising work—not desire for profit. The absence of any clear definition of the kind of response that is expected from the target is more a failure of imagination. Yet it is here that a creative guideline is surely needed. And advertising research needs it too.

We spell out what we mean by defining the response early in Part 1 of the book. This is critically important because it binds advertising research into the main thought processes that are propelling a brand forwards, and it makes it far more likely that advertising research will be central, rather than peripheral, to the problem.

Part One

Before the Campaign

1

Towards an
Advertising Model

Having chided others for not bothering to work out an advertising model, the burden is on us to make some suggestions
about how to develop one that will stand up to scrutiny, and
provide a meaningful framework for advertising and for advertising research.

First of all, it is worthwhile examining what others have
worked out by way of laws on how advertising should work.
In themselves, such laws offer little practical value for the individual marketing team assembling their own model, but they
give general ideas that are worth remembering in case they
should happen to apply in a particular situation. And the
arguments made against some of them have sometimes been
more instructive than the laws themselves.

1.1 Advertising: general theories

A division can be made between theories that mainly reflect a
marketing interest and those that spring from advertising
men's hunch and experience. In the first category came the
principles of AIDA and DAGMAR, that were born of a careful scrutiny of available information at the time, assembled
with an objective attitude which was determined to introduce
logic and rational sequence into an area which was at the time
threatening to become a motivation guru's paradise. Very
briefly:

AIDA = Attention—Interest—Desire—Action

This purports to show what happens when advertising starts

3

to take effect, and how it works through to the point where somebody actually buys a product.

DAGMAR (an acronym for "Defining Advertising Goals for Measured Advertising Results") was more complex:

Awareness—Comprehension—Conviction—Action

Neither of these systems is totally implausible in certain marketing contexts. Both tend to assume a conscious, rational sequence, which does not really stand up to examination. Consumers are not necessarily "convinced" *before* they buy, for example. Further, both imply a kind of conversion process.

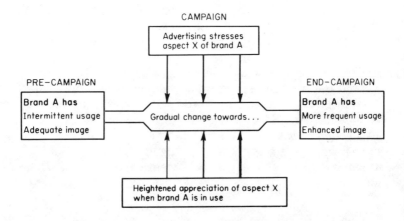

Figure I.I THEORY OF ADVERTISING: HEIGHTENED APPRECIATION

The idea that advertising brings about conversion from not knowing about something to buying it seems more acceptable where a new product is concerned. But what happens after the first purchase? It is arguable that most advertising is involved with the fortunes of products that have already achieved penetration of a large proportion of the target market. Here the task may be much more a matter of *reminding* people of the existence of a brand; of drawing attention to a feature of the brand that may have been underemphasised, or changed for the better; of investing it with distinction, or more interest, than the rest of the field, in order to help it justify a premium price, or space on the shelves next to its competitors; of supporting promotions that will help the brand, etc. All these functions do not fit easily into either of the compact schemes above.

One simple attempt to summate the main ways in which advertising influences the consumer in the above model is to seize on the commonly observed aspect of successful campaigns: namely, that they tend to emphasise a particular aspect of the brand's characteristics on performance that is appreciated by consumers. (See Figure 1.1.)

More recently, analyses of brand-switching, and purchasing patterns in general against measured exposure to advertising, have encouraged a view that most advertising works by encouraging an increase of the frequency of purchase of one brand against others. This suggests, in a simple form, a model like that shown in Figure 1.2.

Consumer's relative likelihood of:

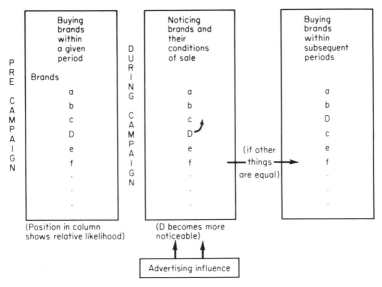

Figure I.2 THEORY OF ADVERTISING: BRAND DIFFERENTIATION

There are, of course, a number of questions that have to be asked about the box at the bottom—mysteriously called

"Advertising Influence." This is a Black Box, in fact, and some have been content to leave it at that. But if advertising research is to be at all precise in its work, it needs to be levelled at *certain ways* in which the advertising is believed to exert its influence on a target population.

1.2   Advertising models for a brand

You may not get it right. But at least, if you try to prepare a model, based on what you know and believe, you establish a frame of reference for subsequent argument, in terms that are understood by the parties concerned. This gives you the opportunity to learn from mistakes.

The first stage is to consider the extent to which a general model of the kind we have just described fits the conditions of the market as you understand them, and how far it is consistent with the advertising strategy being devised.

Now how realistic a marriage does this seem to be? Only *you* can answer this question.

Then there is a useful discipline which requires examining precisely where the brand stands at this time in relation to what can be expected for it and what can be hoped for it. Setting down the answers to some simple questions (as shown in Figure 1.3) can indicate a great deal about what advertising can be reasonably expected to achieve in the short term and in the long term. It is also worth noting down in detail what conditions will need to be fulfilled if the advertising is going to be able to reach these achievements.

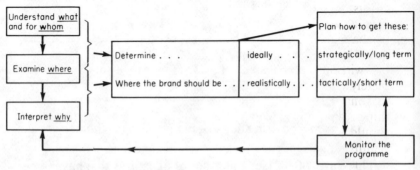

Figure I.3 USING RESEARCH TO DEFINE ADVERTISING TARGETS

UNDERSTAND WHAT AND FOR WHOM—For example: What *is* the product exactly? Original, or a copy? Superior? Inferior? A brand within a brand? A representative of a corporation—for example, a brand used to exemplify a corporation's leadership, etc? What kind of people buy it? What kind of people need it?

EXAMINE WHERE—For example, where does the product stand in relation to its market? Do people think about it and about the individual brands? *What* do people think about the brand? Do they know the brand and understand its difference from others? Are these people loyal to the brand? How many? Is usage slipping?

INTERPRET WHY—For example: Why do so many (or so few) people know of, use, or stay with the brand? Are there certain natural restrictions on its growth—limited distribution, high premium price? Are there strong beliefs about the brand that encourage or dissuade buyers? How well founded are they?

Finding out these things, is a basic task of market research. This becomes "advertising research," as soon as it is applied towards defining advertising strategy. Separating the "ideal" from the "realistic" is worthwhile at this stage because it helps get people in the right frame of mind for ascribing a realistic role to advertising.

"Ideal" is used here in a special way. It may, for instance, be consistent with the long-term aims of a company to have an ideal aim of growth for a brand over five years, if an increase of share from 10 to 20% within a market whose growth will increase at 3% a year. Any greater growth might not be possible without, perhaps, driving some competitors out completely or pushing productive capacity beyond what is reasonable, either of which could be counter-productive. Anything that is completely impossible, as opposed to ideal, should not be entertained here. Cloudcuckoolandish aims require similar means and, since one of the points of this procedure is to encourage a comparison between tactical ideals and long-term aims, it does not help in the slightest if the latter are so grandiose as to wither any practical motives placed next to them.

The realistic aims are a question of the immediate future —that which can be planned within a scenario that is a continuation of current trends and which deals with marketing variables, including how much marketing investment is feasible in the near future, in the form which can be seen today.

Ideally, the intention might be to get the growth outlined above by means of expanding the penetration of the brand from, say 50 to 70% and aiming at getting a higher proportion of regular users among those who have tried it than before —one in three, perhaps, instead of one in five. Advertising might need to attract more attention to the brand in this context—to tempt those who do not use the product to give the brand a try and to encourage users to continue by underlining some of the benefits that are individual to the brand (or which the brand may appropriate to itself by being the only one that is telling about them).

Advertising may need to signal the advent of promotions, and help these seem desirable; or, in joint campaigns with retailers, show where the product can be bought at bargain rates. All these might be necessary, over a long period, but there will be negative requirements too—for example, avoidance of cheapening the brand in the long term, if the loyalty of status-conscious premium-brand buyers is demanded.

When the short-term realistic aims are being worked out, the advertising tasks can be made more precise. Possibly, in the current year, the only viable aim in the face of heavy competitive expenditure, it to try to hold or regain the brand's position. This could be by announcing promotional activity in such a way as to keep the name more in people's minds, with perhaps a simple reminder message of its quality, possibly in slogan form. Planning for, or expecting to measure brand image shifts may *not* be realistic in this example as described, but if these have a part to play in looking at progress over the whole five-year period, some check of the extent of possible slippage may be important, against the time when a more positive attack on the market is made.

The information arranged by this time, allows for further decisions to be made, this time on the nature of the intended advertising effect. This is the point when the black box is, effectively, opened. The result is a two-part exercise, as shown in Figures 1.4 and 1.5.

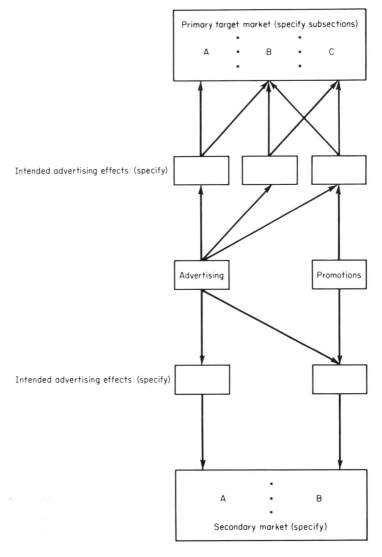

Figure I.4   MODEL OF THE EFFECTS OF ADVERTISING

In Figure 1.4, it might be decided that for a food product, subsection A of the "Primary target market" is "Non-users who have never bought it." The first box in the row that reads "Intended advertising function" might include phrases such as "Tempting a first trial by showing how much it is enjoyed by children" or "Tempting a first trial by suggesting that the family deserve a pleasant change, and that this product would make a pleasant change of diet for them."

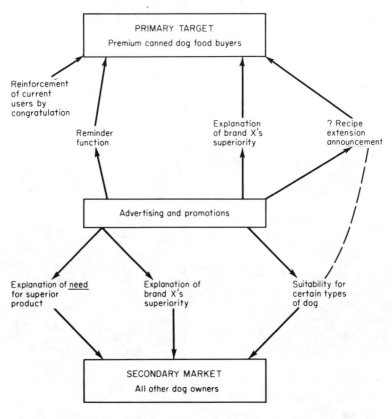

Figure I.5   MODEL OF THE EFFECTS OF ADVERTISING: DOG FOOD

Figure 1.5 presents an elaboration of this principle for a premium product in the canned dog-food market. Here it is worth noting how different a proposition it is to influence users as opposed to non-users. Specifying what has to be done against separate targets in the market is vital. This shows what kinds of *different* demands might be made on the advertising. "Might" because this is the moment when all the challenges lurking within the original advertising brief become clear; it must be decided, then, whether or not all the challenges can be taken up within a single campaign, or whether different pieces of advertising and promotion should be concentrating more exclusively on particular targets and effects. It might be considered, for example, that a campaign intended to convince premium dog-food buyers that brand X is the best for vitamin balance and dog-appeal, would not be so effective if it had also to do an educational job among scrap-slingers that prepared dog-food, of which brand X is the supreme example, is best for their dog. Some would argue that a really brilliant campaign might well accomplish both tasks; others would say it is an example of "yetism"—that is, "We must concentrate on A and B, yet without forgetting C . . ." which has been stigmatised as the bane of creativity. But that is not the point. Once the intended functions are decided, among the relevant targets, it becomes possible to work out:

1   The kinds of mental effect that would be consistent with accomplishing those functions, and those that would need to be avoided.

and subsequently:

2   The kinds of research evidence in concept testing and pre-testing that might reflect those mental effects.

Figure 1.5 shows a portion of that work for the canned dog-food. It could *not* have been completed without the full collaboration of the creative team.

In other words, the way to make sure that advertising research becomes more helpful than simply a witchdoctor's brew is to work out, step by step, what makes sense for it, and what makes for *relevant* sense. This is going much further than saying blandly "Structure your pretest according to the aims of your advertising." Nobody can disagree with this but it is much easier to claim than to achieve. *Our* method takes some time, and some trouble, and it also means involving everyone who is working on the advertising. But then so does most professional activity.

1.3 Decision-chain analysis

Inherent in these principles we have discussed so far is the need to establish a thorough decision-chain analysis for the product or service that is at stake. A very obvious example is airline advertising: who actually decides on the purchase of a ticket for a particular flight? A boss? A secretary? A travel clerk? A travel agent? What are the main ways in which each of these might combine to make it a case of flying by one carrier or by one route rather than by another? When you have decided, on the basis of research, what the answers are, then the advertising model can be built.

This kind of research can often point the way towards some positive ideas for strategy as well. Knowing that somebody with a critical role to play in the decision to buy is liable to be answerable to others in terms like these: "Will my boss react favourably if I tell him I've given a big buying order to X?" or "Will my husband feel he is getting the kind of beer he likes if I get Y, instead of Z?"—makes it possible to develop an advertising platform which will pre-empt or allay fears of a bad reception.

But advertising research can go further than this. It can help determine:

1   What there is about a brand that needs to form the nucleus of an advertising campaign.
2   What there is about consumers in the target market that can be successfully appealed to on behalf of your product.

1.4 From the brand to the consumer

It is desperately easy to find out what a consumer expects from a product, decide that this is what you must say about your brand, and design advertising on this basis that is a complete waste of time and money. A typical result might be a headline such as "Now, Brocklebourne Dairies bring you butter that spreads evenly on bread, and tastes really nice." This is the classic misuse of research that yields a gutless, me-too approach.

The diametrically opposite approach is to look for a gap in the market. Nobody has ever thought of saying about his butter that it comes exclusively from cows that have been kept in fields with a high clover content so the butter is richer. This might be a break-through, or it might prove just as uninspiring as the Brocklebourne Dairies campaign.

To succeed, it must be true: "richer" would need definition that could be supported by fact. Richer than what? It must be relevant as well. If the target consumer does not care for richer butter, this cannot help. Another point is that it must be distinctive. Is another brand claiming extra richness? If so, is it worth fighting a "richness war"? Further, it must tie in with the other points being made about the product in marketing. Richness could not go with a drab pack. It probably could not go with anything but a premium price, either. And does clover-richness tie in with what has to be told about the region or country of origin?

Finally, there is the question of "believability." Contrary to some opinions, we hold that complete credibility is probably a disadvantage, and for the advertising to take hold on the imagination—which it must if the campaign is to be effective in the long term—a phenomenon known as "curious disbelief" is desirable. This means that although the consumer feels that what is claimed for the product may be rather improbable, he is intrigued about it nonetheless, and eventually may try it out. (Obviously, this is different from generating a feeling that it is a damned lie.) The first campaigns for After Eight chocolates were brilliantly successful and changed a large slice of the confectionery consumption pattern in Britain—but their suggestion that this is what the upper classes pampered themselves with at the end of a dinner party probably aroused much more curiosity than outright belief. Ideally, the claim or group of claims being made should reflect *perceptible* benefits: if Brocklebourne butter actually tasted richer in use, or looked richer in use, this would underpin the campaign.

To recapitulate, the following are the criteria on which research would normally be expected to examine new suggestions for advertising strategy, and for the advertising platform to be used for developing treatments. Is what you want to communicate convincingly to the target market:

1   *Relevant*—Is it desirable? Has it anything to do with specifying, or preferring a brand?
2   *Distinctive*—Does it suggest a stance for the brand that sets it apart from and superior to others?
3   *Consistent*—Does it tie in with appearance?—with how the brand is sold?—with all other promotional activity?
4   *Credible*—Does it avoid being unbelievable without becoming banal or boring?
5   *Perceptible in use*—Does it reflect what consumers actually derive from the product when they know it better?

Some of these points might seem to be a matter of factual verification. But that which seems logically, from facts and figures, to fit all these criteria perfectly, may not do so in the consumer's eye. A strategy might look distinctive in the agency, when competitors' campaigns are scrutinised on the wall, but the consumer might still suppose that the strategy is only typical of what everyone is saying.

One other criterion is important here, too:

6   *Avoidance of serious negatives*—Does it avoid suggesting any attributes or associations that the consumers will resent or shun?

There are numerous ways in which research can be mounted to do this job. But most of them, whether they are a few in-depth interviews among users and potential users, or a large-scale quantitative exercise, have one kind of lowest common denominator. This is that they rely on consumers talking about the product and how they use it. Some advocate a systematic exploration of the repertoire of consumer language by one variation or other of "Kelly Grid Technique." Others prefer to have group discussions, in which the talk is guided round and through a chosen series of subjects related to the product field and the brand in question. "Paired interviews" are sometimes recommended to give an opportunity for opposing views to be aired, for instance of loyal and lapsed users of a brand. "Elicitation techniques" have their supporters, notably those influenced by Fishbein, for determining beliefs about a product and its use, whether these are personal or "normative"—that is, what a consumer feels that others may be expecting him to believe—and what their influence on attitude towards using a brand might be. Individual in-depth interviews are sometimes favoured, so that a group's normative influences can be discounted and so that an interviewer can delve below a superficial level of response.

In most circumstances marketing people prefer to have this work quantified so that they can be clear about how many people might be involved when fixing upon a particular strategy as likely to have a strong appeal. (For example, how *many* people are likely to feel that a "richer" butter is important to them?) But research that is to help formulate advertising strategy has to be sensitive as well as comprehensive because it has a *stimulus* job to do—goals for an advertising campaign do not spring out, fully-armed, from a set of tabulations. There is no doubt that a great deal of the flavour of consumer comment is lost when one proceeds from qualitative to quantitative work. This applies particularly where differentiation between brands in a product field is an elusive matter and depends more on "added value," or extrinsic characteristics (for example, associations with good taste or rich living), as opposed to intrinsic differences (for example, paler colour or stronger taste). Brand image measurement for both these kinds of attribute is perfectly possible with a tightly structured questionnaire, and may be accurate—within its own terms. But these terms tend to be stripped of overtone because the structured interview situation does not favour elaboration of feelings.

This is not a book in which to start analysing advantages and disadvantages in market research techniques in general, but only insofar as they are going to be helpful to advertising. All the methods described above can be useful on occasion, depending on the problem.

Sometimes a difficult problem may need a complex research design at this stage. An example is given to show the kind of considerations worth bearing in mind when devising or assessing a research proposal.

The work done for Brylcreem prior to development of an extremely successful new campaign in 1970 is a case in point. This programme included:

1   *Group discussions*—with Brylcreem users; with users of

other hairdressings; with ex-users of Brylcreem; with (older) non-users of hairdressings; (each subdivided into age categories, and split north/south).

2   *Individual depth interviews*—with young users and non-users of hairdressings.

3   *Individual Kelly Grid interviews*—with hairdressing users.

4   *St James' Model*—attitude study among hairdressing users to classify and quantify images of hairdressing brands, and assess the relation of these to brand choice.

5   *Individual interviews*—with psychologists, who were shown the qualitative and St James' data and asked for their interpretations and suggestions for creative briefing.

Some observations are worth making on this programme, which was followed by establishment of clear advertising strategy, creative briefing and concept research to aid creative development. First, the groups were a very convenient, economic and time-saving way of tapping the views of a variety of different market segments. They gave a good impression of the different social forces requiring some to use this kind of product and forcing others to abandon it.

It provided a broad set of contrasts of how Brylcreem users talked about *their* product and how other brands' devotees spoke of *theirs*. In short, it was an easy and fertile field to plough. But there was perhaps too much pressure to conform on the young informants, and individual depth interviews helped show how far this factor had been influencing the results. It also enabled some questions to be put for individual consideration and answers, unaffected by a strong expression of feelings by the biggest extrovert in the group.

At one group discussion, the suggestion that they might try to discuss "What sort of a man do you think is likely to be using ——— (a competitive brand) on his hair everyday?" was met by a dirty laugh from one informant, who cried "A bleeding ponce!" It was rather difficult for the others to speak objectively about the brand's users afterwards. Individual interviews were more rewarding on this point. But the individual interviews by themselves would not have been so helpful in suggesting what product performance areas needed to be avoided because of associations that were made between them and implications of homosexuality or a threat to the male role.

The *St James' Model* work showed clearly what sort of product attributes were desirable and which were associated with which brand, by users and non-users. It also showed what kinds of attribute tended to co-exist in the mind. This was largely confirmatory work, but gave useful data on what strategy areas would be more and which less *distinctive*. It was weak on the importance of extrinsic variables. Part of this might be due to overreliance on the Kelly Grid Method of triads (that is, very briefly, getting informants to consider every possible grouping of *three* brands in the field and indicate which is different from the other two and *why*) to get the consumers' "repertoire" of language. But we believe it is more a problem of the basic methodology.

Interviews with psychologists exposed to all the data can be very helpful. They prevent in-breeding of interpretation that can bedevil an otherwise sophisticated qualitative research programme if it is under the thumb of a single intransigent personality. Individual interviews are best here—when in confrontation with each other they can be more competitive than productive.

Throughout the qualitative work it can be helpful to raise the subject with informants of advertising they can remember, and to show parts of your own and other brands' past advertising as stimuli. This is not strictly concept research—rather, it is getting a feel for the kind of message or overtone that starts to make a genuine impression. This is obviously supplementary to what has been learnt in campaign evaluation research.

Another useful aid is to have plenty of packs around. At this stage, there is often a question of what exactly *is* the product field—should the strategy be to develop out of it or within it? What is the *real* competition? Getting informants to make their own groupings of products, in terms of what they would expect to see going together on a shelf, either at home or in a shop, is an easy way to help solve these questions. It requires little articulation on the informants' part, although of course probing reasons for clustering products in a particular way can be important.

Finally, there is the technique which is called "brand personality" in certain agencies. This depends on asking informants to describe the kind of *person* they would imagine a brand or a service would be if it were to become a human being. "Miss Woodpecker Cider is young, bouncy, full of fun and she enjoys life more than others" is an example, which says something about consumer expectation of what is to be associated with this brand. It can suggest subtle differences between brands when sensitively used and interpreted, but the technique falls down when a particular figure is too strongly associated with the product in the advertising. Thus "Mr Kentucky Fried Chicken" might tend to evoke a misleading response like, "an elderly gentleman in a white jacket and black tie," referring to the founder, Colonel Sanders, *despite* the fact that the informant may actually associate the brand with young families.

1.5   From the consumer to the brand

A lot of the work described in the section above can help describe the consumer. In fact, advertising agencies on a new assignment sometimes commission a few groups at speed among a brand's users, as a start towards "finding out what the hell these people are like."

Qualitative work can take one a long way here, but sometimes a target market may require definition by reference to a large usage and attitude survey or, once it is defined, it may need to be looked at in sufficient numbers for everyone to be clear just how distinctive its needs and aspirations are, and how homogeneous a target it really is.

Lucozade provides a very good example of the value of understanding the consumer thoroughly before determining advertising strategy. Its user profile has for a long time shown that, although the great majority of British housewives have bought it and tried it on some occasion, it is dependent for a high volume of sales on a small fraction of these who are regular buyers. Knowing who these buyers are is crucial for strategy. When most housewives buy Lucozade—if they or their children happen to be ill—these housewives take home a bottle a week. These are the kinds of question that need answering:

1   Are the heavy users of Lucozade unusual in:

a   Their health and their family circumstances?
b   Their use of the product and their history of experience of it?
c   Their anxieties about health, energy and children's growth?
d   Their belief in what the product could do?
e   The advice given them by doctors, etc?
f   Their use of other tonic products and flu aids?
g   Their general psychology (for example, outlook towards looking after themselves, etc)?

2   How did these heavy users differ from:
a   Medium users?
b   Other users?
c   The whole population?

With this kind of product, it is important to know these things before the relationship of these consumers with the product can be understood. The comparative data is important—to know whether, and how, new recruits could be attracted to the heavy users category, or whether it would be easier to recruit users in general, and how this might square with advertising to encourage the heavy users to continue.

Paired interviews, in which a heavy Lucozade user was paired with a light user, were helpful aids towards preparing a set of hypotheses about what the answers to those questions might be. Groups were also useful, but the atmosphere was less provocative.

One important drawback about restricting oneself to small-scale qualitative work is illustrated by the fate of a very attractive hypothesis that came out in the early stages. This was that heavy Lucozade users might have been mainly those who were themselves given the product as children, during convalescence after a more serious illness than the influenza that would accompany most people's introduction to it. It was an attractive idea, because it seemed to explain their marked dependence on having Lucozade in the house. Obviously, this would have had serious implications for advertising strategy had it been true. But subsequent quantification showed that it was a sampling quirk that had provided us with more heavy users with this experience.

Other psychological differences suggested by the qualitative stage were shown by a quantified usage and attitude study, backed up by a battery of personality scales, to be a more viable basis for interpreting the part played by Lucozade in the lives of the separate market segments. One particular point was a greater likelihood on the part of heavy users to be particularly concerned, if not anxious, about whether they were fulfilling their roles as wife and mother as well as they should. This, too, had implications for the way advertising should be used to strengthen the brand's position.

This example was of specific research mounted to throw light on predetermined market segments. Determining those segments is by itself an important function of research during this part of the build-up towards advertising. There are many techniques which have been developed to do this in ways which avoid too much influence on the part of the man organising the research. This usually means applying a computer program, so that individual people in the particular data bank (for example, the respondents in a large usage and attitude study) are divided into segments according to any combination of behavioural (for example, brand usage), demographic, attitude and personality characteristics. When this can be done mathematically, as opposed to by arbitrary clustering, it obviously gives reassurance that everyone is being objective about it. For a comprehensive introduction to clustering methodology, you are referred to Tony Lunn's chapter "Segmenting and Constructing Markets" in *Consumer Market Research Handbook* (1972, edited by Bob Worcester).

More recently there has been considerable interest in "life-style" research as a means of combining within one data bank the information necessary to derive a precise picture of the nature of the market for a large number of different products and services. This has the great advantage that a big new usage and attitude survey is not required each time a new market has to be investigated.

The Leo Burnett UK Life-Style operation is a continuing survey in which 1250 informants are interviewed every six months. Blocks of informants are combined, and sometimes compared, so that there is a check on how the population's life-style may be changing with time. The data picked up from each informant is usage, frequency of usage and brand preference in approximately seventy-five product fields, demographics, media exposure, and programme preferences, and a battery of over 200 "A10 scales," measuring attitudes, interests and opinions.

This last component is the life-style part. Including it means that if, for example, the target market for a brand of cider is outgoing, extrovert, fun-loving and confident, and if it gravitates towards pop music, discotheques, and a desire to break away from the ethos of their parents—all this will become apparent from a straightforward examination of correlations. Media exposure and preference, however, can contribute a great deal to a life-style portrait too. It shows how close a target market is to particular media, and what they get out of them. This can be an important help in deciding how to design the advertising for a brand within particular media to reflect the mood of the target.

That belongs to a later part of advertising development than is being considered here. The main task of life-style research is to provide evidence of the kind of relationship that exists between a target (given the kind of people they are) and the brand or service being advertised; also the kind of relationship that *might be fostered* in order to achieve growth. (For more information on Life Style research see Broadbent and Segnit, *European Research,* January–February, 1974.)

2

Pre-testing:

Introduction

By pre-testing, we mean research conducted on consumer reaction to advertisements, to campaigns or associated material, or, alternatively, to ideas for advertisements and campaigns presented in some intermediary form—*before* anything is exposed to a major part of the market in real-life conditions.

The basic principle of pre-testing is easy enough. Its main concern is to establish whether the advertising is likely to perform its allocated tasks efficiently and whether the advertising can be improved in any way. This involves showing the ad to a relevant sample of consumers and seeking their reaction to it. The circumstances in which the advertisement is shown, the information obtained from the consumers and its interpretation varies somewhat, but the central idea is simple enough. Despite the possibly bewildering details all one does it to arrange that an ad passes in front of a person's face and then either observe reactions or invite them to comment on it in some way, whether directly or indirectly. The hope is that this evidence will indicate some useful lines of action. Some approaches are more subtle than others, and both skill and experience are needed in making sense of consumer reaction. But there is no magic about these processes that should deter any client from demanding a full explanation of what is being proposed or interpreted.

Before outlining details of the various methods of pre-testing, it might be as well to consider the objections of those who believe pre-testing to be a waste of time and money. Although heretical, their views are not entirely implausible and in certain limited circumstances they may well be right.

Objection 1—*A judgement on whether an ad is effective or not, should be left to experienced and talented specialists in advertising. There is no need to seek amateur advice of consumers.*

Many people (including, of course, some experienced and talented specialists in advertising) incline towards this view quite wrongly. In pre-testing one is not trying to substitute amateur for professional judgement. One is trying to obtain data which will make professional judgement more effective. An aeronautical engineer does not seek the advice of a wind tunnel; he uses the information he gets to modify the design of his aircraft. The analogy is exact. An experimental approach is by no means incompatible with professional expertise. If you think your ad will describe the characteristics of a new product—its uses, price and brand name—why not check that it does? Informants in the test are not usurping the functions of the creative director, they are simply being used to help one understand how far the advertising is doing what it is intended to do.

Another problem with specialists is that their cultural and social life is completely different from any of those who will be exposed to their advertising. Their standards of aesthetic taste or humour, for example, are quite different. This is not an airy-fairy theoretical issue. One of us once attended a meeting at which an American marketing director of a biscuit company was discussing the merits of a commercial with a socialite creative director of a large London advertising agency. The point at issue was whether a Geordie accent would be acceptable to viewers in Manchester. To our certain knowledge, neither had been further north than Welwyn Garden City and the unreality of the argument had to be experienced to be believed.

Jack Potter once conducted research into the reaction of creative personnel in advertising agencies towards ten press advertisements, and compared the results with the reactions of ten non-specialist consumers, matched for age and social class. Both groups rated the ads on whether they liked them or not and whether they thought they would be effective. The results were interesting. There was no correspondence between the rank orders of the professional and consumer judgements. If anything, there was a slight negative correlation, with ads which consumers rated highly tending to get low ratings among professionals. Although we are far from advocating the substitution of amateur for professional standards, we believe that consumer tastes are relevant in creating advertising and they should be known and taken into account.

This research example is slightly misleading, although it makes its point. In it, consumers attitudes *towards ads* were being checked; meaningful pre-testing usually means checking consumers' awareness and attitudes with regard *to what is being advertised.*

Objection 2— *The techniques used for pre-testing are unvalidated. No one can point to any hard evidence that ads which perform well in pre-tests sell more of the product than others.*

Some practitioners would take issue with this claim. They could point to whole series of case histories and experiments, where advertising, which has pre-tested well, has in fact delivered the sales when used. Examples can be found from all types of product field and in many different countries. Both press ads and television case histories can be found. Sometimes the new campaign has been associated with more sales than the old campaign, which was defeated in a comparative pre-test.

Unfortunately, to a sceptic with a scientific training, these claims of validation are suspect on the following grounds:

1   The practical difficulties of running a validation study in the market-place cannot be overestimated. Advertising is not the only factor affecting sales—competition can hot up or decline, new products may intervene, a new incentive scheme may galvanise the sales force, the whole market may change. Advertising can interact with other advertising. General economic circumstances and even the weather can put a spoke in the wheels. It is rare for any validation study to be completely uncontaminated so that the effects of advertising content are isolated for interpretation.

2   A case history is all very well, but what about the failures? Instances of pre-testing successfully predicting sales are immortalised in charts and slides, but inconvenient examples are quietly suppressed.

3   Thorough validation should mean turning out ads that pre-test *badly*, too. As this approximates to commercial suicide, it is not surprising that few practise it.

4   Worse than suppressing inconsistent findings is to make them consistent, so as to show a pre-testing technique in a favourable light. It is sufficient to say that some have suspected it.

Although 4 is the exception, not the rule, we would side with the sceptic with the scientific training. Validational studies are difficult to run as controlled experiments. Case histories are highly selective and we have met instances where validational studies were orchestrated, if not rigged. The case of validation is not proved.

Having said this we maintain, nevertheless, that pre-testing is an essential part of the advertising process. The ultimate test of sales validation is too rigorous a requirement—marketing life must go on. While evidence of likely sales effectiveness is welcome in an advertisement under test, the main concern is usually with intermediate objectives. The question "Will it sell?" is seldom heard, because most realise that it is a contributor, not a sole cause. People want to know the answers to questions such as:

1   Is it better to feature a hand-rolling brand of tobacco in a social situation, or simply to show the pack? Is one too limiting? Is the other too dull?

2   Is one presenter better than another for a launch commercial? How do they compare for getting attention and for being believed?

3   Can a claim for service with a smile be accepted for company X—given the unfriendly and truculent nature of their staff?

4   Should the copy for a shampoo ad have a cosmetic or a medicinal overtone?

5   In a commercial for cat food, is one set of kittens preferable to another? Which will be distinctive from

competitors' presenter cats, and thus help the commercial?

The list is endless. A couple of examples might make the usefulness of pre-testing clearer (despite lack of validation):

1   A spirit ad Jack Potter once tested sought to establish the quality and exclusiveness of the product by describing its origins and manufacturer in great detail. Consumers of the product rejected the ad because they felt it gave unnecessary information and thought it would be more suitable for occasional drinkers who might be new to the product. Occasional drinkers, on the other hand, felt the ad was intended for connoisseurs because it gave so much information. Both groups therefore were to some extent alienated by the ad. The agency decided to try again. Nobody can *prove* that the sales effectiveness of the ad would have been affected by this alienation but, on commonsense grounds, most advertisers prefer to know that their customers desire something more than simply brand awareness from the advertising.

2   This illustrates the purely technical value of copy research. The test advertisement was for an airline. A seat by the aircraft emergency exit was featured, with the headline "This is the best place to sit, when you travel with us." The copy explained that a little extra leg room could be found in the seats near the emergency exit—a sign that the copy writers understood the problems of regular long-distance fliers. Naturally, there was some trepidation about the implication of disaster and unreliability in the headline and illustration. High-powered research was set up to discover the possible effects of this striking but potentially dangerous approach. In the event, the ad produced virtually no effect at all, other than a feeling of slight bewilderment. People looked at the photograph, and the fact that the door was marked emergency exit just did not register. For them, the shot was simply of an aircraft interior and the emergency exit sign was an overlooked part of the background. The ad did not disturb anyone, but it proved to have no drama either. Once again, there is no *proof* whether the ad would have worked for the airline or not. But sensibly the agency took it back to the drawing-board.

Intermediate effects therefore can be examined quite

legitimately, to ensure that for good or ill, the advertising works in the way intended. Exclusive concentration on intermediate effects, though, is not defensible in the long term. Eventually, relationships between pre-tests and post-tests have to be hunted down.

It can also, at a personal level, leave one vulnerable to the lifemanship ploy of the experienced adman. In the middle of a complicated debate on the pre-test, in which he suspects he is losing, he will say in a slightly, but only slightly, patronising way "Look, I am not trying to educate the public, or create status symbols, I am only trying to sell the product." This can be devastating, unless one has an answer prepared—for example, a hammer!

Objection 3— *Much advertising takes time to work. A good campaign improved attitudes to a brand over months, or years. How can a pre-test, with a brief exposure, pretend to replicate this situation?*

Right—it can't. But there are many pre-tests where you are left with a distinct impression that the long-term image improvement that is hoped for is inconsistent with the initial reactions of your test sample. Sometimes there is a clear indication of the reason for this inconsistency, and the ad can be changed accordingly.

One of a series of tactical advertisements for a British Airways campaign dramatised the headline by printing it in white out of black across the top of an 11in triple. This device communicated the tactical message (that you could take your wife with you for half price on a BA flight) very quickly and clearly. But it was noted that a minority, in each country where it was tested, saw the black rectangle at the top of the advertisement as sombre and funereal. This was obviously inconsistent with the long-term aim of linking BA with a sense of security. The layout was redesigned to keep the tactical message vivid but make the setting more optimistic.

Sometimes one gets asked to pre-test a campaign, bearing in mind that exposure to each of a series of ads is required "before the feel of the campaign comes through." There *are* campaigns that need to be examined like this, although our belief is that in a really strong campaign each ad will speak for itself. A really good psychologist can throw light on the likely cumulative effect of a campaign after qualitative research, but it must be admitted that the results of this kind of inquiry are much less clear-cut than when assumptions have to be made of average likely exposures to combinations of ads over time.

Objection 4— *It costs too much and it takes too long.*

The pay off from pre-testing cannot be measured accurately. But with the cost of advertising being what it is, even a marginal improvement would pay for the modest cost of research. Take the airline ad in the example just given. Is it worth £250 to save running a virtually pointless full-page colour ad in the Sunday supplements for several months? The cost equation can never be properly drawn up, but common sense makes the question rhetorical.

If you are in the big league, the cost of pre-testing in relation to your appropriation and the possible avoidance of disaster makes the proposition particularly attractive. Disasters apart, the feedback of consumer information makes long-term improvements in the advertising inevitable.

If you are not in the big league, the ratio of pre-test costs to billing is smaller. But even for a small advertiser, a fairly simple inexpensive checking operation can be beneficial. One can argue that the smaller the campaign, within limits, the more important it is to get it right. This does not mean you should look for cheaper research—you get what you pay for. Finding the time for pre-testing should not really present a problem. Part of the ritual of marketing and advertising is to work under timetables that flirt with the impossible. Often this involves long periods of unnecessary waiting, interspersed with bouts of frenetic activity. There are profound psychological reasons why advertising and marketing men should behave in this way, which merit a book to themselves.

The cardinal mistake made by most of those who get squashed into a narrow time box is to plan pre-testing along the lines of Figure 2.1.

This may look professional, but what *really* happens? The creative director is on holiday during part of the first month, the first presentation of agency recommendations is a curate's egg; the salvaged ideas, or a new one, need to be disentangled,

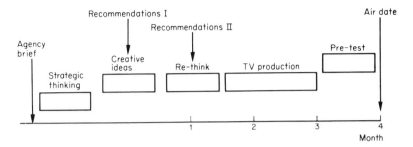

Figure 2.1 CREATIVE DEVELOPMENT SCHEDULE (a): RISKY

argued, sold; then, at the TV shoot in the Crimea (where else?!) rain falls in June for the first time this century. The retakes in the Essex marshes eat into the research time available. On the day the prints should be delivered to the ITV contractors, the first pre-test findings arrive—doom laden.

The earlier that pre-testing is organised, within reason, the better. This means that the benefit of consumer reactions to rough work can be put into restructuring, or reslanting the scripts, or can indicate points that need stressing at the pre-production meeting. That way disaster at the eleventh hour is far less likely.

The kind of time scheme that usually makes sense is like the one shown in Figure 2.2.

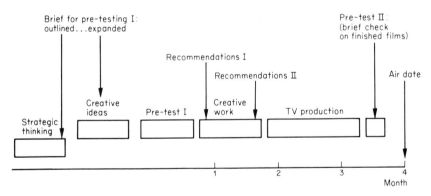

Figure 2.2 CREATIVE DEVELOPMENT SCHEDULE (b): CAUTIOUS

There are two points that should be made: pre-test I may suggest a strategy reappriasal; pre-test II is a briefer operation than the pre-test of the finished film envisaged in the first time schedule. It concentrates on points of importance decided on after pre-test I and during the subsequent further creative work. If a serious doubt exists, the work can be expanded and the air date may again be under threat. But the chances of this are greatly reduced by (a) knowing one is on the right lines after pre-test I, and (b) feeding through the implications for production from pre-test I into the pre-production meetings before casting and shooting are finalised.

But even if there *is* something wrong with the finished commercial, and the only changes you can make in time are to the titling and the voice-over, isn't it better to *know* you have a possible turkey so that you can start planning again?

2.1   Criteria and measurements used in pre-testing

Leaving the major objections to pre-testing to murmur quietly in the background, we now want to discuss the measurements that are made in pre-testing. If the exercise is to be useful, both the criteria against which ads are to be judged and the measurements used for those judgements have to be defensible.

Really, there are only two rules: first, each advertisement should be pre-tested on criteria that relate directly to the aims behind that advertisement; second, the measurements must be reflections of consumer reactions that mean something for those criteria. Choosing is important.

Here are some of the more frequently used criteria, with their respective measurements:

1 IMPACT—If an advertisement merges into the background of surrounding ads and editorial, without a fuss, then it cannot be thought likely to work hard at attracting the target market's attention. This is probably the criterion about which there is the least argument in pre-testing work. If it can be demonstrated that a particular ad draws consumer attention, gets them talking about it and lingers in their minds afterwards—this has to seem positive. Others would go further and say that it is a *sine qua non* of effectiveness. "If they don't notice it, how can it do any good?" But sometimes, depending on the nature of the product field, a fairly high level of impact, rather than a high level, seems more appropriate to success. This is probably true, for example, of lavatory paper campaigns and some medicines, where a dramatic thrust in an ad may bring the brand too close to notoriety and put some consumers off. But usually advertisers want more impact, and are right to do so.

Reported noticing, in a folder test, is an obvious measurement which usually comes close to what one requires. Similarly, when several ads are displayed at once and a group discussion concentrates, spontaneously, on two out of that set, those two may be said to have impact. Variations on these approaches are countless.

The main problem with these measurements is that informants may, sometimes, be hesitant about revealing interest in a particular ad. Possibly it is offensive to them—an offensive ad can have great impact—or it may raise points that are difficult to talk about with an interviewer. Ads of this kind need a cautious indirect test, run by a psychologist.

2 INVOLVEMENT—This is different from impact, in that it assumes that a personal chord has been struck with a consumer by the ad. There is a lot of difference between gaining impact with, say, a picture of a nude and inducing women to have this reaction: "I wish I could look like her—so cool and fresh!" If the ad is for, say, a bath additive, this involvement may be very relevant to an ad's success. In simplified terms, it is making the involved consumer think of the benefits of the product and the brand at a personal level.

Obviously, impact *with* involvement is usually preferable to impact by itself.

Sometimes involvement is very elusive to measure. This is typical of ads which major on a situation which *might* occur to a consumer, but does not apply at the moment of the test—for example, an announcement that businessmen can now go by train from London to Bristol in two hours. A businessman interviewed in the pre-test may not have a contact in Bristol at the time of the test. He may say "Well, I don't often go to Bristol, you know." But he may also be thinking to himself

"Train services are certainly getting faster; I must compare the flight times with road and rail times for getting to Newcastle."

Involvement usually has to be deduced from spontaneous comment. Questions such as "What thoughts or feelings occurred to you when you were looking at this ad?" or "Tell me something about the ad—was it different in any way from the others you saw in the folder?" or "Was it different in any way from others you have seen for products like these?" usually supply material from which to elucidate whether there is involvement or not. Some advocate a content analysis procedure which counts the number of personal references made in the answers, and compares this against a norm or results for another ad tested at the same time. (A "personal reference" could be something like this: "The girl was getting into the bath and I thought that's what I feel like doing—having a good soak," or "The cat was looking at his tin of food. I thought he didn't look as well fed as my Sammy.") If time and personnel resources are available, content analysis certainly helps provide a more objective basis for calculating involvement. But in most cases individual answers or the tape of a group discussion give a good indication by themselves if there is a lot of involvement or too little.

3   RECALL—Some very "impactful" ads, which made the consumer's mouth water (with involvement) are still defective when it comes to communication of the brand name and the basic brand benefits. Ads like these are usually the subject of pleasure in the ranks of competitors, who rub their hands and gloat, "Those —— ads are doing a great job for the industry."

The possibility of advertising being mistaken for that of the brand leader or a brand with a similar name is always worth ruling out if there is the slightest doubt.

There is a difference, however, between testing how well an ad *communicates*, and how far it has good *recall*. The difference is greatest when it comes to recall of messages; least when it is simply recall of the brand name. Recall usually means contriving an exposure to the ad, then, when it can no longer be seen, asking questions to see whether it was remembered at all (see Impact); remembered by name of brand and product; remembered for its detail, pictorial and verbal; remembered for what is was trying to say.

Because they are so easy, recall measures have long been popular with advertisers. But there are so many problems with them that Mark Lovell has summarised these in a paper, writen with Judie Lannon of J Walter Thompson, called "Difficulties with Recall." In an interview people tend to recall what they know well and what they feel that the interviewer wants to hear. Anything difficult, such as trying to explain the point of an ad that was not easily put into words or encapsulated in a neat slogan, stands much less chance of being played back. And yet the feel of the message might well have got through—as is shown by some studies which compare image measurements against recall scores. Motivation affects recall. So also does interest in the product field concerned. If someone tells you that a Ford had scored $x\%$ in a recall test, ask immediately how many of the sample were owners, especially recent owners of a Ford. If an ad for fig roll scores $y\%$, how many ever bought fig rolls or associated products? This is particularly important if any attempt is being made to relate particular recall scores to norms.

Although there is little doubt that really bad or really good recall scores must mean something, this is a much less sensitive tool than many have made out. The work done by Haskins in the USA for the American Research Foundation showed that recall scores do not correlate well with sales results when area tests can isolate the effects of copy change.

As far as the question forms go, there is some evidence that direct questions such as "Do you remember what was said in the advertisement?" can be limiting, in that they put off some respondents, especially older ones. "Can you tell me all you noticed about the advertisement?" followed by individual probing—for example, "Can you remember any words or phrases from it?"—takes you further into what the informant actually *knows*. Psychologists will tell you that each individual needs to be approached in an individual way to get at what he actually has available for recall. In a way they are right.

4 COMMUNICATION—A warning has already been given that questions about communication always get better results if the answers are easy for the respondent to put into words. But communication is at the core of the advertising business. If the agency cannot promise increased sales, surely it can promise a better informed consumer? Whether the consumer gets the point of an ad is possibly the most widespread common feature in pre-tests. If a particular piece of communication is what the agency believes is the road by which the advertising will attract the consumer to buy, or to buy more, then it is reasonable that this should be so. A communication check will in any case give the opportunity for any misunderstandings to come to light, as well as giving the degree to which the points are understood correctly.

Questions to check on communication need to be worked out so that they fit the kind of communication that is being put across. A straightforward ad with a direct message such as "Angel Delight tastes just like strawberries and cream mixed together" or "Eat at Joe's" can be checked by asking what the main point was that the ad was trying to get across. But something such as "Only the Austin Allegro has hydragas suspension" needs a question like "What did the ad say about the Austin Allegro? Did it mention any special features?" This is because recall of "hydragas suspension" may conceal complete lack of understanding (or misunderstanding) of what this means as a consumer benefit; conversely, the consumer benefit may have been understood but the technical description may have been forgotten. (See Figure 4.1.)

Sometimes, as mentioned above, brand image questions—"Which of these adjectives do you associate most with Bulmer's Woodpecker Cider?"—can show more sensitively when a treatment that suggested but did not *say* "refreshing" actually got this point across in association with the brand.

5   *IMAGE*—You cannot alter the consumer's image of a brand by showing him one ad, once, in a pre-test. There was a vogue not so long ago for image batteries to be administered at a pre-test, before and after exposure to a test ad. The vogue was based on a misconception. What this measurement was doing was *not* to check attitude change but communication.

Consumers are not fools. They do not alter their opinions of a brand they know at all well within the space of a few minutes.

Furthermore, they have an inkling of what the game is about. Asked to decide which of the adjectives "sparkling," "refreshing," etc, applies best to Woodpecker cider before and after an ad showing someone enjoying a cool drink on a summer's day, they may well switch from "sparkling" to "refreshing"—but this means only that they have understood one of the points of the ad. It is, in fact, that bane of consumer market research: the consumer trying to be helpful. But once this is understood for what it is, brand image measurement can be used as part of a communication check.

It is with new products, or very little-known products, that brand-image measurement comes into its own. The pre-test may be a consumer's first encounter with a new brand—what does he think it is *like*? Good or poor quality? Beloved of connoisseurs or tramps? These questions tell you how the advertising is likely to be influencing brand positioning.

Many of the more successful brand-image measurement procedures are indirect. For example, asking about the people shown enjoying a cup of tea in an advertisement may tell you more about how the ad is likely to affect brand image than asking about the tea itself—always assuming they are people and not chimps!

Really good clues about the likely influence of the ad on brand image over time are most likely to come from qualitative work—where the *overtone* of an informant talking about the ad can be studied carefully and interpreted, as well as the words he actually uses.

6 *CREDIBILITY*—There are instances where it is crucial to find out whether consumers believe what an ad says. A medicine must be believed to contain what is claimed for it; an investment trust guaranteeing a certain income irrespective of market conditions must also be believed. In these cases, a question on the lines of "Is there anything here that you find hard to believe?" will serve, provided the answers are carefully probed.

At the same time, there are many examples of ads where belief is out of the question—for example, a fantasy sequence showing the magical world you enter when you eat a chocolate bar or try a particular drink. Obvious hyperbole is another kind of advertising style that sidesteps the issue of credibility completely.

There is also a case for having an open mind about the desirability of everyone believing implicitly what you say. A rival school of thought will hold that (particularly with rather banal products where few seem to care greatly about brand differences) a certain amount of incredulity is no bad thing. The argument here is that by making a claim that sounds a bit far-fetched, consumers may be jolted into this kind of thought process: "That can't be true. Or can it? Perhaps I'd better try it sometime. . . ." The trick, then, is to sound far-fetched without overclaiming, and without going too far and seeming outrageous. This is a view of advertising that cannot be proved, although in some cases it seems plausible.

The implication is that for this situation, a psychologist's verdict on the basis of depth interviews or group discussions is needed to gauge the kind of belief/disbelief vibrations that arise.

7   LIKE/DISLIKE—Some informants are polite in research interviews: some are critical. An experienced psychologist can usually distinguish a polite "I like it" from genuine enthusiasm. Similarly, he can distinguish between automatic dislike of an ad *because it is an ad*, from a situation where somebody is riled.

Does it actually *matter* if the ad is liked or disliked? Very often it seems that it does not. Or rather, it depends very much on the market concerned. A self-indulgence produce—such as a beer or a chocolate bar—probably does itself no good by having a commercial that excites dislike. It is a *personal* product, and therefore establishing a personal wavelength seems important. Certainly the most successful campaigns for this kind of product have generally been liked.

But in many cases abrasion of some kind is needed to get the brand to be intrusive and to stand out from the rest of a drab field. Soapers will sometimes point to a climb in a sales graph of a detergent and say, "That's when they were saying how much they hated our advertising."

Figure 2.3 shows the ratio of like/dislike for nine campaigns studied at Leo Burrett, London. It is clear that, although some seem to obey the rules of apparent logic, there is no real correlation between liking and success in sales in areas where the effect could be observed separately from other factors. But *if* the products are divided between those that consumers enjoy, or take an interest in, as opposed to mechanical or grudge purchases, the findings make more sense.

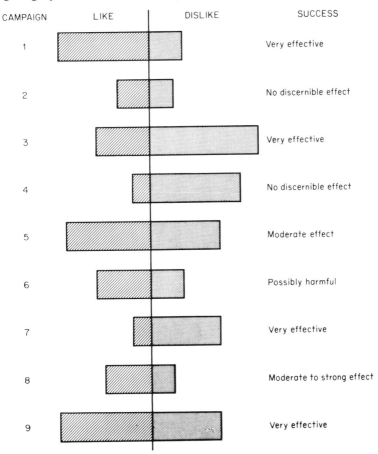

Figure 2.3 LIKES AND DISLIKES COMPARED WITH SUCCESS

There is no doubt that some informants will *always* express dislikes if asked directly. It is important to find out how deeply felt these are. Degree of like/dislike is often well worth studying, especially if the amount of involvement (in terms of personal references—see above) is high. Spontaneous comments should always be analysed for signs of this, wherever it occurs in the course of the interview.

8   NEW LEARNING—When Dr Paul Lyness hit London in the mid-1960s, one of the key measures that he claimed could distinguish the effective ad from the strip of wallpaper was whether the consumer felt he had learnt something new from it. "Something new" has to be taken in a broad sense—it can include a fresh way of looking at a brand, or its performance, that was already well known.

This is an attractive criterion on logical grounds: if a consumer has had his frame of reference altered, or the data at his disposal increased, he presumably has been affected by the advertisement instead of it passing him by. But it is a hard concept to apply to many campaigns. Some of these—such as the evocative TV campaign for Dubonnet, for example—give the consumer something to think about, rather than "new learning." Whether the criterion makes sense or not for a test must depend on whether there really is anything new that is being put across.

Next, it is important to measure whether new learning has happened; this is best done by reference *both* to general comment about the ad *and* to an answer to a direct question: "Has this told you something about the product that you feel is new to you?" It is also important to find out whether it *means anything* to the informant. Useless new learning is neither here nor there. A feeling that a new point is valuable may influence future purchase.

9   INTELLIGIBILITY—This is one aspect of communication: measuring the one, you generally get the other too. But there is also the question of perceived intelligibility. Somebody may get the general idea of what an ad is trying to say, but still think that it was a damned tortuous way of getting to the point. This can be a prime cause of irritation, which is less healthy for a brand that needs to be liked (see 7 above). It can also lead to a lot of consumers simply not bothering to pay it a second glance if it passes in front of their eyes, which could be even worse. People at least notice an irritant, but they do not give themselves the chance of noticing something that seems dispiritingly difficult at first sight.

Intelligibility of this kind is, therefore, worth covering in tests where there is any reason to doubt it. But a direct question such as "Is there anything here you found difficult to understand?" is self-defeating. Nobody wants to be thought a cretin by an interviewer. Better to probe any spontaneous comment that hints at difficulty over understanding.

10 DISTINCTIVENESS—Does the ad seem new, original, or otherwise out of the ordinary? It is almost invariably, in our experience, a good sign for an ad or a campaign that it should seem fresh and distinctive. It is a suggestion that at least the ad will not be mistaken for a rival's. The exceptions to this rule come when distinctiveness is bought at the cost of apparent professionalism for example, a television commercial that has all the trappings of a romantic saga and very little about selling a car—or at the cost of evident strain. When a respondent informs you in a pre-test that "they're trying very hard to be funnier than anyone else," you know that it should be reserved for amateur night.

This is also a difficult area to be tackled directly. The following dialogue reveals very little except a certain defensiveness on the part of the respondent:

Interviewer   Would you say this commercial was different from others for shampoo in any way?

Respondent   It was just like all commercials.

But if she were asked to compare the test commercial with others she has seen recently, and to say whether she saw anything different about it, she would very likely have been much more forthcoming. The commercial might still have emerged as no better than run-of-the-mill but the reasons for this impression, and the strength of it, would have been clear.

11 PROPENSITY TO BUY—Pre-tests of advertising for new products, in particular, tend to include a measure of consumers' propensity to buy the brand after exposure. There are two main reasons why this criterion is difficult to apply with any sensitivity: first, (a point made earlier) many informants in market research are polite—they would like to help the interviewer, and express some approval of the product they now partly identify with her; second, they simply *do not know*. Buying a household product is fitted into a shopping ritual and a shopping budget. Outside the context of comparing prices in a supermarket—and determining what extras can be afforded this week or what has to be sacrificed for what—a housewife is thrown back on very general feelings about the product: does it seem nice enough for her to express approval? Or is it out of the question? Or does she simply (and honestly) say "Maybe"?

It is still worth applying a scale to measure this where new consumer products are concerned, but not with a view to a sensitive reading. Over time, you can judge whether the level of response keeps an ad for a product launch in play or raises serious doubts. As a comparative measure between ads, on matched panels, it can discriminate between them, although not particularly sensitively, and an examination of the reasons behind the choices made on the scale can tell you more about reactions to the ads from the point of view of personal reference.

It goes without saying that when matched panels are compared in this way they have to be matched in terms of purchasing habits in the relevant product field, otherwise the measurement may be partly of pre-existing differences. This criterion does not seem at all attractive when expensive items such as consumer durables or services are concerned. Here answers would reflect personal circumstances and aspirations rather more than impressions gained from an advertisement. Concern to impress the interviewer also enters into the reckoning in these fields.

12   PERSUASION—You still sometimes see persuasion scales used in pre-test questionnaires. Heaven knows why. Even if a consumer senses that she is being persuaded by an advertisement to buy a product—and this is unlikely except in unusual cases—why should she admit as much? This seems to be different in countries where selling and being sold things arouse less emotion. Many Americans' reactions to being asked how far they feel they are persuaded by an advertisement seem, after probing, to be much more objective than many Britons' reactions. The latter often seem to feel that admission to being persuaded by advertising is like declaring oneself a fool.

The whole concept of persuasion is probably wide of the mark for most advertising. Advertisements are not studied like brochures as a rule; they are the source of incidental information and casually acquired impressions. This is not the stuff of which persuasion is made, even if the emotive overtone in this word is discounted.

A psychologist may be able to deduce from respondents' comments, and their content analysis, that one advertisement is more likely to encourage people to buy more of x, or to try it for the first time. But this is too elusive, in our opinion, to quantify. The best guide on this "encouragement" is probably "involvement" (see 2 above).

13 EMOTIONAL AROUSAL—At different times in the 1960s some powerful claims were made for the use of physiological measures to get an objective reading on emotional arousal. The main problem with arousal as a criterion is that it may be good or bad in character. A stripper, a beautiful cross-section of a Chateaubriand and a view of Castle Dracula might all be equally arousing, but one or all might give entirely the wrong impression of the product. The ironmongers' tools do the measurement job perfectly well, but it seems like misplaced effort to substitute mechanical for human diagnosis of the *amount* of arousal when one is happy to leave interpretation of the *kind* of arousal to a human research instrument. (See also Chapter 7.)

14 SIMULATED SALES, OR INQUIRIES—Some very ingenious arrangements have been attempted for getting informants to be exposed to a test advertisement and then having the opportunity to go through a supermarket (or part display of foods) and choose products they would like to buy. The attraction of such schemes is that one is getting back to basic *sales* as a criterion.

For durables or services one counterpart to this idea is to show a test ad among others in a folder test (this is dealt with in Chapter 4) and give the informants the chance to pick up brochures afterwards, or arrange for interviews with salesmen "if they are interested."

This kind of criterion makes sense if other variables can be controlled. These include:

1   The number of women who intended to buy the product anyway, on a particular day.

2   Awareness by the informants that they are intended to shop for particular items, and that this is being recorded.

3   How far there is an incentive to buy *less-usual* products or brands, because free coupons or money are being offered for participation.

Controlling these points is important if the criterion is going to be sensitive enough to distinguish between ads or to show that one ad seems to attract more sales than most of those tested. It is doubtful if the results should ever be used to suggest by how much sales could be increased if a test ad were used nationally. But the basic purpose of a test of finished material can be served in this way if there is very tight organisation of the research situation, plus oversampling so that matched samples can be compared with comparable purchase behaviour profiles. It is only worthwhile if it is done very well, and it costs money.

Some ready-made panels exist for this kind of work. The Research Bureau's test market operation, involving a mobile shop calling once a week on each member of a pre-selected panel, or Trutest, organised by Audits of Great Britain, offer this kind of opportunity. The test ad can be tried out within a sheaf of material which is left with each panel member on a weekly basis, including order forms and a catalogue. It is use of the catalogue, naturally, on which the use of this facility for pre-testing purposes depends. Experience suggests that this does provide a realistic basis for testing the extent to which an advertisement may influence buying behaviour, but it should be noted that it takes time for this influence to make itself apparent. It is also expensive, relative to pre-tests dealing with intermediate criteria, and it may not evade the need to do *diagnostic* research which shows *why* a particular ad may have such and such an influence, if pre-testing is to be an aid towards improving campaigns.

Inquiries can be checked as a measurement of buying interest aroused by an advertisement. Advertisements incorporating coupons or invitations to ask for brochures can be posted or otherwise distributed to samples of consumers. However, the people who fill in coupons and reply may not be typical of those who might buy the product advertised. They form what is called a self-selecting response group. For this reason this kind of test can be very insensitive. But in situations where coupon response is virtually the only means of obtaining the product, and the market is reliant on stirring the interest among coupon-cutters, there is a case for adopting this measurement, as it replicates the criterion. (See also Chapter 9.)

15   ABSENCE OF NEGATIVES—Sometimes the use of this criterion has been described as "a trawl for red herrings." This is a criticism of the determination among some researchers to ignore nothing in a desperate hunt for something that can be shown to be bad about an advertisement. Their puritan zeal has often dismayed creative teams, who feel that the search for negatives results in every bit of originality and character being threshed out of their efforts. But this is a question of degree. It must make sense to check whether there is not something so misleading or offensive in an advertisement that it promises to sour expectations of the brand.

Not that sheer absence of negatives ever made a good advertisement. But there is a difference between being calculatedly provocative and suddenly finding that your headline has outraged a proportion of the market because of a double-entendre that sounds more like an insult than a joke.

If a negative is serious it will almost always come out most clearly in individual interviews in spontaneous reactions to the advertisement. Bandwagon negatives are a problem in group discussions—where one housewife may unfurl the flag of consumerist protest and the others promptly salute it. But there is sometimes a layer of politeness that has to be penetrated before the negative is voiced; typical of this was a group discussion conducted among middle-aged lower-class men, where a test commercial for a hairdressing was greeted first with silence, then with mild enthusiasm and more silence—until the woman psychologist realised that these men were inhibited about expressing their strong conviction in front of her, that the male presenter was an undesirable kind of homosexual. Probing is in order, then, as it is part of increasing the rapport between the interviewer and the test informant. The better the rapport, the less misleading or reticent the informant is likely to be about negatives. But direct questions tend to *invite* informants to be critical (as discussed under "like/dislike"—see 7 above) and they themselves will require probing to determine the degree to which they are really felt.

2.2 Sampling considerations

All market research is dependent on competent and accurate sampling if the results are to mean anything. Advertising pre-testing is no exception. There are also some particular problems with sampling in this field of research that require careful watching.

First, it is not much use investigating reactions to a test advertisement among people who are outside the target market. The definition of the target market is crucial. Demographic characteristics are a guideline but do not help ensure that the sample is appropriate. Usage of the product may be an important quota control, or being in a situation which means that you could use the product if you knew about it.

One of us once arrived to take a group discussion which was one of a series. Each group was to consist of C2D men; half married, half single; age range thirty to fifty. One group was to be of Brylcreem users, one of those who had never used Brylcreem and one of past users. On arrival at the last group, it was found that three of the men recruited were bald. They fitted the quota perfectly. But for the purpose of judging whether a new advertising approach might tempt them back to Brylcreem they were singularly ill-equipped.

It might seem pedantic to insist that sampling briefs should include details such as "Must have at least half of his natural hair remaining." But this example should underline the fact that interviewers do not necessarily supplement from their imagination what is missing from the piece of paper in front of them.

Sometimes the position of the informant in terms of likelihood of being interested in a market has to be established very precisely. Car advertising is designed to attract motorists to buy a particular make of car next time. The timescale in mind will vary, but the model in most advertisers' minds is that somebody who is influenced by the campaign will buy the car concerned within about a year. Some car advertising is more protective, some is more orientated towards conquest sales, but the principles tend to be similar. Some categories of people who might be appropriate subjects in a test of the advertising are these:

1   Motorists, with a car that they bought new, which is now between two and four years old, who were responsible for the choice of their current car and for the financial transaction.
2   Young men and women with no car, but with a driving licence, who intend to buy their first car.
3   Secondhand car owners who indicate in answer to a scale question that they are seriously considering buying a new car next time.

Certain other categories of motorist might be quite inappropriate, for example:

4   Motorists who drive a company car, the choice of which rests with the office manager.
5   Motorists who intend buying a secondhand car next time.
6   Motorists who are committed to a particular make or country of origin—for example, those told by their wife or office manager "You may order anything you like, so long as it is made in Japan."

One could expand these lists indefinitely, according to the particular nature of the marketing and advertising problems. Obviously there comes a point at which insistence on further precision of the sample constituents becomes uneconomic. But with small-scale qualitative work, in particular, it seems vital to us that all the necessary requirements should be analysed and spelt out clearly.

The next problem about sampling for qualitative advertising research is that of *informant set*. The first time that an informant appears at a group discussion, she may not know much about what she is going to see, or what her role is expected to be. Her reactions to a test advertisement may be described as naive, in that she is unlikely to have a prepared view of how to react to it or what to say. On her second visit and on subsequent visits she is likely to anticipate more and to say to herself "Ah! They've reached the point where they're going to show some ads. I wonder what they're going to be like this time." If she is asked to look through a folder she may even consider memorising each brand name so as not to be at a loss when the recall question arrives. She is no longer naive. She may even start (making even the toughest researcher flinch somewhat) by saying "As I was explaining last time. . . ."

Informants should *not* be overused. There are, sometimes, exceptions. For instance, for a very early check on some rough creative ideas it can be useful to have an entirely open discussion, after the manner of a brainstorn session, in which a few consumers known for their garrulity and fertility of thought associations are asked to take part. But this is exceptional.

Nor should informants come expecting to test advertisements. They should be recruited as respondents, "to talk about . . ." (the product field or an area that includes the product field) *not* enrolled as jurors. Ideally they should be in a frame of mind in which they can react to the product or service advertised as presented in the advertisement, rather than setting out to pontificate about artwork and headlines. When listening to tape recordings it is usually possible to spot the consumer-as-critic and put his contribution on one side. But if recruiters, and interviewers asking screening questions before interviews, can be persuaded to stick to procedures which minimise the chances of getting inappropriate informant set it can save a great deal of trouble.

This boils down to training and to standards applied among the interviewers and the companies supplying them. It is in everybody's interest to find out what these are like and how far they are maintained.

The other kind of informant set that can do a great deal of harm to an advertising test is the militant attitude that all forms of marketing and advertising are detrimental to society. Over the past decade the number of those who take a strong consumerist line on such matters has climbed to the point where roughly one in ten middle-class or lower-middle-class housewives recruited for a group is likely to fit this category. Irrespective of whether one believes she is a force for good or evil, she must be spotted at the recruitment stage or very early in the interview.

In 1973 Mark Lovell presented a paper to ESOMAR showing the results of some pilot work, comparing the results of advertising research when conducted among "consumerists," and "permissive" (in the sense of *laissez-faire*) housewives. Even communication checks can be affected by the nature of the sample in these terms. A series of screening questions is used at Leo Burnett when recruiting informants for their Creative Workshop, so that identification is possible. It is not always desirable to *exclude* consumerists; sometimes it is important to know what kind of extreme reaction an advertisement might meet and what form the criticism will take. But it is important to be forewarned.

One issue that is usually side-stepped in advertising research is whether the informants can actually *read*. This problem is worth taking seriously—especially as the proportion of children leaving school in Britain without the ability to read unaided seems to be climbing each year. The figure in the Greater London area for illiterate or semi-literate fifteen-year-olds in 1973 was 17%. Clearly when an interviewer notes that "He scarcely looked at ad B, and said it was boring," it is perfectly possible that the informant saw a lot of difficult-looking words, quailed at the thought of struggling through them and dismissed the ad summarily. Pictures may be important to these people—which has a certain validity as a finding, given that semi-literates still buy products. But a conclusion such as "The body copy was tedious, without appeal and needs to be made more pointed and amusing" would obviously mislead. The researcher needs to decide whether he wants this kind of informant in his scheme; if not, appropriate screening is necessary.

This can also be the case with colour-blind individuals. Not so many women, but about one man in twenty is likely to have some degree of colour-blindness, usually involving a confusion of certain green and red shades. When advertisements that are very reliant on a clever use of colour are being tested, these people, too, should be screened out.

There are problems about discriminating between potential informants on grounds of race, religion, etc, under the Race Relations Act. But it only makes sense to foresee the possibility of a difficult interview with, for instance, a coloured person on certain cosmetic ads or with a Jewish person on an ad for Danish Bacon. While there is reason to believe that coloured people, in particular, have been too often ignored or left out of the reckoning in market research surveys, there is a case for sparing ethnic groups particular embarrassment, as well as for making sure of getting viable research information.

3

Concept Testing

Some people will say, categorically, that they do not believe in concept testing. They will add, sometimes, "We've all read Stephen King's article explaining why it doesn't work."

The same people, however, may admit to doing some "exploratory creative development work" to get an idea about how an advertising campaign might evolve for the best. Part of this research might include showing the informants some ideas or sketches in a rough form. A newcomer from another agency observes that one of these picks up the idea of "extra flavour," and another may major on "convenience." "Aha!" he cries, "A concept test?" His presumption is resented. It may take him time to grapple successfully with the local patois.

Stephen King's original article deserves consideration as an important contribution to the literature on advertising research. It is "How Useful is Proposition Testing" (see the Bibliography, reference 11). In it, he develops a logical argument about the pointlessness of advertisement concept testing. To oversimplify his viewpoint, he suggests that if Scylla doesn't get you, then Charybdis will: Scylla being the mistake of presenting an advertising concept in so blunt a form, stripped of any advertisingese, that the consumer cannot react to it; Charybdis standing for dressing up the concept in a way that gives a more meaningful reaction, but one where the influence of the treatment elements cannot be disentangled from the concept itself. He argues this well. But our viewpoint is that he is indicating the problems, not the impossibility of navigation between the two perils.

Those who would avoid concept testing as a research operation in itself, sometimes claim that they do just as well by analysing what might make a good concept for advertising at their desks, from the results of interviews with consumers who have used the product, picked up either in consumer surveys or in product tests. Maybe, but there is a gap between determining strategy, and developing an advertising concept to the point of a rough treatment test, which concept testing can sometimes usefully fill.

This has to be qualified with the word "sometimes," because "concepts" are palpably absurd when presented crudely, without the benefit of some supportive creative work. An example would be some of the brand identity campaigns developed in the past for petrol companies—the idea of associating a petrol brand and some product benefit would be very difficult to compare seriously with the idea of associating it with holidays, blondes and fast cars, until you actually have some evocative pictures.

At this stage, some examples may help of exactly what *we* mean when we describe this or that process, or test. Figure 3.1 shows parts of the procedure that could be expected to lead up to a campaign, with examples from case studies of the kinds of problem tackled at each phase. This expands what we mean in the early stages of the chart at the end of the preceding chapter.

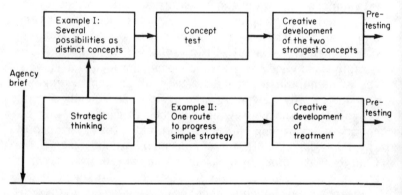

Figure 3.1 TWO ROUTES IN EARLY CREATIVE DEVELOPMENT

3.1 Airwick Solid

The preliminary research for the 1974 campaign for Airwick Solid pointed in the following direction. Housewives needed to be shown that this product:

1   Gets rid of smells by neutralising them rather than just masking them with another smell.
2   That the product is safe to use anywhere even in a child's room or in a kitchen where there is food about.
3   That Airwick Solid is a "natural" product and contains only natural ingredients (regardless of how it works).

There were clearly a number of different creative routes that could be chosen to achieve this desired effect. Of the series of concepts produced by the creative team, two in particular commended themselves:

1   *Flowers*—This approach majored on neutralising, rather than covering up smells, with subsidiary mention of safety and "naturalness."
2   *Trees*—Majored specifically on the "naturalness" angle with subsidiary mention of safety and the neutralising action.

These were advertising concepts, rather than the product concepts mentioned before. The concepts were researched through the Leo Burnett Creative Workshop, by means of expressing them in the form of TV commercial storyboards. Apart from the fact that television was the chosen medium, this seemed the best way of showing the two complexes of intrinsic and extrinsic consumer benefits, in order to get a meaningful reaction. Briefly, the more *extrinsic* the benefits that are enshrined in the advertising concept—for example, "for modern people" or "smart," as opposed to "tastes good" or "leaves no mess"—the more something closer to advertising is required to elicit reactions that can be interpreted as auguring well, or badly, for that concept.

Here it was not so much a question of checking what was likely to be communicated by each concept, as what sort of overtone to the communication was likely, and how relevant it would be. Group discussions, therefore, seemed right for assessing this, and each was presented an equal number of times, to different groups, in first position. Any assessment of this kind has to be qualitative. One is relying on the skill of the convenor to determine what part of a groups' reactions are conditioned by treatment considerations, as opposed to what is inherent in the concept, and by the dynamics of the group as well. Sometimes, it has to be said, there is an equivocal result. But in this case, the results were relatively straightforward:

Figure 3.2 END-PACK SHOT FROM THE COMMERCIAL
DEVELOPED FOR AIRWICK SOLID

1   *Flowers*—overemphasised the disadvantages of aerosols, which were recognised as occasionally necessary for rapidly counteracting smells. This undermined confidence in the message being communicated. "Flowers" also threatened to encourage misinterpretation—that the product had a sweet flowery scent.

2   *Trees*—proved more positive as a representation of the origins, advantages and uses of the product. The desired communication was clear, and the overtones seemed right. (See Figure 3.2.)

3.2   BP corporate campaign

During the sessions at which the advertising strategy for this campaign was discussed and defined, it became clear that one aspect of the company's recent successes, above all, could and should be the focal point for getting the target market of opinion leaders in industry and economics to take a new look at BP. There were other achievements which could have been worked on as well, but none had the stature of Alaska.

The discovery of large deposits of oil in the frozen wastes, working out ways of getting hold of it and putting it to commercial advantage was a significant victory. *Not* to make use of it would have seemed perverse. An analogy would have been the first airline to offer a transatlantic service: it was crying out to be advertised.

A big question remained, however: *how* exactly, should Alaska be used? And could it be used in such a way as to give a chance for other BP successes to be dramatically brought to the fore? Concept research consisted of a series of depth interviews with a small but representative sample of the target market. As this was to be an international campaign, interviewing took place in England, France and West Germany.

The idea itself had to be examined in relation to expressed attitudes to BP. Therefore the first part of the interview, and an important part, not just the lead-in, consisted of tapping informants' attitudes to a series of large multi-national organisations, among them BP. They were asked to say what they had heard of recently that was at all interesting, about these companies and what they were doing. The level of expressed spontaneous interest in Alaska, even among those who were critical of BP, lent support to the campaign idea. Had Alaska provoked merely a polite yawn, a very urgent reappraisal would have been needed.

Then a rough press ad layout representing the "opener"—an ad based purely and simply on the theme of exploration, and how Alaska was but an example of the BP exploratory spirit—was shown in a series of other layouts for corporate campaigns. The latter were the results of collages, in which segments of recent campaigns were cut out and fitted onto boards. The interest here lay in seeing how far informants would become naturally drawn into talking about BP and Alaska, as opposed to feeling more involved with other material, and whether there was any sense of banalisation once they were shown a genuinely interesting subject in a particular *advertising* form. Later, the hand of BP was disclosed fully when a series of further layouts showing possible juxtapositions of new BP successes against Alaska scenery and the motto "BP Do Things Alaska Style." The rest of the concept test explored reactions to this *adaptation* of the theme.

The results of this research helped campaign development in several ways, notably, they confirmed that:

1   Alaska as a theme was involving.
2   It put BP in a desirable light in terms of campaign objectives.
3   Interest in the campaign would be likely to be maintained when it was used to feature other BP achievements against the Alaskan background.
4   "To do things Alaska style" meant something useful in this context, as a link between Alaska success, and BP's stance in other fields.
5   Some "achievement combinations" worked much better than others.
6   Certain points had to be made clearly in the body copy if full value was to be derived from the campaign.

To sum up, this is an example of a situation in which only one advertising platform was considered for testing, because it was the only one that seemed likely to do justice to the strategy.

Concept research has to be considered separately from *both* advertising strategy definition, *and* treatment testing. It does not *have* to happen at all.

There are good reasons for examining very carefully the creative options that are open, before a lot of creative time and money is committed to treatments that major on what might be at a tangent to what will really arouse public interest. The most infuriating kind of pre-testing is that which casts a shadow over a finished treatment, and at the same time raises serious questions about what the advertising concept really ought to be. This is what concept testing is designed to avoid.

Here are the main considerations to bear in mind at this stage:

1 Concept research is there to *help creative development*. This will be regarded as a help only if the creative team is involved in the work, and has some respect for the operation. This is not the same as agreeing with the findings: arguments are often fruitful, provided they are in the open, objective and informed.

2 Asking the creative team to think up concepts, merely so that there should be a kind of "competition" in the research, is counter-productive. So is the inclusion of concepts in which the team, as a whole, has no faith.

3 It is not necessary that any single concept tested should emerge a triumphant winner. The best concept research sometimes throws up the finding that an unlooked-for balance of two claims might be the best route to explore further.

4 In our experience, most advertising concepts fail because they are too complex, or too far removed from the consumer's ordinary perception of the product. For example, those preparing the input for research on a good product sometimes unaccountably play down or ignore the simple principle that it tastes nice.

5 There is no magic formula for preparing concepts in the perfect way for exposure to a concept test. The simplest rule is that when a concept is based on *intrinsic* product benefits- —for example more vitamins, quicker to prepare, etc—a flat statement of the concept may be sufficient, but when the concept relies on *extrinsic* benefits, or "added value"—for example, beloved of connoisseurs, etc—some kind of embellishment to suggest the required overtone is usually necessary.

Individual researchers often have their preferences here. But be wary of the man who says something like "I always insist on plain statements typewritten on pieces of paper." This smacks of subordinating the problem to a technique. Most researchers will take the nature of the target consumer into account here, too.

6 There are some advertising concepts that are extremely difficult to present in a way that makes useful research. Those which anticipate production values are obvious cases—for example, a concept for a new car that is the one favoured by intelligent, well-heeled bloods who have a habit of attracting scantily clad hitch-hikers on the Côte d'Azur. If there is sufficient belief in this kind of concept, it should be the object of a rough treatment test, with sufficient by way of professional technical aids to make it possible for the idea to get across.

From this is should be clear that our view is that while concept testing can be a help, it should not become a fetish. It is also worth bearing in mind the strictures of Stephen King (first page of this chapter) and working out exactly how preparation of material and interpretation is going to make the research a success notwithstanding them.

3.3   General Accident campaign

Let us visualise a solution in which everyone is clear on the strategy, but not on the advertising concept. There are several kinds of consumer benefit, which may be tidily enshrined in a "consumer proposition." But the choice is difficult.

This was the situation for General Accident, in 1973. There was a range of possible concepts that could, separately or in combination, provide the basis for a theme campaign.

The advertising strategy was to increase awareness of General Accident among the public as a major insurance company that caters for all possible insurance needs, and with whom it was most desirable to do business.

The series of concept boards was advanced, each covered the spectrum of different ways in which both General Accident and their agency believed that the company could be advertised. Here are some examples:

1   Because General Accident is one of the largest insurance companies and has been established for nearly ninety years you can rely on us whatever your insurance needs.

2   General Accident, the pioneers, are always looking for new ways to give you a better deal.

3   General Accident is a world-wide company; big enough and experienced enough to give you secure insurance that covers everything from your car to your life.

4   Because we're a Scottish Company you can trust General Accident to look after your insurance interests carefully and conscientiously.

5   Whatever General Accident policy you hold we give you fast reliable service right up to paying out on time.

It should be noted that each of these concepts is in fact saying more than just one single thing. While it is not so desirable to bracket concepts in such a way that one can be sure what people are reacting to in a test, this made sense in this instance because certain claims seemed to mean very little when presented by themselves and much more when in combination. For example, the fact that General Accident is long established means a great deal more, at least in the context of insurance companies, if it has also become very large. Hence the wording used in the first concept board.

The first concept test work produced for General Accident made use of concept boards where there was an illustration as well as one of the headings above. This was done in order to give character to certain of the concepts which otherwise seemed arid—for example, a boardroom scene, redolent of success, size and long establishment, seemed right for concept 1 above.

When, the findings were presented, there was a feeling that the lack of success of concept 4 might have been due in part to the picture of a Scottish scene, which included a man in a kilt. This might be portraying a popular tourist view of Scotland, the argument went, but it was hardly likely to convey a suitable balance of Scottish characteristics of frugality, forethought and the rest.

The concepts were later retested by identical means (combination of individual depth interviews and group discussions) as in the first concept test, but using plain boards, stripped of their pictorial interest.

The interesting point in theory is that there was virtually no difference whatever between the findings of the two concept tests. This cannot be ascribed to the use of the same convenor, anxious to replicate his original interpretation.

It seems to come down to the fact that, illustrated or not, people will tend to react in a consistent way to key thoughts or phrases that strike them as being significant in a concept statement.

From the point of view of General Accident, the concepts that did best out of the five given above were numbers 2 and 3.

These were found to be more relevant than concept 1; more desirable than concept 4 (at least in the South of England while concept 5 was highly desirable but not the kind of criterion on which informants are prepared to believe that individual insurance companies differ significantly from one another.

This should make is clear that the terms on which one can draw judgements from concept tests are a long way away from simple findings giving which concept people *prefer*. From many points of view informants preferred concept 5—that on an ideal plane, is how the best insurance company should behave. Unfortunately it is not entirely feasible as an advertising advantage over competitors.

It should be noted that comments made about concept 3 were easier to interpret in a positive way. For example:

a   A world-wide company—that's good. That means they are much less likely to fall into the difficulties of those insurance companies that fold up.

b   It is very convenient to be able to deal with an insurance company that you can talk to about anything; when you know they have got the experience that means they can set up policies that are exactly right for you.

It is obvious that there is a good measure of personal relevance implied in this comment. This is much more important than liking. But comments about concept 2, which was judged to have come off about as well, were more oblique. For example:

a   There is not so much competition between the insurance companies nowadays as there should be.

b   There are lot of ways in which people ought to get benefits like the no claim bonuses—on house insurance, for example.

Both these comments seemed to be at a tangent to the concept itself. But the important point is that this was the kind of discussion that was generated by the concept stimulus. This encouraged the researcher to believe there was value in exploration of new insurance possibilities as a way to appeal to the consumer when it was clear that General Accident was also believed to be progressive in this way; the potential importance of this concept became even more clear.

A great deal depends, here as in all advertising research, on the way in which the concept is introduced.

Perhaps the most important point is that the informants should not be given to understand that they are being shown *advertising*. If they are, they are likely to be critical of matters of layout and illustration (or the lack of it), and to be reacting to treatment more than is helpful for the purpose of the research.

> I am now going to show you some rough ideas, on boards. They are *not* finished advertisements. They are simply saying a few things about the company.

This is how the General Accident concepts were introduced. By the time that the concepts were shown, the interviews (and the group discussions) had already been going for some length of time. It is important that the ground is adequately prepared, both in terms of knowing how much awareness of the client's company or brand there is and so as to establish an understanding or rapport between interviewer and informant. The interviewer needs to know—if he is going to interpret reactions correctly—whether the informant has ever *heard* of General Accident before, whether he has ever bought a policy from them, whether he has any prejudices about them and whether he has strong preferences for *other* insurance companies. All these things could influence reaction to particular concepts, and the interviewer needs to get the perspective right. Similarly, he needs to know if the informant is on the whole helpful, or snide; suggestible, or dominated by fixed ideas. In short, he needs to know what sort of person the informant is, and he needs interview time to develop an understanding of what his hesitations or gestures might mean, as well as how articulate he is and how he uses words.

There has to be a careful build-up towards concept presentation. In the case of the General Accident concept research, this preparatory stage included discussion of:

1   Insurance:
a   What the informant felt about insurance.
b   The importance of different kinds of insurance, etc.
2   Awareness of insurance companies.
3   Policies held with insurance companies.

4   Attitudes towards using one insurance company or several.
5   What qualities are looked for in an insurance company.
6   General Accident:
a   What is known of this company.
b   What is felt about this company, etc.

Only then did one get on to the concepts themselves. It may seem a long way round, but we believe that this is good practice. Apart from the reasons given above, this procedure allows the interviewer to glean ideas about *why* a particular concept should go down well and why another should be off-putting. When concepts fail utterly, the preliminary information can provide more grist for the creative mill. Finally, it gives an opportunity to see whether the same concepts tend to arouse those who are in favour as well as those who are antipathetic towards the company. When part of the strategy is to help extend the company's business among new or lapsed users this last point can be a crucial one to check.

The campaign that was developed for General Accident succeeded in gaining a great deal of attention; and it communicated the main parts of the advertising strategy for the company. The sign-off line "Is there anything we haven't covered?" came logically out of the concept research and proved to be cautiously exploitable.

3.4   Conclusion

It is worth stressing that good concept research *does not make a campaign*. It may make a campaign that is correctly on strategy more easy to produce. It does not guarantee creative brilliance for a moment, however well it is conducted and reported.

Some concept research practitioners like using shuffle board techniques. There are times when card-sorting operations can be helpful, but our experience suggests that these are comparatively rare. Nevertheless, the following is an example.

Forty adjectives describing the possible consumer benefits of a new cleaning product were written onto pieces of cardboard. Informants were asked, individually, to allot eight of these adjectives to the kind of product that they felt would help them most when cleaning floors (tiled floors, linoleum,

We don't let a spot of bad luck keep you off the road

Sometimes, even the most careful driver finds his car off the road for accident repairs. And being without a car is no joke.

You could always go to the expense of hiring a substitute, of course. But you'd be most unlikely to get your money back.

Well, that's a problem any motorist with a General Accident Keep Motoring policy just doesn't have.

Because, with Keep Motoring, you get a Godfrey Davis car of up to 1600cc if your car is damaged. All you pay for is the petrol. You have the car for up to fourteen consecutive days whilst your own is off the road, regardless of whose fault the accident was. And the same applies even if your car is stolen.

So, when your present comprehensive policy is due for renewal, impress upon your broker that you want the best.

Hopefully, you'll never need us. But, if ever you do, we'll put you back *General* on the right road. *Accident*

Keep Motoring. Honestly, it's the best policy

Figure 3.3 AWARD-WINNING ADVERTISEMENT FOR GENERAL ACCIDENT This has come a long way from the preliminary concept research but the message delivered is consistent with what was learnt in the early stages

etc). "Easy to put on," "No smell," "Disinfectant included," are examples. This sorting exercise allowed the researcher to see what kinds of qualities might be promoted for the new product; in terms of what it could justifiably claim, what went together in the housewife's mind, and what had most appeal. The rest of the interview was devoted to exploring why these choices were made, and resorting to see which descriptions best fitted brands that were already available. This last point meant that a *distinctive* advertising platform, as well as a popular one, would be developed.

Card-sorting works best when all the items are no-nonsense factual points and when they are homogeneous.

An elaboration was used for National Benzole in helping to decide what concept should be pursued for National petrol stations. Informants had ten points to allocate to "The petrol station you yourself would like to find locally and which you would tend to use."

The awarding of points was a private event between the informant and the board, rather than with the interviewer. This had one significant result: whereas in open discussion the cry is "Down with promotions—just take some money off the basic price," when using the board, greater interest in promotions and trading stamps was shown than could ever have been predicted from ordinary interviews.

This kind of device, and a preference for individual interviews as opposed to group discussions is recommended in concept test work whenever there is a legitimate fear that the conventional wisdom of the consumer is likely to overwhelm other considerations. When consumers are determined to appear rational there is nothing that will stop them—except, perhaps, for the little sign saying *Get your double stamps here.* . . .

4

Pre-testing
Press Advertisements

4.1 Rough treatment testing

When a brilliant press campaign is launched, people tend to wonder how it could ever have been the object of an argument. But it often is. Sometimes, when it first appears in rough form, it demands imagination to realise how brilliant it might become when it has had the benefit of one of the best photographers.

Equally possibly, however, it is regarded by the account and the brand group, and sometimes by the creative team themselves, as one of several runners; or they may doubt whether it will really deliver the message intended. Later, they may well forget or disclaim any such indecision because memory tends to filter out any thoughts that are inconsistent with a sense of foresight.

It is decided, then, to check one or more creative ideas for the campaign, before a lot more time and money is spent. The crucial thing, as with all advertising research, is to think out carefully what the brief for this research should be. And then —*everyone in the team must be clear in his mind* about that brief.

It would be legitimate to ask research to answer any of these questions:

1   When a rough prototype of the advertising is exposed to a sample representing the target market, are the informants' reactions consistent with the kind of job that the campaign will be intended to do?

2   Are there any reactions which suggest that very careful efforts need to be made—either by changing the

campaign, or the copy, or by taking particular steps in production—to avoid a misconception or another undesirable effects?

3   Is there any evidence in informants' reactions that suggests ways in which the creative team could develop or improve their work on the campaign?

4   Is there a suggestion that one campaign might be particularly stronger than others being tested?

5   Is the test campaign likely to appeal right across the target market, or is it restricted in some way? For example, does it appeal to women but antagonise men?

6   Is the communication straightforward or will the intended message only get delivered once it has the benefit of considerable "production values"?

7   In the context of the campaign idea, does the communicated message seem relevant to the product and to the use of that product?

In addition, more specific questions about details of the campaign might be included—for example, on reactions to a presenter named as an authority figure.

But don't expect a test of this kind to do *everything*. Overloaded research is almost always suspect and unlikely to give value for money. A clear, uncluttered brief, which concentrates on the main points at issue is by far the best. There are certain questions which are, in our opinion, *not* legitimate at this stage. Here is a selection of the more notorious ones:

1   How good is the new campaign going to be?

2   Will it be better than the current campaign?

3   How much impact will it get?

4   How likely is it to persuade or sell?

It is, in fact, very likely that a competent researcher will have some *ideas* about these points, after the test. But they will be heavily qualified, as each depends very much on execution. The last question is extremely difficult, and sometimes unanswerable, even with *finished* press ads.

The next point to sort out clearly is who is supposed to be benefiting from the research. Some of the "legitimate" questions are more of concern to the account and brand side, while others are aids to the creative team. Some large agencies allow a budget to be set aside for use by the creative team. A creative director determines the brief; the researcher reports to him; he and his team will see the results and use them—they *may* or they may *not* be passed on to the account and brand groups. This gives a creative team more confidence in the work being done. But on some occasions, the whole team might share a very deep concern that they do not proceed further before getting a check done. Here the researcher needs to probe carefully what, exactly, is in the creative group's mind with regard to how the campaign is intended to work. This is specially important where the brief to do the work comes from an account executive who knows some but not all the creative thinking.

The methods that will be applied will almost certainly be qualitative, if much value is to be derived from the job. Qualitative does not necessarily (contrary to popular imagination) imply small samples. What it does mean is reliance on skilled researchers—whether interviewers or interpreters or both—to elicit and analyse informants' reactions sensitively, and flexibly, without the trammels of a structured questionnaire. This allows for the individuality of a particular informant's reaction to be observed and the evidence of this to be combined with other interviews in a way that is also individual. Good qualitative work makes few assumptions about what is likely to be important: it permits surprise. Obviously, the pressure put on the quality of the personnel used in qualitative work is enormous—which is both a weakness and a strength.

Why insist on qualitative work at this stage? First, because the creative work is in a rough state, which means that a researcher has to be very much alive to the possibility that an informant may be reacting at one point to the campaign idea as a whole, and at the next to a detail ("I don't like this drawing") which would certainly be changed when the idea is developed further. Informants are not consistent in this. A researcher will often need to note whether and to what extent a test is being biased by the quality of the artwork, and what precisely is wrong. Next, qualitative work can be observed or listened in to by members of the creative team. They get the flavour of informants' reactions, and their language, at first hand. Sometimes they can be involved in presenting rough creative material to informants, and answering questions about its unfinished state. "When I did this once," said a creative director at a large London agency, "I could sense from the faces of the people in the group exactly what they found difficult to grasp. And then I *knew* how we had to change the ad—virtually before anybody had said anything."

A further reason is to allow exploration of "negatives." The answers to the question "Is there anything you particularly dislike about this ad?" are bold and uncompromising when they appear in tabulations. Perhaps 20% said they disliked the look on the girl's face. In the ad she is raising a bar of chocolate to her lips. What exactly don't they like? She might look too upper class; too lower class; too coy; too sexy; alarmed; stupid; unsophisticated; proud—and whichever it is, it might not go with the informant's feelings about eating a chocolate bar. A qualitative approach would find out what was wrong, how serious this was, whether it was central or peripheral to the idea, and whether it is something that could be easily rescued in the final execution.

An advertising researcher might decide that his qualitative approach should take the form of:

1   Group discussions.
2   Mini-groups (about four people in each).
3   Paired interviews.
4   Individual depth interviews.
5   Semi-structured interviews.

Our experience is that the researcher will tend to react badly to being asked bluntly "Please do some groups." Give him the research problem first and he will propose the method he thinks best. Obviously, he should be prepared to argue his case for his choice. This will usually rest partly on the way he feels the material should be exposed and partly on the comparative difficulty of getting the desired sample.

While all market research depends for its viability on good sampling, there is no question that qualitative work, as it does not rely on numbers, must have even more attention paid to getting precisely the right people. Quotas can be set in demographics, product usage, media exposure or in personality terms.

There is an advantage, even at this stage of development, in exposing the test advertisement in a way that does not disclose immediately what it is that the researcher really wants to know. This can mean including the test advertisement in a folder, or a dummy newspaper or magazine. The point to remember is that if the test ad is *obviously* different from the rest of the material in the folder, it is simply a waste of time. It is sometimes worth adapting currently appearing ads so that they can be used as "controls" which are indistinguishable in finish. This is not always practicable, however.

The interview should in most cases be designed so as to encourage the informants to react automatically to a test advertisement, revealing something of the impressions it makes on him at the moment of exposure. This is more relevant for interpretation of the likely effectiveness of the advertising than a considered opinion given in response to what is obviously a carefully framed question. Krugmann's work on advertising research led him to complain that researchers are too often concerned with question-and-answer to tap mental events long after first exposure, and pay scant attention to feelings during the event of exposure itself.

This view, which we share, is backed by observations made by experimental psychologists that most advertising is for the great majority of people a matter of *incidental learning*, rather than what happens when you read a book. There are exceptions—the perusal of car advertisements by prospective buyers is an obvious one—but for the most part the principle must be right. Therefore what is happening at the moment of the "incident" is worth examining if you can. But can you?

Advertising researchers believe (and we believe some of them) that they can get at least an inkling of what is going on in the mind of the informant when he first sees a test ad. They also believe that they can usually, on the basis of their experience, tease this out from attitudes that are subsequently assumed and later rationalisations of first comments. The following are some of the procedures that help them to do this:

1   Watching informants' faces when they turn to the test ad in a folder.
2   Encouraging free and open discussion (either in a group or in an individual interview) before the moment of exposure, so that the informant feels in a voluble, communicative mood and is used to saying what he feels.

3   Establishing a pattern of immediate reply, before a folder or an individual test ad is shown, so that a question at the time of exposure is actually unnecessary.

4   Probing in an indirect way for elaboration of a response—or of non-response. Some examples:

a   Did you smile, then, or was I wrong?

b   No comment?

c   Anything more?

d   You turned the page rather quickly.

The important thing is to have the right tone, as well as to avoid phrases that are leading.

5   By asking questions such as:
     We haven't much time: is there anything here you'd like to comment on *first*?

6   By asking, at a suitable moment, if the informant would like to see the test ad a second time—and noting the reaction.

7   By noting differences in comments on a second exposure, which may suggest communication problems on the first. For example, "Oh, I see now, it means. . . ."

8   By using recording apparatus to check the informant's memory of the first comments made.

It must be obvious that very defensive, uncommunicative and inarticulate informants are very difficult to the researcher in a qualitative exercise. Yet they buy goods and services, and are part of the market. Even the best qualitative research expert will meet the occasional bad group. But he will usually find a way of forcing even the tightest clam to disgorge something of value. Sometimes he achieves this by switching off the tape recorder, and saying something such as "OK, that's it. Everybody can go home now. What did you think of it all? . . . . And the ad? . . . ."

Another problem that is growing is the emergence of informants in all social class groups who take a rigid attitude of disapproval of advertising. Their views may not be apparent at a conventional recruitment interview. What then happens is that early in the group discussion one dominant character declaims "I think advertising is downright immoral. It's a waste of money. The manufacturer ought to be made to cut their prices instead."

The effect on the rest of the group may be considerable, and inevitably it influences the test results. This problem has already been discussed in section 2.2, where it was pointed out that screening questions on consumerist attitudes are a useful discipline because they forewarn the researcher about the kind of sample he has got. This is done not necessarily to exclude extreme consumerists, although this is often desirable, but to *know the background* of attitudes against which the test advertising will be regarded.

4.2   Case history

A series of advertisements were tested in rough form for the Austin Allegro, before the decision was taken to progress a particular campaign to its final form.

A car is perhaps a special case in advertising research as the number of points of its character and performance that could legitimately be featured in advertising are far more extensive than in the case of the average product. Styling, safety, miles per gallon, reliability, convenience in use, associations with particular types of people. . . . There is a very long list of points on which, it can be argued, an individual advertising approach that will commend the car to potential buyers should be made.

For Allegro, with models ranging from 1100 to 1750cc, there was a strong rationale for approaching the consumer with the reliability story: an honest car which does an honest day's work and which required less expenditure on fuel and maintenance over time. This much had been established clearly before work was done preparing rough treatments.

At the same time as bringing the car more forcibly to the target's mind in these terms, there was a strategic job to be done on behalf of the Austin marque in general. This was a secondary consideration to the task of preparing the ground for selling more Allegros. But it was still important that the advertisements should give a sense of greater dynamism and overall quality for Austin—this would be to the marque's advantage across the range of Austin cars and, naturally, for future launches.

The method used for testing six rough advertisements was to introduce them in the course of group discussions, after a preliminary talk about cars in the low to medium price range and their advertising.

The group discussion is not a perfect vehicle for this kind of work. It is worth specifying what it could and could not do. In this context it could:

1   Give a chance of seeing which of the rough ads tended to attract attention, and in what combination, and which ones were ignored.

2   Provide a situation for assessing comments, to see how far the ads were likely to provoke the kind of consumer response at which the creative team were aiming.

3   Suggest ways in which each ad needed some kind of improvement if it was to be more likely to position the car in the mind as reliable, etc.

4   Show which of the ads were more likely to prove coun-ter-productive, by making people think in other terms about the car.

Throughout this, it should be stressed that *interpretation of reactions* was important. Surface reactions could be mislead-ing. The discussion leader was a psychologist, and had to be in this case. Even respondents who are anxious to tell you how to write ads can yield some valuable information—provided somebody is there who can sort the wheat from the chaff.

A group discussion could *not*:

1   Show precisely what each ad would communicate to each respondent.

2   Indicate the extent to which the ads might change entrenched attitudes to the Allegro or towards Austin.

Essentially, then, this research was providing information to help creative development by showing what kind of dramatic potential each of the roughs might have, how each might be developed to advantage and what potential dangers should be avoided.

The choice of sample was difficult for several reasons. It had to relate to the spread of the target for the Allegro, in terms of the make of car already owned. They had to be new car buyers, too—habitual buyers of old secondhand bangers were of no interest. Cars, as a subject, are difficult for a mixture of ages, social classes and the two sexes to be combined in individual groups. This meant careful selection of a larger number of small groups (six in each) in order to cover the target without running risks such as a battle between the sexes over what women and men want out of cars which can distort reactions to individual advertisements. Finally, the market divided more or less into three groups: those who automatically think of buying British; those who are poised between British and foreign cars; and those who would not consider buying or going back to buying British. The latter category had to be excluded: no doubt Allegro advertising *might* have some effect on them, in time, but it made sense to avoid including anyone whose overt prejudice would lead him to give the same raspberry reaction to *any* rough ad for any British car.

In any event, there were some cases where basic antagonism to Austin had to be taken into account—as revealed in the early part of the discussions—when assessing reactions to the test ads.

Layouts were used, which meant that careful explanation had to be given that these were "the kind of first design that an advertising agency might put forward for discussion before taking photographs, getting everything printed, and so forth." An example of a layout that was *not* in the test ad series was shown first to make the principle completely clear.

One of the series, A, was headlined *No Shocks on the Road, No Shocks at the Garage.* The illustration featured two scenes with two views of the Allegro—moving at speed along a rough country road and on a garage forecourt. The copy explained that the Hydragas suspension in the Allegro car protects the traveller against a bumpy ride while cutting down on motoring costs by not requiring specific maintenance.

Another, B, was headlined *The Law and their Order* (see Figure 4.1) and featured an Allegro at rest at a crossroads in Soho, where two policemen were interviewing someone who appeared suspicious. The text explained that for the London police to order a large number of Allegros—as they had done—meant they were convinced of its reliability, its endurance, its need for little maintenance and its value for money over many miles.

Both attracted a reasonable amount of attention, by comparison with most of the other advertisements. This was

The law and their order.

After months of testing, Her Majesty's Police Force placed an order for the Allegro.

Soon, a full 657 of them will be doing the law full justice.

Now, it's all very well to have the law on your side. But maybe you'd like to know some of the things that went down in their notebook.

First, the Allegro 1100 De Luxe boasts a touring mileage of 35.9 mpg. (Motor Magazine, 19.5.73.) When you're spending public money, you mustn't spend too much of it.

Second, all Allegros have front-wheel drive. This makes for more disciplined handling and road-holding.

In a tight corner, any persons bent on a get-away will be summarily outmanoeuvred.

Third, there's the Allegro's electric cooling fan. This aids the engine's efficiency by cutting in only when needed. And, because it operates off a thermostat, it cools the engine even when it's loitering.

Fourth, there's the Allegro's Hydragas® suspension.

Hydragas® is a unique system. It rides on gas, absorbing any form of assault or battery the car might have to take from the road.

On your way to the station, you'll get a ride as good as some cars costing twice the price.

What's more, Hydragas® needs no regular maintenance.

The way it's sealed, it's locked up pretty well for life.

Fifth, the Allegro goes quietly. So now, when the law come, they come quietly.

No wonder they made their order.

Vital evidence always leads to conviction.

Austin

Austin Allegro

When you're travelling economy, go first class.

Figure 4.1 AUSTIN ALLEGRO ADVERTISEMENT

judged in terms of the spontaneous attention paid to each rough when they were all displayed on a table; the respondents in the group could walk around them, look more closely at whichever caught their eye and start to discuss them as they pleased.

Ad A, however, was felt to be trying to link together two aspects of the car in a way that sounded forced, if not actually false.

Anti-Austin voices made comments such as "Just the kind of thing you'd expect from them—they can't make up their minds what kind of car they're trying to make."

Those who were more favourable towards British cars, and to Austin, wanted to know either "What *else* can you say about what it's like to drive?" or "What *else* can you say about costs and economy?" in a way that suggested that the double point suggesting why this should be a good car for them was unconvincing or restrictive.

Ad B, on the other hand, commanded a kind of respect that made one feel that a serious and unexpected point had been made on behalf of the Allegro. The message was discussed as if it were *news*, as opposed to contrived argument on behalf of the car, for example:

> I didn't know the police had ordered Allegros. I wonder why . . . .

> This isn't so much like an advertisement is it? I mean, it's like an announcement . . . . The police decided it's all right—so it's worth anybody's while giving it a try.

Later, when the ads were cleared away, conversation kept reverting to Ad B. Even those who were anti-Austin were prepared to concede that the Allegro must have some basic advantages. It was felt that these were crystallised in terms of "reliability." The other parts of the advertising task seemed to be as well answered by this ad: it made sense that the police would want a car that did not require extensive or expensive servicing, and the feeling that the police had to have a car that gave quick acceleration seemed likely to contribute to the long-term aim of making Austin more "dynamic."

ALTERNATIVE METHODS OF PRELIMINARY PRE-TESTING include work done on particular aspects of the press campaign being developed. A visual device may be intended to "brand" the ads in a campaign—does it, in fact, communicate the brand name successfully on its own? A campaign may be going to be built round a particular word or phrase describing the brand or the function or individuality of the brand—how do people react to this word or phrase? Has it the kind of associations on which the campaign can really make capital? These are the kinds of questions in which specific question-and-answer research, often quantified, may be legitimate.

As an example, some years back the word "Butch" was felt by the creative team to symbolise succinctly the rugged characteristics of a small car due to be launched. If it was to be used, this word would be right at the core of the campaign. Two parallel series of interviews were mounted, therefore, to investigate:

1   Reactions to the word "Butch" by itself.
2   Reactions to the word in the context of a picture of a car (unidentified) of the appropriate kind, with brief explanatory copy.

Two sets of fifty motorists were given very brief individual interviews. Those who saw the word by itself were puzzled by the situation. Their associations with the word were vague, and on the whole unflattering. The second set of interviews (in which there was a context to the word) revealed this picture of the car so described:

1   Something for Bonny and Clyde to get away in.
2   A woman's car, masquerading as a man's.
3   A dangerous car (butchery).

The idea was dropped—rightly, we believe.

4.3   Testing the details of a press ad

Before proceeding to research finished press advertisements, it is worth considering briefly the kind of test that is sometimes conducted to check on particular details. These can be variations in the pictures used in illustrative examples, in headlines, the strap line or even chunks of body copy.

The premise on which such research is usually based is that

the format of the advertisement is probably right and that the test is to try to optimise its effectiveness or to suppress variations which may militate against its effectiveness. Essentially this is taking a somewhat atomistic view. A logical extension of this view might be to conduct research in such a way that one emerges at the end with an optimum headline, an optimum picture and the best format of body copy and layout and then it is merely a matter of putting it all together. It is extremely doubtful whether many good press advertisements have been constructed in this way. The creative man's skill in preparing appealing advertising is a matter of devising successful total effects in which the way that the different parts interlock is a matter of felicitous harmony rather than a formula which will stand chemical analysis.

In the past we have seen press advertisement tests involving a round-robin approach. In one of these the creative team had been asked for six photographs and three combinations of headline and strap line. It had been determined that the layout and the basic points of the body copy should be standard from the start—and in fact equivalent to those used for the brand concerned in the United States. ("What has been good enough for American mothers must be good enough for. . . .") An ingenious research design was worked out whereby other possible combinations of picture and headline were produced and inserted in a folder containing other advertisements. Thus there were eighteen folders which were identical except for the version of the test advertisement. Interviews were conducted on 270 mothers, using the folder test technique and divided into equal cells of fifteen.

By combining and recombining the evidence from these cells one could see the effect of forty five situations where each of the photographs was exposed; and ninety situations in which each of the headlines was exposed. This enabled the research to find out a lot about the relative impact of the photographs, in terms of how many mothers described them accurately after looking through the folder and handing it back, and a lot about the short-term recall value of the headlines. The research, however, did not leave one with a great deal of information about the advertising itself. Somewhere along the line the people concerned had chosen to forget that the elements of the advertisement followed dynamic not static principles. The creative team was told little about the total effects it might have achieved. It is, however, perfectly possible to devise a research programme which allows experimentation of alternative elements, but does not lose sight of the primary objectives which must be to try to get the advertising as such to work as hard as possible to achieve the advertising objectives. How the advertising is seen *as a whole* is crucial.

A very good example illustrating this point has been provided by Ann Burdus of McCann Erickson. The 1973 campaign for the Milk Marketing Board had various illustrations which make it quite clear that one is talking about *milk*: the headline (used in posters and press) asked "Are you getting enough?" Getting informants' reactions to the headline by itself is to ensure a very different response from getting reactions to it in the illustrative context. Divorced from its context it can appear rather coarse, rather insulting. In context, however, it appears to be entirely acceptable humour with a valid consumer point—which means an effective result.

4.4   Testing finished ads

Encouraged by reactions to the early work on the rough ads, print advertisements are prepared in their finished form. They are then tested for any of the following reasons:

1   To check whether the promise of the campaign as revealed in the early research has been borne out at this stage—that is, have the points in the campaign's favour been carried through and perhaps improved?

2   To check whether serious negatives suggested in the early research have been avoided—or whether there are any serious negatives.

3   To see whether each of a set of ads is contributing promptly and consistently to the effect of the campaign. Or is there a sore thumb? Why?

4   To see that certain basic points are communicated, clearly and meaningfully, by the finished ads—for example, the brand name, the kind of product or services, the range of products (if applicable), etc.

5   To check whether the campaign will appeal to all

sections of the target market, without alienation of important groups of consumers.

—and similar variations on the "legitimate questions" outlined in section 4.1.

It is worth stating again that although we are dealing here with finished ads, it is still not legitimate to talk of pre-testing them for their persuasive effect.

4.5 Interviews: showing v concealing your hand

You have an advertisement, with finished artwork and the copy typeset. Before it is irrevocably committed to production you feel that testing consumer reactions would be useful, in case something is seriously wrong or there are important improvements to be made. To simplify the choices before you, either:

1 Interviewers can be asked to confront consumers with the test ad alone.

2 They can show the test ad to consumers in and among a sequence of other ads.

In situation 1 it is difficult for the consumer not to feel that the whole purpose of the interview is to get his comments specifically on the test ad and on what it says. This does not necessarily mean that the information derived from the interview is going to be irrelevant. But, obviously, if there is a greater likelihood of identification of the research purpose, the personality of the interviewer (who is the interface between the consumer and the advertiser) is liable to play a bigger part in influencing reactions.

In situation 2 the consumer need not—at least in the initial stages—be aware of the research purpose. Occasionally there may be a suspicion that the interviewer is concerned with *all* the ads, but follow-up research among informants who have recently taken part in folder tests suggests that this is rare. Here, the interviewer's personality will undoubtedly still play a part, but as he is not specifically identified with the test ad this is likely to be a smaller part.

Experienced interviewers can usually tell whether, and in what way, an informant is playing up to them—for example, by exaggerating his or her disapproval of a racy suggestion perceived in the test ad. But relying on interviewers' skills to the extent of adopting situation 1 in all research is questionable. Some precautions against this can be taken (and, in fact, the best interviewers often insist on this) by showing a test ad only after a fair amount of discussion has taken place or after one dummy ad has been exposed. This means that the interviewer will have a better understanding of the informant's way of talking and it is to be hoped, thinking, by the time the ad is tested. Probably there is also some doubt in the informant's mind about what exactly is the point.

When there is a comparative test—that is, several versions of an ad or several campaigns for the same product and brand are being tested to determine which has the greatest promise —the time factor is sometimes held out as a reason for diving straight into the main business of the test. *This is the abnegation of planning, in favour of convenience.*

Situation 1 is defensible, but it demands the best interviewers (preferably psychologists), it puts a premium on interpretation and it can always do with application of some of the principles of situation 2.

Situation 2 often takes the form of a folder test, and deserves a section to itself. In addition to increasing the chances that informants will not be reacting overconsciously to a test ad, it allows the chance of a better measurement of *impact*, or the degree to which, if other things are equal, a test ad attracts attention to itself and its content.

4.6   Folder tests

In this book we use the term "folder test" in a broader sense than is often accepted. The basic definition must be a research situation in which there is exposure of a test advertisement within selected material that forms a background, with the result that no informant who is shown this, with a request to look through it, is aware of the test advertisement's identity. *Usually*, this material may be gathered together, bound or stapled in the form of a folder. There are other forms that it could take, however, while still achieving the function of disguise. One is a dummy magazine or newspaper. It would theoretically be possible to extend the term "folder test" to a solution where informants are asked to press a button to get slides of press advertisements appearing on a screen before them. But this might be a little too misleading.

The prime requirement of a folder test must be that the disguise *works*. Otherwise there seems no point in organising a complex rigmarole, when it would be possible simply to show a test advertisement individually and note reactions. This means that obvious qualitative or intrinsic differences between the test advertisement and the rest of the folder, which might signal the identity of the test advertisement, need to be avoided. An "intrinsic difference" means having the test advertisement as the only one of its kind in the folder—for example, the only ad which is aimed at men. A "qualitative difference" refers to the state of finish of the test advertisement—for example, the only ad which has "printers' Latin" instead of body copy. When the test advertisement is in the form of a photographed layout, instead of being a printed "pull," there is an obvious problem when it comes to choosing competitive or background material for the folder. (Few have access to layouts of competitive ads, in an earlier stage of development.) Occasionally some ingenious solutions can be reached by photocopying competitive material, or by making a collage by cutting up several copies of a competitive ad and sticking the pieces together to give a deliberately unfinished look. Ingenious—yes, but it raises two questions:

1   How realistic should a folder in a folder test be made to seem?

2   Is it worth testing unfinished material by means of a folder test?

The case for "realism" has often been urged; particularly by companies offering services involving the placement of specially prepared copies of magazines and newspapers which are accepted by an informant as normal. The emotional appeal of the argument that an advertising pre-test should be made to be as much like real life as possible is perhaps greater than the logic behind it. There is no doubt that most researchers feel more confident when they are introducing something to an informant that is demonstrably ordinary, as opposed to extraordinary. But a pre-test is an extraordinary event anyway. There is nothing whatever natural or realistic about asking somebody a series of questions about what they have been looking at or reading—either in a normal magazine or a made-up folder. In either situation the same kinds of interpretational problems arise in analysing their replies. The argument that greater realism in the folder aids the disguise of the researcher's purpose is a fair one, but this is very different from claiming to have a more realistic test.

Finished test ads quite obviously need to be used for insertion in a made-up magazine or newspaper if they are not to stick out like sore thumbs. This is a useful format for a pretest. But it is not a prerequisite. The point must be repeated that a finished ad may require extremely expensive photography; pre-testing a layout can help to indicate whether the confidence in proceeding with such photography may be justified. This may require a drawing or a photograph from stock that conveys something of the mood and the point intended. Many creative people will tend to argue that a drawing may be less misleading, given that photography, which may have been used before, may have too precise associations for the research audience. In any event, the rough ad for research would normally be submitted as a layout or a photographed layout.

In this case, it is almost always better to have the copy typeset and to include the advertiser's logo exactly as it should be. There is a big difference in reactions that consumers are apt to express when confronted by something that they feel is the preliminary work of professionals and something which they feel looks rather amateurish. This is clear from many test situations when they are asked *after* the test to talk more about their feelings during the test. The visual treatment, then, may be rough, but the copy should be as finished as possible.

A *real* "folder" is what this kind of test ad is going to need. A dummy magazine of sorts is still possible, however. This is a series of stiffish pages which may be on a ring or spirally bound. Sometimes the material fastened to each page is covered with acetate to give a more attractive feel and gloss to the finished product. The cover may be an actual cover from a magazine. The interior pages are also largely taken from magazines, including some editorial material of a timeless variety, such as cookery features, knitting patterns, etc. There are control advertisements and, of course, the test ad. The material can be shifted around the folder, and substituted according to the nature and interests of the target consumers for any particular campaign. Provided no attempt is made to publish the resulting folder outside the test context, there should be no problem over copyright.

Other kinds of folder may dispense with editorial material altogether. The last links with the concept of a dummy magazine may then be severed. But there are always control advertisements. The choice of suitable controls is often vexing. How many should there be? Does it matter mixing black and white with colour? Should they be all the same size? Do they have to be competitive—or should *none* of them be competitive? How about their relevance to the target market?

Our view is that the main purposes of a folder test can be satisfied with a wide range of folders, and that it is pointless looking for exact answers to these questions about the controls. For example, the same conclusions about a test ad for Macleans toothpaste, with regard to impact, communication and the likely influence it might have on consumer associations with the brand, were virtually identical in either of these two test folders:

FOLDER A

Competitive toothpaste
(colour, 11×3)
Frozen peas (colour, 11×3)
Macleans (colour, 11×3)
Cooking fats (colour, 11×3)
Canned peas (colour, 11×3)
Margarine (colour 11×3)

FOLDER B

Eye cosmetic
(colour, half page)
Car (b & w, double-page spread)
Toilet paper (colour, half page)
Macleans (colour, 11×3)
Biscuits (b & w, 10×2)
Canned meat (colour, dps)
Furniture (b & w, 11×3)
Cosmetics (colour, 11×3)

It is important to notice that the overall number of informants who mention the Macleans ad spontaneously after exposure to the whole folder is certainly different, between the two situations. The relative position of the Macleans ad on this impact measure against the other ads also varies. But the conclusions: that the Macleans ad had a high number of spontaneous mentions, with correct brand identification in most cases; that particular points had stuck in the minds of the informants, in a particular order of importance; that the aims of the campaign were likely to be achieved except for one negative, which could be changed once it was identified—all these were common to both tests.

If it is the intention to compare brand name registration, or to make some other comparison between the test ad and a competitive ad, then standardisation is a must; comparing ads with different basic features—for example, black and white versus colour—in folder tests makes no sense. Another inducement to standardisation would be a strong desire for the figures to *mean* something. Some advertisers feel more confident if they know not only that they have an advantage over a competitive ad or a previous ad in seizing a sample of consumers' attention, but also by *how much*. In other words, not just—"this ad gets more people talking about it than our last one," but "74% mentioned us spontaneously and 42% voluntarily broached discussion of at least one point, as opposed to 68% and 30% respectively last time." Our view is that figures as such contribute very little, by comparison with interpretation, in advertisement pre-testing. But, obviously, if you want them and need them, you must have a consistent and logical attitude towards controls if they are to be at all defensible.

Here are some points about what to include in the folder, in summary form:

1 Some, at least, of the controls must be of known interest to the target at which your test ad is aimed. Otherwise, the results of a "Which would you prefer to talk about?" question, or "Did anything strike you as interesting?" or "Do you remember any names of products you saw advertised?" are only meaningful if they are *bad*.

2 Some, at least, of the contrasts must be as likely to catch the eye in sheer visual terms as the test ad—if the test ad is full page and in colour, some of the controls must be as well.

3 Some, preferably all, the controls should be in the same or a very similar state of finish as the test ad.

4 Some of the controls should reflect a similarity of style to the test ad. A creative's objection would be that *his* ad is unique. But this precept is to avoid situations where a test ad in a poster style with a headline and no body copy is tested among four solid blocks of pseudo-editorial advertising. The rule is, avoid extremes.

5 Some of the controls should be for *different* products, if the test ad is the kind that requires any kind of study. This sounds more obvious if you imagine a situation where a respondent is asked to consider several very detailed ads, all for oil filters, at one sitting; by the time your ad is reached, enthusiasm for reading body copy about the principles of oil filtration, never very high at the best of times, may be entirely satiated.

6 Include, if you have a choice, control ads about which you are genuinely curious—either because they are by competitors or because they express a mood or a way of speaking that you may have considered for your brand.

7 Include competitive ads knowing that you will find out *something* about them, but *not* so much as you will about your own test ad; this is because you cannot assume that your criteria or your understanding of the target market are the same as your competitor's.

8 If part of your test involves observation of how the informants react to your test ad, include some editorial material; alternatively include rather more ads (about ten) than might normally be used, of different kinds and sizes. These measures reduce the chance that a high proportion of the informants merely flick through the folder and hand it back, muttering, perhaps, "Just some ads."

9 Do not include as controls *only* ads which have received a great deal of exposure, and have become talking points. This lends directly to frustration if the test ad is a new one. It is a fair argument that *some* controls might indeed be of this mind, as this will be the situation in which a new ad will have to appear, and as the test *cannot* be an investigation into long-term as opposed to short-term effects by its very nature. But no new ad should be expected to seize attention in competition with nothing but the strongest and best-known of the past year's campaigns.

10   Include as many control ads as you like. Fewer than two does not make much sense. More than eight, and the main problems will be with interviewers and control of the operation in the field. This is a very real limitation: "*Every* interviewer," so a very wise and reverend field controller once declared privately, "will return a quota of filled-in questionnaires, but whether they are any more than tarted-up rubbish depends on whether they feel you are imposing on them or not." Carrying an unmanageable 3 by 2ft folder with twelve stiff cardboard pages, and being responsible for rotating the pages before each interview, will give even some of the better interviewers a Bolshevik attitude.

Now for the test itself. Here are two examples, which yield good information if the purposes of the advertising and of a particular test correspond to those specified below.

4.7   Variation A: semi-structured interviews

BACKGROUND—A campaign has been developed to launch a mini-greenhouse which can be assembled at home by an average do-it-yourself enthusiast, under the brand name Crystal Palace. Research is required to see if the campaign (represented by one leader introductory ad with three follow-ups) will effectively seize the attention of potential purchasers (the target market), inform them of the main features of the Crystal Palace and suggest that it has something they might want to buy. Because of the possibility that many kinds of resistance might be involved if informants rejected the idea of getting a Crystal Palace—for example, price, size, diffidence about blowing up the polythene shell with a bicycle pump, etc—it was felt that qualitative work was needed to disentangle reactions in such a way that improvements to the campaign could be worked out logically.

METHOD—Fifty   semi-structured   interviews   to   be conducted by specially trained interviewers (these should ideally be interviewers who can give an articulate account of their impressions at a debriefing, as well as probing pertinently and objectively in the interviews themselves). The informants to be recruited by checking on readership of specialist gardening and d-i-y magazines. Folders to be prepared, consisting of five advertisements (four controls, chosen from gardening and d-i-y magazines, and a photograph of the leader ad, all acetated) and three articles on making sheds, conservatories and frames for the garden.

The procedure is to ask the informant, after establishing his eligibility, to sit down and look through the folder while the interviewer "gets through her paperwork." The interviewer must position herself in such a way as to note colour codes on the backs of each page of the folder, so that she can note how studiously each item in the folder is looked at. This is an "ad lib" folder situation. It makes sense here, in that the time taken on the test ad will give an indication of how curious or serious a proposition it seems to be. Not the whole story, but *part* of the information.

Then the folder is requested back. The rest of the interview goes like this:

Q1a "Did you see anything interesting in the folder?"

PROBE: Details of editorial/ad mentioned. What was interesting about it? . . . Why? . . . Serious idea for the informant or not . . . why?

b "Anything else that struck you as interesting?

PROBE AS ABOVE

Q2 "What other things were in the folder? Can you remember them? . . . Anything else?"

PROBE DETAILS

Q3 "Sometimes when you see an article or an advertisement for something new to make or build for the garden, you might feel instinctively 'Yes, I might try that' or 'Not on your life.' Did you get either of these feelings about anything you saw in the folder?"

PROBE FULLY—IF NECESSARY ASK Q4

Q4 "There was one advertisement in the folder for a mini-greenhouse kit. Do you remember seeing anything like that?"

PROBE: Name, Details of ad. Details of product. Feeling about it.

Q5   "I'd like to show you this page again. (SHOW CRYSTAL PALACE AD) Could you please try to say what sort of thoughts passed through your mind when you first looked at it?

PROBE: Did you look at part of it first? . . . Which parts did you look at? . . . What were your main feelings about each part? . . . What were your main feelings about the whole ad? . . .

The question form for Q5 works quite well, although one must not expect every informant to introspect honestly and accurately and give you back exactly what went through his mind. What it *does* do is act as an aide-memoire to some strong impressions he may have had, and as a spur to examining the details and saying what he thinks of them, without guiding him one way or the other. Other researchers may prefer a completely open question—for example, "Please look at this again. . . . " (LOOK AT INFORMANT INQUIRINGLY) This may work just as well in many cases, but the more standardised question reduces the chances of interviewer bias.

From this point on, the role of the folder declines. The informant knows, or should know, what the purpose of the interview is. He might, however, make some comment to the effect that another ad or piece of editorial explains construction detail much more simply. Having the folder there to refer to is then helpful. A good qualitative interviewer will sense when it might be a useful aid to show another page of the folder again, without needing to be asked. Further questions would be specific, for example:

Q6   "The headline says 'I'll huff and I'll puff and I'll blow your greenhouse up.' What do you feel other gardening men will feel when they see this?"

It depends on the copy and the illustration!

Later in the interview, the follow-up ads are introduced and reactions to them are probed. Do they tell the same story about the product? What do they contribute? Are they consistent? Further questions will be needed in those areas.

It might be noticed that nowhere is it proposed to ask whether the informant *likes* any of the advertisements in the folder or which he likes best. This is of doubtful relevance at the best of times and certainly can be avoided in this field where a challenge to the imagination is probably more important than a warm, cosy feeling.

4.8   Variation B: structured interviews

BACKGROUND—Let us assume that the leader ad tested above was shot down in flames. (Given the headline, it would hardly be surprising!) But the research suggested what was wrong about the campaign. Having qualitative work helped sort out those instances where antagonism towards the idea of the Crystal Palace itself was the primary influence on informants, and others where communication as such was inadequate or misleading. With this information the creative team is briefed to produce an improved version of the campaign that will communicate the following, clearly and winningly:

1   The name of the new product.
2   Its basic features and purpose.
3   How it differs from others.
4   How it is assembled.

On top of this, the advertising would have to attract attention to a campaign—to be filled in, torn off and sent to the Crystal Palace manufacturers requesting a free demonstration at home, without obligation.

The team delivered a new version, called Campaign Y. This crystallised the above information, with a big illustration to help everyone understand both assembly and use. But another idea emerged while this was being prepared: why not use a presenter—the familiar features of Handy Grist, the well-known d-i-y and gardening pundit of screen and radio? The argument for this development (Campaign Z) was that keen gardeners would read more attentively what the incomparable H Grist had to say and, if they saw him urging everyone to cut out the coupon, they would reach for their scissors that much more quickly.

Research is required to see which campaign meets the campaign objectives more satisfactorily, how effective the better of the two campaigns is going to be and whether any further improvements are possible.

METHOD—Numbers are going to mean more in this piece of research than they did in the last. Two panels of 150 informants are recruited on the same basis as before. "But this costs money!" cries the advertiser. So it does: approximately 0.5% of the advertising budget in the first year. Big deal.

To keep unnecessary expenditure down we recommend sequential sampling. This is a procedure which allows for systematic analysis of the findings as soon as the first results come out of the field. When it is obvious from this analysis that there is a clear-cut result, whatever the remaining interviews yield, the fieldwork is halted. The more homogeneous the sample, the safer this procedure is likely to be. Some research and fieldwork companies dislike working on this basis because it demands greater flexibility. But for any organisation that does a lot of work of this kind, being able to apply the brake can save a lot of money and time.

There are two folders this time. They might as well be the same as those that were used before, but the editorial could be missed out. Observation will not play so much of a part in this exercise as recording evidence of communication. The folders differ in that the leader ad for Campaign Y appears in one and for Campaign Z in the other.

Informants are recruited as before. The quota for each interviewer comprises *equal numbers* in Panel Y and Panel Z (corresponding to the folder each one sees). This is crucial. Interviewer bias most certainly affects folder tests, particularly the recall questions. It can be reduced by the training and briefing that the field team receives. But it cannot be ruled out.

Hold it. If interviewer bias exists, doesn't this mean that the whole practice is questionable? No. It means that it is less rigorously scientific than many prefer to believe. But it still produces meaningful data, for all that. This is the case with consumer research *as a whole.*

Subsamples forming key quota controls should also be divided in such a way that each interviewer has equal or near equal numbers of interviews to conduct within each. Otherwise you may end up with intriguing artefacts such as "Nonusers had more to say about the benefits perceived from the ad than heavy users"; this *may* be the case, depending on whether both non-users and heavy users were interviewed by the same interviewers. Regional comparisons, for obvious reasons, are often suspect.

In the Crystal Palace test, equal numbers will be in each panel at each sampling point; a north *v* south comparison on reactions to Y as opposed to Z will be legitimate, although the base will be low.

The fieldwork supervision will analyse product name recall in the interviews received back, by interviewer; if an interviewer is consistently lower or higher than the rest in terms which suggest lack of probing or misuse of lists—for example, "Did you see an ad for Crystal Palace? . . . for Traumatic Woodsheds?" etc—her quota can be replaced.

The interview starts off the same for both panels. The interviewer offers the informant a folder which he is asked to look through. After one minute's inspection it is requested back. (If he returns it sooner, that is his choice: you can take a consumer to the advertisements but you cannot make him drink them in.) Stipulating one minute has the advantage that the interviewers are more likely to be all applying the test in a similar way and that the questions afterwards are a check on what is communicated during a quick look at the ads rather than a studious contemplation. When comparing advertisements for their delivery of clear information at speed, this latter point means greater sensitivity.

Some researchers—for example, Dr Paul Lyness in the US—have advocated the exercise of greater control over exposure of sucessive pages in a folder. Interviewers have been trained to mutter to themselves "One hippopotamus, two hippopotamus, three hippopotamus," before whisking over the page so that there is a standard three seconds per advertisement. Our view is that this gives a false sense of advantage through greater precision. Even with very carefully trained interviewers it tends to make the informant feel he is undergoing a test rather than being asked to look through some advertisements in anything like a normal way. Of course, the situation is unreal anyway, but irritating or unnerving the informant must be self-defeating. Research studies in which informants are interviewed *afterwards*, about how they felt during a pre-test, show that this is a real danger.

One last point before the questionnaire itself: should the ads in each folder be rotated? If you are anxious only to test Campaign Y *v* Campaign Z and to get a general idea of how they compare with the other ads, you might leave each in the same place, provided this is the same for both test ads. The usual practice in this case is to put the test ad between the middle ad and the last ad in the folder. Psychological laboratory tests show that such a position—for example, seventh out of nine —is at a slight disadvantage for recall, compared with material in other positions. (Therefore, when the results are presented, no one can complain that the test ad was specially favoured.) But should you be anxious to check the performance of Y and Z against particular ads, as well as against each other, then you must make sure that there is an adequate rotation system, so that no ad in the folder is favoured by its position.

QUESTIONNAIRE

Q1   Here is a folder with some advertisements in it. Would you please have a quick look through it?
SHOW FOLDER: WITHDRAW AFTER ONE MINUTE

a   We have not got a great deal of time. Is there a particular advertisement that you would like to talk about? Which?

b   Please tell me all about this one.
Product
Brand name
Manufacturer, etc
Details of product
Details of ad

c   What specially struck you about this one?

Q2   Are there any other products you can remember seeing advertised in the folder? Which?
PROBE: Did it have any other name? . . .
Products
Brand names

Q3   Did any of these ads strike you as being:

a   Difficult to understand?
PROBE: Which? . . . Any others? . . . Why? . . .

b   Particularly useful to somebody like yourself?

c   Difficult to believe?

d   Rather stupid?

Q4   Were any of the products the sort of thing:

a   You might want to have yourself?

b   You might like to make or put up yourself?

Q5a   Did you notice any coupons that somebody reading the ad is supposed to clip out and send off for more information, or for a demonstration?
IF YES

b   What products were these coupons for? Any others?

Q6   Here is a list of products. Can you tell me which of these were in the folder, and which were not?
SHOW LIST CONTAINING NAMES OF FOLDER PRODUCTS AND SPOOFS

Q7   IF NECESSARY: There was an ad for Crystal Palace mini-greenhouses in the folder.

a   Please describe the Crystal Palace product in your own words.
PROBE: What is it like? . . . What does it do? . . .

b   Please tell me all you can about the advertisement for Crystal Palace.
PROBE AS NECESSARY: What did it say about the product? . . . What did it say about construction? . . . What did it show? . . . . .

Q8   SHOW CRYSTAL PALACE AD AGAIN
Is there anything else that occurs to you about this ad, now you are looking at it a second time?

Q9   SPECIFIC QUESTIONS ABOUT DETAIL OF CAMPAIGNS Y AND Z ACCORDING TO PANEL

E.g.

Q9   (Y) What do you think about the picture?

      (Z) What do you think about Handy Grist?

Q13   What do you think about the product in terms of value for money?

Q14   Are there any other questions you would like to have answered about Crystal Palace? . . . Any others?

Q15a What do you feel about filling in the coupon? Would
you do so, do you think, if you saw the ad in the paper?
RECORD WORD FOR WORD—IF YES OR UNCERTAIN:

b   Would you like to fill one in *now* (SHOW SPARE COUPON)
and I'll pass it on for you?
SHOW OTHER ADS IN Y OR Z CAMPAIGN, ACCORDING TO
PANEL

Q16   Here are some other ads which might appear after the
first one that you saw. Please tell me anything that
occurs to you about them. . . .
PROBE—SHOW Y OR Z LEADER AD OF DIFFERENT PANEL:

Q17   Here is a completely different introduction to Crystal
Palace. Please tell me what you feel about this. . . .

It should be noted that Q15a and b is used as a test of persuasion, rather than the conventional "Now what do you feel
about buying brand X? Please show me on this scale how
likely or unlikely you are to buy this product in the next few
days." This scale question has the advantage that you can
probe the answer (although respondents are often tongue-tied
about it) and it is more natural for fast-moving consumer
goods. Q15b gives a relevant (and a tough) *behavioural* measure. A behavioural measure at this stage is always to be
engineered if possible. One method is to say something like
this:

> I could arrange, if you like, for your name to be passed
> on to the manufacturer for you to receive a packet of
> this product. You would have to pay the recommended
> price for it. I can't sell it to you myself, but if you give me
> permission, I will pass your name on.

Obviously, a positive answer to this question must reflect a
desire to buy. The interviewer *may* have sounded persuasive,
but the inference to be drawn from a higher positive response
to one ad over another is that one ad is more persuasive, even
if it is only reminding the informant that the product has been
found reasonable in the past. When such questions are being
worked out, great care must be taken to keep within the Code
of Practice of the Market Research Society, which forbids the
use of surveys for the purpose of selling.

When considering impact measurement, it is worth checking through for a mention of Crystal Palace at *any* point during the answers to Q1 to 5. The perfect success, of course, would be for everyone to mention it at Q1 or, failing that, Q2. But there are other opportunities, before the prompt card appears, and all the evidence needs to be inspected together. Furthermore, it is important to compare panels Y and Z for the *average* number of brands and products that they are capable of mentioning at Q2. Should there be a difference here, weighting might be necessary before the raw figures for Crystal Palace are compared from each panel.

Sometimes, the results of this kind of test are not clear-cut to the point of one campaign being clearly the better on all points. But it will show the strengths and the weaknesses of both on the criteria specified. It will also, *if* the probing is carefully done and full answers are recorded on the open-ended questions, indicate more about how the target is reacting to the advertising. This is always valuable—even when it is obvious that a new campaign has to be developed.

5

Pre-testing
TV Commercials

When a new person joins a firm he is often an embarrassment to his superiors until he is integrated into the work flow. Junior executives in advertising agencies frequently find themselves in this position. "What on earth can we find for him to do until he can safely be entrusted with actual work?

Once he has read all the back reports he is often given the task of assessing the techniques for pre-testing television commercials on offer at the time. This entails collecting all the brochures from the research companies, talking to some of them and producing a report. Literally hundreds of young executives must have been asked to undertake these studies. Their advantage is that they are not urgent but time consuming, thus keeping the apprentice occupied but readily available for the real action when it arises.

Several important considerations connected with commercial pre-testing are implicit in this ritual activity and it is worthwhile looking at them.

1 Pre-testing television commercials is a subject of enduring interest to advertisers and their agents—much more so than any other advertising research. Mainly this can be attributed to the greater expense involved in making and showing TV commercials. Important too, though, is the glamour associated with commercials. Here the scope for creativity is greatest and consequently so is the opportunity to score and lose points. Reputations, both individual and agency, are more at risk. That goes for the brand manager's reputation, too.
2 There are lots of techniques to assess. One implication of this is an absence of agreement on how commercials should be

pre-tested. Controversy is more common than with other types of research and people are prepared to go to the stake for their beliefs. Principally this state of affairs is due to the complex functions of a commercial and the absence of any generally accepted method of validating pre-test predictions in the market-place.

3 The combination of a high involvement activity (commercial making) and a poorly validated research (commercial pre-testing) means nervousness and uncertainty. Hence the periodic need to see what is happening in the research world and whether the answer has been found or indeed whether the question is worth asking.

In these circumstances the uninitiated need to tread very warily. As a first and vital step one must be clear-headed about why pre-testing is being undertaken. The following are the main categories of pre-testing rationales.

5.1   Systematic development and assessment

Advertisers who are in the big league usually undertake more or less routine pre-tests of their commercials. With the huge expenditures involved in regular television advertising even marginal improvements pay for the cost of the research involved.

The basic philosophy of such testing is, first, to reject any commercials that are not up to standard and, second, to isolate the strong points of a commercial or campaign with a view to exploiting them further. In practice the first aim predominates. Some kind of normative yardstick is established and commercials are viewed with suspicion if their pre-test scores do not measure up to the norms. "Norm" to many people, particularly creative people whose work is being judged, is a horror word and the relevance and validity of norms is questioned.

Certainly uncritical use of normative data has been responsible for the destruction of many excellent commercials. It has also encouraged the production of cliché, or safe commercials, that meet the norm. On the other hand, the systematic pre-testing of a large number of commercials on the same measures yields a bank of information which is of obvious value in picking out the sheep from the goats. A sense of perspective is required because small differences from norms are often artifacts. But many advertisers use this kind of data to good effect in their campaign development—*if* there is diagnostic follow-through to indicate *how* norms are being passed or missed.

5.2   Creative feedback

Here the basic orientation is to research a commercial, primarily with a view to getting a reaction from consumers which can be fed back into the creative process at a practical level. Whereas normative systems tend in the nature of things to be quantitative in orientation, feedback research tends to be qualitative—that is, usually carried out by group discussions or, less commonly, depth or semi-structured interviews.

At a technical level both types of research and both broad objectives can be accommodated in the same basic research framework but there is a genuine difference in orientation. A normative system is more likely to find favour with a manufacturer that wants to make sure that the agency is doing its job. Smaller-scale qualitative research is viewed more sympathetically by advertising agencies that find the more vivid findings ("straight from the horse's mouth research") of greater value towards understanding consumer reactions (as opposed to having them filtered through computer printouts) and therefore towards actually improving commercials—which after all is their main concern.

There are exceptions to this general picture but the two themes will be clearly recognised in practice. It is also generally true that normative systems find their institutional expression in specialist independent research operations and feedback systems in the creative workshops of advertising agencies. Creative Workshop accurately describes the philosophy of pre-testing of this type.

5.3   Ad hoc pre-testing

As its name implies this is something of a rag-bag category but covers a large proportion of day-to-day commercial testing. In so far as categorisation is possible at all, often commercials fall into two types:

1   Normal problem commercials.

2   Unpleasant problem commercials.

Among the first group are to be found commercials for new products, and the object is to assess how accurately and correctly the product is presented. Clearly it is important with a new product to make certain that consumers get hold of the right end of the stick at the outset. Communication is covered in greater depth than with commercials for an established product and questions of usage and attitude more akin to market research than advertising research are often included.

Other commercials which are researched in a similar way are for those products which are advertised heavily but infrequently such as those for highly seasonal items.

Commercial testing in the second category usually means trouble. Something in a commercial bugs somebody with enough influence to matter and research is ordered to sort it out. The client thinks a small child shown eating an ice-cream will turn the stomach of his customers; the chairman's wife thinks a girl is showing too much bosom. A pre-test is tailor made to allay fears or have the commercial altered—or in the grisly extreme, to have the account moved.

To use the rubric of market research, before embarking on a commercial pre-test, you should decide which of these descriptions best fits you:

1   I want a quality control system to make sure my
       commercials are up to scratch.

2   I want to hear what viewers get from commercials, and
       what they think about them, so I can make them better.

3   This commercial is particularly important for the
       product and it must be right.

4   In my/his opinion there is something wrong with that
       commercial and I want my/his doubts allayed/confirmed. (Cross out whichever alternative does not
       apply.)

       None of the above categories describes me.

       What I want is

Honesty in completing this questionnaire helps everybody —especially the outside research agency. Having decided why you are testing, the next questions are when to test and how to test.

Tests should be carried out as early as possible, preferably in rough form. Commercials are expensive to make and alterations take time which runs out fast when air dates are fixed. When a considerable investment has been made in making a commercial, and reshooting would take a superhuman effort, there is a strong vested interest on everybody's part to leave the commercial alone so long as the pre-test isn't an unmitigated disaster. Research at an early stage before personal and financial commitments are too great, and while there is time to take remedial action, should be the aim.

How rough, it is frequently asked, is rough? Can all commercials be satisfactorily tested in rough form? Principally pre-production commercials can take the following form:

1   At simplest, a static storyboard showing scenes from the commercial with the script in written form.

2   One degree more sophisticated, slides of selected scenes from the storyboard shown in synchronisation with a soundtrack linked to the slide projector.

3   Slides of selected scenes put on film and shown with synchronised soundtrack on a machine resembling a television set. La Belle Courier machines are an example. Cassettes can also be used, as with the Sony.

4   Drawn scenes from the commercial photographed with a movie camera to carry some impression of movement with an added soundtrack. Occasionally genuine animation is used.

5   Videotaped commercials using non-professional actors and fairly simple visual devices—the ingenious can produce quite spectacular results.

There are some variations on these themes but those described above account for the bulk of "rough" commercial treatments that get tested.

As a general guide, the more "meaty" the commercial is in terms of its directness of communication of consumer benefits, the easier it is to test in the more primitive forms (1 and 2 above). The same can be claimed of visual situations which are obvious (e.g. South Seas, jungle, frozen north) rather than subtle (e.g. children's adventure playground). This is fortunate because it is precisely in these situations that an early warning system is most needed. For example, with a genuinely new product it is easy to see whether people understand what it is for and what further information about it is needed. Further, in a field such as beer advertising, humour is currently the accepted idiom; rough treatment testing allows the kite of a serious factual approach to be flown, or an appeal to virility.

For the majority of commercials shown, some form of animation is preferable. Conventional wisdom says the soundtrack itself should be of professional finished quality and our experience bears this out. Informants seem quite willing to make the imaginative leap with the visual but can be irritated and confused by a poor soundtrack.

Some commercials, particularly those of the mood variety or dependent on subtle photographic effects, are clearly more difficult to pre-test in rough form than others, and some are impossible. However, most commercials are amenable to useful checking before final shooting. Drawing the line is largely a matter of experience; if in doubt, objective advice should be sought.

As mentioned in Chapter 2, at Leo Burnett, London, creative directors sometimes introduce their rough treatments to group discussions in the Creative Workshop. They are often the best people to explain what kind of picture behind the pictures needs to be imagined. They appreciate the implications for finished production that come from puzzled looks or questions at particular points. From a research point of view, this procedure works well, provided the creative director doesn't argue the toss with informants afterwards.

There is always a nagging doubt that test results from a rough commercial test will bear no relation to a test of the real article, making the whole exercise an irrelevance. Doubts of this nature entered the minds of J Lyons & Co which undertook a study designed to settle the matter. The research convinced them that storyboard results correlated strongly with those of the finished product. Over a series of commercials all evaluation scores for the storyboard commercial tests were lower than for finished commercials but the rank ordering was virtually the same.

ASI, a specialist pre-testing company in the USA with considerable experience in the field, also finds this general correlation. American agencies, incidentally, are much more likely to devise several treatments for a commercial and sort them out with pre-testing than are European companies. In Europe and Britain agencies tend to commit themselves to an approach early on and prefer to develop it rather than scrap it. Economics and a different timescale determine these attitudes rather than differences in professionalism. Much greater media expenditure in the States means that production costs of commercials are a much smaller proportion of total advertising expenditure than in Europe.

Even if a commercial cannot, for whatever reason, be researched in storyboard form all is not lost. Tests of finished commercials can expose faults that are inexpensively remedied. Often some of the material needs to be picked up again from the cutting-room floor. An alteration in the soundtrack or additional titling could be all that is required. With more fundamental faults the cost of giving expensive air time to a dud commercial against remaking must be grimly assessed.

5.4   Mechanics of pre-testing

Unfortunately, for purposes of exposition, the categories of commercial testing problems set out above do not nearly correlate with the techniques available for solving them. All quality control testing is quantitative and most creative feed-back research is qualitative but it is difficult to go much further than that. Perhaps the easiest way is to consider quantitative and qualitative techniques separately.

QUANTITATIVE METHODS—Although all quantitative methods are concerned with relatively large samples of people answering a structured questionnaire, there is a great divide in format—namely, theatre testing against hall testing.

5.5   Theatre tests

With theatre tests informants are invited along to a studio or cinema, ostensibly to give their opinions of pre-release feature films—indeed, sometimes they do. Interspersed in the programme, however, are television commercials and these are assessed by means of questionnaires completed by the participants under the direction of a master of ceremonies. Showings last about two or three hours and eight or so commercials are tested.

ADVANTAGES—There are some advantages to a test structure of this kind.

1 Informants are available for a longish period which makes some measures such as recall and attitude changes much easier to handle. There is time to explain the use of apparatus.
2 Because several commercials are tested at each session costs, theoretically, can be lower.

DISADVANTAGES—The following must be set against the above advantages:

1 Sampling is difficult. The invited audience tends to approximate in its age and social composition to that of normal cinema goers. Young ABC1s are easy to lure to the session; C2DE housewives with four children are not. Although 300 people normally attend a session, the target group for a commercial may be much smaller than that. Much effort is required to ensure that those attending sessions have some relevance to the research requirements. Regional facilities for testing are also hard to come by as a rule. The personality of those accepting invitations is skewed towards those with a not very active social life, for obvious reasons.
2 Questionnaires are completed in a body by informants themselves. Quite apart from the inherent limitations of self-completed interviews (semi-literacy, etc) there is the danger of collusion which can be particularly damaging with measures such as recall of the commercial.
3 It is sometimes argued too that the large screen usual in theatre testing is not suitable for TV commercials, although the evidence is limited. We do not know exactly how and to what extent this shortcoming manifests itself. But certain eating shots are undeniably less appealing on a big screen. This much has been clear from informants' comments.

5.6 Hall tests

The hall can be a church hall, a room in a pub or restaurant or hotel—any public hall available for hire near a busy centre. Occasionally a caravan or trailer is used. Instead of being invited beforehand to attend the research session, informants are stopped in the street and persuaded to go in immediately and take part in the test. This imposes a limiting factor as it is unreasonable to expect people to break their shopping or whatever for more than twenty minutes or so. The interviewer takes informants in to the hall where they see the test commercial(s), usually on videotape, and then they are taken through a questionnaire. Usually six to eight interviewers work at a test location and, over a period of a day or two, 80 to 200 people might be interviewed. A fieldwork supervisor or an executive is in overall charge of the proceedings.

The balance of advantage and disadvantage is:

ADVANTAGES
1 Sampling can be much more precise. By asking filter questions it is possible to ensure that exactly the right user groups with the correct balance of sex, age and social class are interviewed. Housewives with young children, difficult to inveigle into a theatre session, are easy to pull in. Tests can be set up virtually anywhere in the country at short notice. Interviewing can be extended through lunch-hours and evenings to pick up elusive working informants.
2 The interviewing situation itself is much more controlled. Questionnaires can be more complex and attitudes probed—a valuable facility with new-product or problem commercials. Commercials can be readily shown and reshown much more flexibly than with theatre tests.

DISADVANTAGES
1 Against this there is the difficulty of taking recall measures, much less "attitude shifts" in the comparatively short time available. Not everyone will *want* these measures, but they are distinctly "unreal" in rapid hall tests.
2 Syndication is virtually impossible so hall testing can be expensive.
3 It is obvious to informants from the outset that they are to look at advertising—although in a well-organised session they

will not know which commercial in a reel is the test commercial.

4 Hall tests can *look* rather amateurish. Theoretically this should not be a consideration but where issues of confidence are concerned it counts. Executives of theatre testing companies are anxious to invite clients to test sessions in order to impress them. Because trained people run the sessions several evenings a week the proceedings are slick and well managed. Anyone who has visited the ASI test theatre in Los Angeles cannot fail but to be impressed—it's like something out of a James Bond film. Clients, on the other hand, are normally discouraged from attending hall tests—even by giving them wrong dates, times and directions. A dusty church hall with the Wolf Cubs' totem pole in the corner, filled with untidy people cluttered with their shopping, children and waiting husbands can be an embarrassment. We would not like to overstate this difference but it certainly exists.

5.7 Measures taken in commercial pre-tests (quantitative)

At this point the conscientious reader may experience a *déja vu* feeling as the measures taken in a television pre-test are very similar to those taken in press ad pre-testing already discussed. However, like so many aspects of advertising research the subject does not lend itself easily to neat demarcation. Commercials act in a different way from press ads, although their ultimate aim is the same. Potentially they can inform instantly, more dramatically, with more detail and product demonstration. Questionnaires for commercial pre-tests and experimental designs tend, in practice, to be more elaborate than those for press ads, while some measures only make sense in relation to commercials. At the risk of some repetition, therefore, it is worth considering all the parts of a commercial pre-test.

So with the informant sitting either in a theatre armed with a questionnaire and a pen, or sitting next to an interviewer in a hall, what is to be done?

It goes without saying that the intentions behind the commercial should dictate choice of questions. There are a bewildering variety of questions that can be put but the main variants are as follows.

COMMUNICATION—"What do you think the advertiser was trying to put across to you in the commercial?" is the classic communication question. Here are some typical data from alternative commercials for a floor-cleaning product:

CLEANING PROPERTIES

Lifts dirt off any surface	25
Gets right under dirt	4
Cleans dirt off surface	*
Effective/cleans well	15
Better than others	6

CONVENIENCE

No rinsing needed	19
No mixing needed	13
No scrubbing needed	6
Sprays on	6
No mess	6
Cleans all in one go	11
Easy—unspecified	26
Quick—unspecified	10
Quick and easy—unspecified	5
Easy—specified above	6
Quick—specified above	1
Quick and easy—specified above	*

VALUE

Cleans all large areas	6
Economical/goes far	2
Other answers	1
Nothing/don't know	*

Immediately one can see the general pattern of communication and the relative balance of cleaning properties to convenience elements. But specific evaluation of points is more tricky. Only a minority mention that no rinsing is required, which could be an important product benefit. Does this mean that the majority have not grasped that point? One cannot be sure. Other supplementary questions are needed if a specific point is really to be pinned down. Usually probing is the answer in the form of "Any other things the commercial was saying? Anything else?" Or a prompt may be used: "Do you recall anything about rinsing in the commercial? What did it say?"

Alternatively a battery of questions to check comprehension can be devised.

"Some of the following things were said in the commercial and some were not. SHOW CARD. Could you tell me which are true and which false? . . . No rinsing is required. . . . The cleaner in aerosol form. . . . The price is 27p . . ." etc, etc.

Total recall of all sales points and action in the commercial may not be required—the concern may be with what the consumer takes to be the *main* message of the commercial. Emphasis is placed in the question on the main message or if an alternative form of wording could be used: "Suppose you were to describe the floor cleaner to a friend; what would you say about it?"

Quite apart from specific messages there is a general communication element which is sometimes important. How will a new product be seen in the market context by the consumer —for example, at the cheaper or more expensive end? Any questions can be designed to assess this. What kind of mood does the commercial create—again an area of communication which can be measured with the appropriate techniques.

The extent to which communication is pursued in the questionnaire depends entirely on what job the commercial is designed to do. New product commercials must tell a readily understandable product story and the need for comprehensive communication questions is obvious. Commercials for existing products often say very little in a specific sense: rather, they may be intended to put the product before the eye of the public in a desirable way. In practice, the degree of emphasis to be placed on communication questions is easy to decide— provided it is agreed between advertiser and advertising agency before the test.

5.8 Impact

Whether the commercial will attract attention and stick in the mind is an obvious source of worry to advertisers. Unfortunately both at a theoretical and practical level "impact" is a nasty parameter to measure. Practically, impact is measured in two principal ways:

1 In theatre tests, at the end of the session, informants are asked to write down all the products they can remember having seen advertised in the course of the showing. A decent time interval has elapsed so the question is sensible. However, collusion is a real problem.

2 In hall tests a reel is normally shown containing the test commercial with five or six others (the screen equivalent of a folder test). Immediately after having seen the commercials, informants are asked to recall the products they have seen advertised. They may be asked to say which they would prefer to discuss, too, and to suggest *degree* of impact. Difficulties can be encountered when informants are recruited at differential rates—there is a danger they may come into the hall during the showing of the test reel and see part of it; or they could hear the test commercials again during the course of the interview. Organising flair is required in the researcher, quite as much as interpretation skill.

A percentage figure indicating the proportion recalling a commercial in a theatre test session or from a test reel in a hall is a purely relative measure, being entirely a function of the test as set up. If theatre sessions (God forbid) lasted six hours or the test reel contained twenty commercials not seven, the figure would be much lower. Other commercials shown in either test also affect the issue—if you are up against six drab commercials you shine while the best may eclipse you. Really, therefore, comparisons of effectiveness can properly be made only between test commercials subjected to very similar testing.

Whatever the characteristics of the index of impact, and the difficulties in measurement, how does it relate—if one can be metaphysical briefly—to reality?

This has been touched on already in Chapter 2. But it is worth discussing again in this context.

The supposition is that short-term successful recall of a commercial means that it, and the brand name, are more likely to entrench themselves in the mind of viewers when they see it on the screen at home. As a consequence they will be more likely to remember the product and buy it, or buy it more often. After all, if consumers can't remember the commercial how can it influence their behaviour?

Unfortunately this simple view does not accord with the findings of modern psychology. Attention, learning and memory are peculiarly complex functions, and there is no reason why they should work in the same way for commercials of varying complexity, among consumers of varying intelligence. Suffice it to say here that people may need several exposures to material which seems curious, or has associations with a personal need, before they can put into words the detail in relation to the brand. They can also be influenced by information which they have not consciously imbibed. The fact that a commercial cannot be remembered does not mean it hasn't done its job. Day-after recall of the previous evening's commercials is so low, on average, as to discourage anyone from spending money on television if recall is taken as a measure of effectiveness.

Recall measures have their uses, however, in providing a touch of discipline in television advertising. As a matter of common observation one frequently hears people say "Did you see the commercial the other night with the kittens in it?" or "Did you see the cartoon with the giraffe driving a vintage car? I can't remember what it was advertising, but is was very good." Sometimes the brilliance of a commercial can upstage the product completely. Creative self-indulgence is not only confined to shooting all commercials in the Caribbean, but extends to making interesting films with the product tacked on as an afterthought. Outraged creative men will argue with some justification that pre-tests are single-exposure affairs and that in real life reinforming effects will be achieved with repeated viewings. But whether they are right or not, in a given instance, it seems a better bet to go along with a commercial that is *locked into the brand's identity* and does not risk expanding the sales of competitors.

5.9 Persuasion and propensity to purchase

Earlier we cast doubts on the possibility of measuring the persuasiveness of an advertisement by asking people direct questions on the subject. Nobody has been able to demonstrate a convincing relationship between such questions and subsequent sales effectiveness.

Notwithstanding those inconvenient facts, many pre-test

questionnaires carry questions on interest in buying the product and whether the commercial was considered to be persuasive or not. Why? Several factors operate. Even though sales validation is lacking, many experienced practitioners feel that persuasion questions discriminate between good and bad commercials, at the extremes. Commercials which by common consensus are truly awful get lower scores on all evaluative measures including persuasion, and sometimes they come out *worst* on persuasion. Good commercials, as defined by the gut feeling of those involved in creating the advertising, may get any kind of persuasion score, however. Many of the latter are not *intended* as converters, but as reminders.

Persuasion measures are useful as probes for strengths and weaknesses in a commercial. Consider the following data taken from a test of a commercial for a dessert.

Would you say the commercial tended to increase or decrease your interest in buying the product (a lot or a little)?

	%
Interest increased a lot	14
Interest increased a little	12
Neither increased nor decreased	35
Interest decreased a little	35
Interest decreased a lot	4

Among those whose interest in buying was *not* increased by seeing the commercial the reasons given were:

	%
Did not like the boy (unspecified further)	38
Disliked boy's accent	24
Child greedy, ate too quickly	21
Mother too soft, lax, indulgent	18
Have tried product, don't like it	14
Never take any notice of advertising	5
Just like any other commercial	3
Dull, boring, stupid	2
Don't know	10
Other answers	6

On these figures alone things were looking bad for the boy.

No data from other questions was forthcoming with a counterbalancing advantage. The commercial was reshot without him.

But was this the right decision in view of the suspect nature of the persuasion measure, or of the like-dislike criterion for that matter?

Might not the stimulus of an irritating child have proved at least as sales effective as a bland, unobjectionable child? No one really knows, but in this particular case the creative intention was to produce an attractive scene of a small boy being served his pudding by a doting mum and tucking into it with gusto; is was *not* part of the plan to sear the product into the minds of a nauseated populace by exhibiting an ill-mannered brat pigging down his food, watched by a mother who should have been clipping his ear instead of ladling more of the stuff into him. Doubts on this score had partially prompted the pre-test anyway.

Other measures could have brought the problem into the open; the persuasion measure was simply a convenient focusing device.

Some prefer to put the question into the third person to avoid making anyone too defensive about admitting to being affected by a commercial—for example, "Would you say that other people are likely to be persuaded . . . ?" With certain types of product or commercial—for example, zany or image commercials or products sold for their associations rather than their intrinsic worth—this is a sensible precaution. But the question is still better treated as an introduction to a probe, not as a stimulus for a real response.

Another example, this time of the propensity to purchase measure, is provided by a company taking a product lock, stock, barrel and commercial from the States to put on the British market. Sensibly they pre-tested the commercial. One problem was the rather unusual jokey name for the product (which unfortunately cannot be disclosed). Questions were asked about the name and data analysed by whether it was considered to be suitable or not. The most dramatic difference was found in the propensity to purchase measure as the figures below demonstrate:

	NAME SUITABLE	NAME UNSUITABLE
Would definitely buy	39%	17%
Would probably buy	23%	16%
Might buy	17%	27%
Probably would not buy	7%	20%
Definitely would not buy	14%	20%

For many housewives the name was so absurd that they could not take the product seriously. Again, the fundamental objection couched in terms of ultimate truth is irrelevant when propensity to purchase is used as a probe rather than taken at its face value.

Some indicators of the selling power of commercials, however, are not used diagnostically but claim to deliver the goods and predict sales. The most famous of these is the gift choice method originated in the USA by Horace Schwerin and currently used by Audience Studies Inc, probably the largest and most experienced pre-testing company in the world.

Gift choice can be operated only in a theatre situation and works in the following way. Participants are told that there is a prize draw and they select from a list of prizes (products, brands) which they would like if they won. All prizes are equivalent in cash terms. Some of the products are those advertised in the test commercials. By a more or less plausible subterfuge, participants repeat the process after the commercials have been shown. Invariably, the proportions choosing each product change. Of the samples 15% might, for example, choose £2 worth of a brand of biscuits at the beginning of the test and 20% at the end. The 5% increase is the pre-post shift and its magnitude is said to predict the effectiveness of the commercial. By comparing a particular shift against the shifts obtained from testing commercials of the same length in similar product fields the test advertisement is adjudged to the good, the bad or the indifferent. Experiments relating scores to buying behaviour and claiming a close correlation have been conducted.

No other measure in the entire field of marketing research has aroused such bitterness and controversy as the pre-post shift. Men do not come to blows over the relative merits of a triangular taste test as opposed to paired comparisons. But the pre-post shift has produced the most fearful scenes of violence. Why re-create them, now that the dust has, in most places, settled? Because they *still* cast their shadow over creative attitudes to pre-testing. The main sources of discontent have been:

1   When the pre-post shift was pioneered by Horace Schwerin in the late 1950s and early 60s, marketing men were

unused to handling advertising research data. All advertisers were feeling their way in the business, and thought they had the ultimate weapon. Unfortunately, a fairly widespread practice of rejecting commercials which did not achieve a predetermined magnitude of shift established itself. This undoubtedly caused great distress among those creating the commercials and although many claimed they could always beat the system this was not the case. Pre-post shift became a dread phrase.

2   To make matters worse, at an interpretation level, there were intractable problems: sometimes the pre-post shift was arbitrary and did not relate to any of the other findings.

Advertisers were then in the position of having a condemned commercial on their hands, but not really knowing what to do to improve it.

3   Quite apart from the validity of the measure, there are practical problems in taking it and there is a high degree of experimental error attached to it. To what extent do audience members understand what is being done, and react to it? How much collusion is there in a particular session?

4   Few people found the sales validation data utterly convincing. Any study of the effect of advertising in the market place is intrinsically difficult and the relationships discovered in the published data seemed rather tenuous to many.

5   New products have a curiosity value that seems to transcend differences in commercials' effectiveness; this suggests that different curiosity levels about established products and brands may be aroused by the *fact* of a TV commercial, not by a TV commercial of particular power—that is, the pre-post shift is a function primarily of intrinsic qualities of the brand, secondarily of the commercial.

We are both sceptical of the measure. However, it is still widely used (particularly in the USA) and used much more intelligently than it formerly was. Many experienced and able advertising researchers consider the pre-post shift measures something of value. It is interesting that several ex-Schwerin men with no particular axe to grind (the company no longer operates in Britain) swear that it is useful, although not the final word.

Variants have been designed by at least one major advertiser—sometimes a direct choice is given, after exposure, between several packs of the advertised brand and the equivalent money. Similar objections apply.

5.10   Attitude changes

Creating a brand image is an important function of advertising and it is natural that advertisers should be concerned about the likely effectiveness of a commercial in moulding the product in the desired way. Although it is easy to check on a post hoc basis, brand image effects are extraordinarily difficult to isolate in a pre-test. As we said earlier, the power of a single advertisement to influence a product's brand image—especially established brands—is extremely small. With new products where consumers are looking for clues to place it, matters are easier.

To interpret, from qualitative work, the likely *directions* in which image may be moved by a campaign is difficult, but defensible and useful. To measure the *extent* of such changes is less plausible, in small- or large-scale work.

Essentially, the measurement systems for brand image changes are based on the pre-post gift choice shift technique previously described. Informants fill in a battery of brand image scales before seeing the commercial and the same (or disguised, equivalent scales) after seeing it. Changes are attributed to the commercial.

Scale items are selected in differing ways and naturally vary with the product field. Sometimes the scales are constructed on hunch, background marketing studies or depth research. More sophisticated scale construction programmes giving comprehensive measures and, it is claimed, key motivating elements in the image are also on offer. Proponents of the St James' Model have been known to promise this.

Plausibility is difficult to maintain. Various methods have been attempted to conceal from informants that they are doing exactly the same thing in a short space of time—and the reason for it. But in hall tests this is virtually impossible. An alternative is to have a central sample not exposed to the test commercial, whose brand image choices are compared with those of the test sample. Sampling errors and the problems of accurate sample matching make this a precarious and expensive business.

Whatever method is adopted, the main difficulty to be faced is measuring a tiny, elusive effect with clumsy instruments. Often we suspect that such measurements are of communication, rather than of attitude change.

The experimental error is greater than the influence of the stimulus. Cliff Homes, in a paper given to the 1974 Conference of the Market Research Society, demonstrated that big changes can result simply by taking the same brand image measurements twice in a short period, without any intervening stimulus at all.

Many years ago one of us was concerned with the television advertising of Piccadilly Filter Cigarettes, a brand at that time considered to be too up-market. Commercials designed to rectify this shortcoming were devised but failed to produce any changes in the desired social class attribute, even though *other* image effects were detected. To check the system, the pre-post scales were administered at the theatre test session without the commercial being shown and (are you really surprised?) a significant shift was observed on the one important dimension.

Great caution is needed in assessing the potential of a commercial for image change. For most commercials we believe the task is best undertaken with qualitative research. Not only is the answer easier to obtain, assuming advertising research experts are employed, but it is a much more intelligible and usable answer.

5.11 Liking and disliking

Usually some measure of overall appeal is included in a test and informants are asked to say what they liked or disliked about the commercial. Whether people *should* like a commercial or not was discussed in Chapter 2. Inconveniently, sometimes it matters, sometimes it does not. Most advertisers most of the time *behave* as though the general appeal of the commercial is important. Great care and expense is taken to provide the best actors, sets and photographic work. Tremendous labour goes into animated films, and the country is scoured for attractive presenters—humans, cats, dogs or chimpanzees. Clearly advertisers, and agencies, want to please. One of the tasks of an advertising researcher should be to use his experience of a product field, and of advertising of a particular genre, to tell them when they should worry more, or less, about this.

Watching television, it is easy for consumers to get into the habit of being entertained without actually taking in any information. Basically these are the functional requirements of the commercial: to attract attention; to convey the desired message or impression. The real danger is that unless the entertainment element is integrated with the selling function the latter becomes incidental and lost. The temptation to pursue entertainment for its own ends is to court the video vampire. Some advertisers who are moving goods in the short term feel they have got to hit hard to prompt the following day's sales and do not weep into their pillows if housewives in pre-tests say rude things about them. But consumer expectations are important: if they are used to your brand, or to all other brands (of, for example, beer), saying something amusing on television, you may well run a risk of alienating buyers either by being serious or by straining for humour and failing.

Handling specific likes and dislikes has been covered in press ad pre-testing and there is little difference in approach with commercial pre-tests. Skill and experience is needed to know whether a particular negative is to be taken seriously or not. Often there is a counterbalancing advantage; it is also impossible to eliminate all negative reaction and attempting to do so can destroy the character of a commercial completely.

Qualitative work is more sensitive at detecting the difference between dislike and outrage.

5.12   Creative profile

Here the struggle to impose unity and form on an amorphous subject becomes even more unequal.

We said earlier that communication is concerned with creating an impression as well as conveying information. To master these some form of word association or battery of agree/disagree statements is employed. Take this example:

> I am going to read out to you various words which could describe the commercial; I would like you to tell me whether in your opinion they apply or not.
> Informative   Unbelievable
> Amusing   Destructive

Convincing	Would appeal to people like me (women), heavy beer drinkers, etc
Different	Memorable
Confusing	Suitable for product

Such lists and forms of questioning come in endless series.

For those who like order, measures such as these were grouped into three categories, *attraction, meaningfulness* and *vitality*, by William D Wells, after using factor and cluster analysis to see what kinds of judgement go together. Any single manufacturer operating a quality control system will soon settle on the dimensions relevant to his needs and stick to those. The weight given to each dimension depends largely on circumstance. Amusement might be an important objective to a cigar advertiser but not in road safety.

In practice, profiles of this kind are an extremely useful supplementary diagnostic device. They are open to criticism that attitudes to the brand, rather than the commercial, are what we should be after. But they can provide clues to the problem of *wear-out*, which is discussed below.

5.13 Mechanical devices

A distinguished advertising research practitioner once wrote:

> The cure for anyone who has an excessive faith in the value of consumer research is to go out and do some interviewing. For a long time the personal interview has been recognised as the weak link in the research chain. For this reason, like generals who do not visit the forward casualty station, researchers seldom make it their business to witness normal structured questionnaires being administered. Quite rightly so, too; such nerve as they had would soon be lost. This is particularly true of copy research where instead of giving fairly straightforward factual answers to questions, informants are expected to put into words thoughts which they never verbalise in the normal course of events. The process is sometimes like getting blood out of a stone.

Exaggeration to prove a point. Certain feelings are indeed difficult to express even when the informant is articulate. Suppose the expression on the face of an actor in a commercial at the seventh second is vaguely wrong—will it be mentioned in the interview? How does the rise and fall of interest unfold during the course of the commercial? What one is often looking for is a kind of running commentary from informants which is impossible for most people to give.

Attempts have been made to adapt conventional interviewing by breaking the commercials into scenes and assessing each separately, against agreed aims for each section. E J Clucas pioneered this approach.

Most mechanical methods fall into two categories:

1   Dials or buttons which informants turn or press to record their response as it occurs—a voluntary activity.

2   Apparatus which monitors some psychological reaction—sweat rate, pupil dilation—and which gives an automatic and involuntary response to the commercial.

Among purely mechanical devices, the best known is the ASI interest dial. Members of the test audience are instructed how to use a dial to register their interest in the programmes and commercials as it rises and falls. Responses are automatically summed for the audience by computer and can be seen on a moving graph as they occur. The Alpha Quiz Chair is used in a similar way with informants pressing buttons to record positive and negative elements in the test commercial. There are several variations on these themes. All the techniques have their limitations—not least being the dexterity and reaction times of the informants. Nevertheless, results are usually fairly intelligible and have proved useful on occasions.

Unfortunately this cannot be said of physiological techniques. We have both had considerable experience in this field and disenchantment is probably not too strong a word to describe our attitude. More of this in Chapter 7.

5.14 Norms

For quantitative pre-testing we have covered the way in which information can be gathered and the basic dimensions which can be measured. Others are listed in Chapter 2. Ad hoc problems with commercials predicate many other lines of questioning and test design. Before following these paths we will deal with the use of normative data in quality control systems, as by nature such data are general.

By collecting pre-test data in as consistent a way as possible, comparisons can be made between the performance of various commercials. Average figures or wave-bands of average scores are commonly called norms—a word calculated to arouse hatred and hostility in the hearts of many. This is unfortunate as an intelligent use of norms is extremely beneficial. In any other form of marketing research, nobody would think twice about using back-data as a guideline, but there are historical and practical reasons why the use of norms has such a mixed reception in research. These are:

1 Although in the early days, when the pre-post shift was king, comparatively few creative directors were actually taken outside and shot for failing to achieve adequate performance levels, the shock waves of symbolic executions are still reverberating a decade later.

2 In certain instances the statistical integrity of the syndicated and normative data offered is highly suspect. Reaction to a commercial varies tremendously with the product being advertised. Yet the product groups in some normative data systems we have seen are only vaguely defined. Searching questions need to be asked about any tests included in the averages, the time period covered by the tests constituting the norm and whether the commercials were made for similar advertising purposes—were they the same length and shown to samples of the same size and demographic composition?

3 Quality control systems deal with the *normal* commercial in a fairly standard way. A special problem commercial—say for a new product or one trying to achieve a new advertising task for that brand—is best handled in some other way.

Too many commercials have been mangled by feeding them into the wrong testing machine. Compared against irrelevant norms, good commercials have been rejected and a great deal of mental anguish caused.

Examples for normative data are given on the following pages. The first series are derived from some standard questions from cake commercial tests. Also illustrated are measures referred to earlier in the chapter taken from theatre research.

	VIENNESE WHIRLS	HOSTESS ROLLS	SHOWBOATS	CARAMEL SHORTCAKE	MAJORCA SLICE
	%	%	%	%	%
INTEREST IN PRODUCT					
Very interested	21	7	23	15	22
Quite interested	55	43	39	42	40
Not particularly interested	18	29	27	21	26
Rather interested	1	6	4	10	4
Not at all interested	5	15	8	12	7
SUITABILITY FOR PRODUCT					
Very suitable for the product	59	26	29	21	36
Fairly suitable for the product	34	53	60	36	42
Not particularly suitable for the product	4	17	8	34	17
Not at all suitable	3	4	3	10	6

	BATTENBERG	MINI PIES	FRANZIPAN CRUMBLE	SUMMERTIME TARTS
INTEREST IN PRODUCT	%	%	%	%
Very interested	20	9	13	11
Quite interested	52	36	50	36
Not particularly interested	17	36	28	34
Rather uninterested	4	7	2	7
Not at all interested	7	13	7	12
SUITABILITY FOR PRODUCT				
Very suitable for the product	48	14	22	13
Fairly suitable for the product	37	47	57	49
Not particularly suitable for the product	15	29	17	27
Not at all suitable	-	10	4	11

Figure 5.1   STORYBOARD COMMERCIALS: SOME NORMATIVE DATA

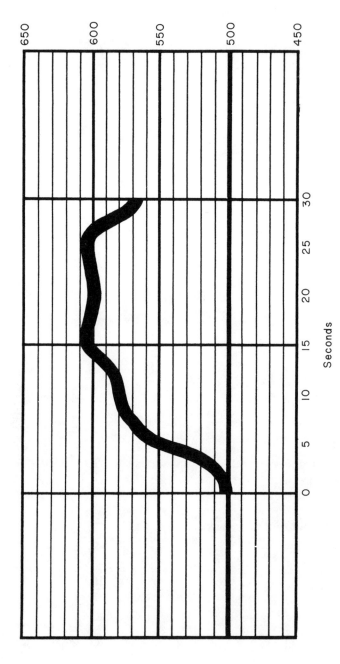

Figure 5.2   MAXWELL HOUSE INSTANT COFFEE "NEWSPAPER" COMMERCIAL
Total housewives audience profile curve, first test

INTEREST SCORE	PERCENTILE	PRE/POST CHANGE
628	99	+ 13
620	95	+ 10
615	90	+ 9
598	85	+ 9
594	80	+ 8
593	75	+ 8
589	70	+ 8
586	65	+ 7
580	60	+ 6
579	55	+ 6
567	50	+ 6
564	45	+ 6
563	40	+ 5
562	35	+ 5
558	30	+ 4
558	25	+ 4
537	20	+ 4
528	15	+ 3
525	10	+ 3
515	5	+ 2
480	2	0

Figure 5.3   NORMATIVE DATA : PERCENTILE LIMITS,
INSTANT COFFEE COMMERCIALS

The pre/post change is the increase in the proportion of
the sample selecting the test product as a prize after having seen the commercial (see page 110). The percentile is
derived by calculation from the performance of other test
commercials and effectively trades the scores.

When a new test is carried out either in storyboard or finished form, the new data is pencilled in and pondered over. Those pondering consist of researchers (company, advertising agency and research agency) and the brand management and the account group from the agency, including a creative man. There is no predetermined level of acceptance or rejection or any fine calculation of the statistical significance of differences. Ocular impact (if a difference hits you between the eyes it's significant) is used for assessment and if a commercial is obviously below par reasons are sought. These may be found in the answers to the open-ended questions or more commonly in the findings of depth research carried out concurrently with the test; they may lie in the nature of the product itself—some cakes being more appealing than others.

Disagreements in interpretation are not unknown; our view is that this is an *advantage* of a quality control system, because it fosters purposive discussion.

The crucial point is that instead of a room full of people arguing about what should be done from hunch or prejudice, the discussion is firmly pinned down to actual consumer reaction. This discipline rather than any mystique or esoteric expertise is the true benefit of the system and it leads to sharper advertising.

5.15   Problem commercials—still quantitative

What about commercials which need special treatment in pretesting and cannot be accommodated in any recognised procedures? Special procedures are indicated:

1   When the problem is highly specific—to an extent which precludes the common practice of adding questions to standard interviews.

2   When the commercial is for a new product. With new-product commercials much attention needs to be paid to the product impression conveyed.

Two examples from cigar advertising are as follows:

1   Manikin, a well-established brand, was becoming dangerously dull and needed a shot in the arm. A commercial showing a beautiful girl running along a beach was devised with a

simple message and pack shot at the end. No overt message was intended. The risk of making a famous commercial at the expense of a product was accepted as advertising was to be heavy and the situation of the brand required the approach. In the event, the commercial worked like a charm, but there came a point when it was felt that a change in girl might be beneficial—she had been running along that beach for a long time.

Research was required to ensure the high aesthetic standards set by the original girl were maintained while checking whether the bounds of propriety were being exceeded. Group discussions were held at which alternative commercials featuring glamorous girls were appraised. (This was one of Jack Potter's more enjoyable research tasks!) There was then a quantitative check on the more promising ones. The key data from a sample of 100 cigar smokers was:

	BEACH	HAMMOCK	HORSE	RAVINE
The girl is attractive				
Agree a lot	93%	80%	82%	88%
Agree a little	6%	14%	14%	8%
Don't know	—	2%	—	2%
Disagree a little	—	3%	3%	1%
Disagree a lot	1%	1%	1%	—

The reigning queen kept her crown in this particular beauty contest, but for present purposes the outcome is less important than the way the job was done. All the paraphernalia of a normal pre-test was irrelevant; the advertising was a known quantity, only technical improvements were required.

2   Another cigar commercial posed an entirely different set of problems. Because the cigar was new it was important to have its characteristics accurately transmitted. Unlike the Manikin cigar commercials, the emphasis was squarely on hard factual communication. The conventional advertising pre-test measures had more relevance and were indeed taken but the emphasis was on the positioning of the product in the market-place and its perceived smoking characteristics. Was the correct impression of size conveyed? Smokers do not like to feel they are being conned. Did smoking expectation match the reality?

Some 120 smokers were shown the commercial several

Figure 5.4   MANIKIN COMMERCIAL
The reigning queen kept her crown

times during the course of a fairly lengthy interview. Data from some of the product expectation questions are shown below:

New product	WOULD LOOK LIKE %	WOULD SMOKE LIKE %	WOULD COST SAME AS %	WOULD BE SAME SIZE AS %
Harlequin	6	5	12	17
Castella	37	31	18	28
Embassy Slim Panatella	23	25	22	23
Hamlet	19	22	20	25
Manikin	13	19	19	5
Tom Thumb	2	5	7	2

There is a danger, avoided in this instance, of making an advertisement test the vehicle for other market research and overburdening it. Basic research into the product concept and product testing should have been sewn up long before advertising is being pre-tested. A good advertising research man should have a shop-steward's eye for demarcation.

Similar concern for product communication was felt by Polycell Products Ltd, when it launched Fine Surface Polyfilla, which, as its name suggests, performs the more delicate filling better than Standard Polyfilla. Was the launch commercial getting the range of tasks across properly? And having established that point, would home handymen do as they were told? Do-it-yourselfers are a resourceful independent body of men and the power of advertising cannot be guaranteed to hold a product in the particular slot in the market that its makers intended.

After being exposed to the commercial and interviewed about it intensively, the informants were accordingly given a sample of the product to take home and try. By analysing the *actual* uses for the product recorded in a postal questionnaire completed by the test participants, further insight was obtained into the overall communication task.

Ad hoc research often involves one in making comparisons between several commercials. Frequently all the commercials will be seen by each informant and the implications of this worry some people—needlessly. Interaction effects do, indeed, occur but they are either unimportant or controllable. Designing the test so that equal numbers see each commercial first gets round most of the problems. Direct communication measures are the real difficulty and are only legitimate when taken after the first showing as progressive learning effects can be strong, assuming that the commercials are saying similar things.

Sometimes one of the commercials in a pre-test has been on the air already and anxiety is created because in comparing an exposed with a brand new commercial, like is not being compared with like. Variously this is supposed to put the new commercial at an advantage or a disadvantage. Usually the test is set up to see whether the new commercial is better (however defined) than the new one. Again the fears are groundless; whatever the *intrinsic* qualities of the existing commercial, exposure has given it certain characteristics; these are the market-place realities against which new commercials should be assessed. But it is worth arranging for more than one showing, where the new commercial is making intellectual or imaginative demands on consumers. This can show whether initial hostility is likely to evaporate or not.

One frequent problem encountered in pre-testing is whether or not a commercial is wearing out. Given the massive increase in TV production costs recently, it would be surprising if more advertisers were not asking research to help them establish for how long they can reasonably keep using their current commercial and put off the evil day of paying for another. In advertising agencies there is often a strong conviction that too many advertisers change their campaigns too quickly: "The marketing manager gets tired of it sooner than the consumer." The argument may be stronger when applied to campaigns rather than individual commercials, but it applies to both.

How can research help? The use of an adjective checklist at successive stages in a commercial's life has been mentioned as giving a rough diagnosis of whether any big change in reaction is taking place. You cannot just ask informants directly to say whether they are tired of something or not; anyone who likes seeing something new on the box is all too likely to take the suggestion and say "Oh yes, do give us something new!" Qualitative research, conducted at successive intervals is useful here, particularly if the same person is used to conduct it. He can discern, from the tone used when informants are choosing which commercial from a reel to discuss first and when the communication of the test commercial is being discussed, whether that commercial is likely to be getting past its best—for example, "Oh my God, not ———— again!"

5.16 Qualitative pre-testing

Structurally, quantified pre-tests of press ads and commercials are very different. With qualitative research, however, the basic format is virtually identical whether the subject matter is intended for press or television. Much of what we said earlier about the nature of qualitative work with press advertisements applies to television commercials.

One or two points of technique need careful watching. Group discussions on television commercials can be easily spoiled by clumsy handling; we know, as we have between us probably ruined more groups than most like to admit. A sure-fire way to kill a group is to show the commercial to the assembled gathering at the beginning of the proceedings and say "Well, what do you think of that?" Unless the commercial is a real stinker there will be a few polite murmurs followed by an impregnable silence; a nasty one to retrieve. Psychologists have been known to resort to farmyard imitations to bring such a group back to life.

The trick is to have a reasonable warming-up period and then introduce the test commercial in a reel of other commercials. By now those in the group have begun to get used to each other and to the room. Then suggest they choose a product to discuss. Most of the necessary reactions to the test advertisement can be teased out indirectly. Then proceed to specifics.

More important than simply technique is the choice of the researcher who will conduct the group. Experience is important; some hostility to television advertising is always present in some degree, even if the precautions suggested in Chapter 2 are taken. The expert must be able to sell the idea that the discussion is worthwhile and to be taken seriously. Personality counts, as well as experience. After group discussions, at debriefing sessions, it is a great help if a researcher knows the scene, knows the particular interests of his audience and can communicate his findings effectively.

At the other end of the spectrum, avoid group discussion hacks who take on more work than they can handle, become stale and simply do not have the time to do the job properly.

Recruitment standards often leave much to be desired. Insist on a check of *informants'* experience of group discussions.

Depth interviews are also used, but less commonly than group discussions. One misses out on the interplay of attitudes to be found in a good group. Admittedly, depth interviews can give a much more thorough view of each person's reactions and there is the problem of broaching taboo subjects in open forum. But most people are used, in real life, to seeing a commercial in the company of one or two others. Press ads are more naturally a private matter. The stimulation of a group helps lubricate comment about commercials.

As well as depth interviews, there are "semi-depth interviews," which take less time but are restricted and usually directed towards specific issues.

There are two main ways of using qualitative research:

1   As an adjunct to quantitative work.

2   As the pre-eminent means of achieving creative feedback.

Taking the first point, most quality control systems make some provision for either group discussions or depth interviews during the course of the structured test. At theatre tests preselected members of the audience are invited to leave the auditorium halfway through the programme and participate in a group discussion about the commercials. Depth interviews are conducted at all test locations when J Lyons Bakery commercials are being researched concurrently with the quantified test. Information from them is often used to help interpret the quantitative data and to give clues as to how the commercial might be improved.

Much of the value of complementary depth research lies in enabling one to understand *how* communication has happened. Not *how much*. It helps particularly in understanding what is going on in the action. Perfectly respectable replies to "What do you think the advertiser was trying to put across in the commercial?" can obscure a profound misunderstanding of what is actually being portrayed on the screen. Often this

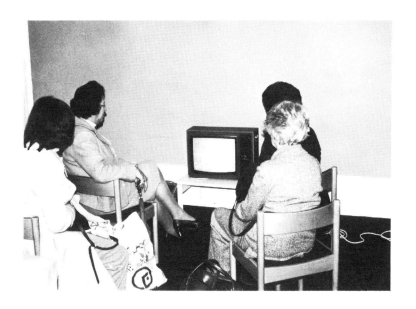

Figure 5.5   LONDON HOUSEWIVES TAKING PART
IN A HALL TEST
Propensity to purchase at 27p

leads to an uneasiness about the commercial which is not arti-culated in the formal interview because the informant does not wish to appear stupid. A good depth researcher can draw the informant out and at the first hint of comprehension difficult-ies can make encouraging noises. "A few people have had trou-ble with this one" or "I find it a bit difficult to follow myself and I've seen it thirty times!"

Special-problem commercials are often preceded by depth research in order to define areas for the quantitative test. Before the Manikin commercial test described in section 5.15, group discussions were carried out and batteries of attitude statements drawn up in the basis of the findings. Group discus-sions performing a similar function for a new product led to the inclusion of a series of questions being included on value for money. This was the hypothesis from the groups:

> Housewives in Leeds were much more resistant to the price of the product than housewives in London, where most considered 27p quite reasonable.

Subsequently, the final pre-test of the commercial threw up the following figures:

Propensity to purchase at 27p	LONDON	LEEDS
	%	%
Very likely	10	11
Quite likely	46	42
Quite unlikely	14	12
Very unlikely	13	18
Don't know	17	17

Egg on face? Not really. The whole point of the quantification was to check hypotheses found in the groups. Groups are not statistically reliable and should not be used for reaching con-clusions to be inscribed on stone. Their functions are quite dif-ferent.

In another test, for example, the perceived value for money of a new product was hypothesised to be lower in Newcastle-on-Tyne than in London, after group work; and this differ-ence was confirmed by quantification.

But the groups showed *why*: in Newcastle, the presenter's genuine Geordie accent was suspect (wrongly, as it happened) of being a crass attempt by Southerners at foisting some worthless trifle on them with pseudo-Newcastle patois. In London, the same voice was received partly with curiosity, partly with a feeling that the man was a Northerner and more likely to speak honestly about an honest product. The obvious change was made. This is when qualitative work really helps.

Everybody concerned in the advertising process should get involved in it, within reason. Certainly it is unwise for those observing groups to outnumber those participating. Nevertheless, it should not always be a case of the group discussion moderator coming back like an anthropologist and telling the creative team what they say and think. Direct participation gives a creative man a chance to judge what changes and what scale of changes need to be made to get the effect that he is striving for.

One-way mirrors and videotaped groups are sometimes used to help here. The Market Research Society's code of practice requires that informants are told about these. In fact, few people object and often seem to forget about them.

One snag with group discussions in particular is that they become the lazy answer to every pre-testing problem. Great mischief is caused when they are used where numbers are needed, as in quality control or some special-problem commercials. "Let's do a couple of groups" has, in fact, achieved the status of a joke. Automatic choice of a qualitative technique suggests that advertising research is technique orientated, instead of being problem orientated, which is crucial for its health.

5.17   Cinema commercials

Returning to his pulpit after having delivered the sermon, the Reverend Spooner once announced to his congregation:

> When I said Aristotle, it should have been St Paul the Apostle throughout.

If, in the preceding pages, cinema commercials are a substituted for television commercials the subject is pretty well covered. Just a few points need watching:

1   Cinema commercials are designed for large-scale projection and all concerned in the research feel happier if the com-

mercial can be shown on a big screen. Normally, for testing final versions of films, a theatre is better than a hall.

2   Cinema audiences are younger than the population average and sometimes hard to come by in large numbers in shopping centres. Again, the invited audience at a theatre tends to approximate to a cinema audience, except possibly in personality terms, and therefore favour the test format. Despite this, in default of a *very* convenient hall, theatre tests are often the best.

3   Pre-test experimentation in real life conditions is more practicable with cinema commercials. Cinema audiences can be interviewed about the commercials they have been shown as they leave after a performance. A large number of interviews and a short questionnaire are practical necessities in this situation.

6

Pre-testing
in Other Media

6.1 Outdoor advertising

Creatively, outdoor advertising hangs on the coat tails of
other advertising. A campaign is devised and researched for
television or press and then its main elements—illustration
and slogan—are embodied in poster form and posted on the
hoardings. Outdoor advertising is occasionally used as the
prime mover in certain traditional areas such as drink, but usually it is a support medium. As far as the attitude and information elements are concerned, the posters can be treated as
press ads. Impact, though, is a different matter.

Outdoor advertising has unique characteristics and these
should be reflected in the pre-test situation. With other media
—press, television, radio and cinema—the target audience is
involved in extracting enjoyment or information from the
medium when the ad hits them. In varying degrees the attention is already engaged and the recipients of the message are sitting ducks. Posters have to work much harder. Wandering
round the streets or driving along in cars we are talking to others, planning our next moves or lost in reverie of one kind or
another. Outdoor advertising has to break through this bar-
rier of inattention and deliver its goods, invariably in a short
time. Impact is the *sine qua non* of posters.

Measures of impact can be taken in various ways. There is
one fairly robust method.

A colour slide of the poster is projected in sequence with a
series of posters for competitive products. Each person might
see a dozen or so slides each held for a second or two. Afterwards the informant is asked what products he can remember

having seen advertised. For the test poster he might be asked to describe it and recall the message ("he" because posters seem to be tuned towards masculine products). In effect, it is a folder test with a tray of colour transparencies. A conventional press style pre-test question is then administered. As far as it goes the technique is quite useful and discriminates between products.

Sometimes the research problem is more specific than assessing product impact in general terms. How much can be put into the poster without vitiating its capacity to communicate quickly? Can we put in another product in the range without confusing the issue? Does the fine de siècle lettering, so perfect for creating the ad's trendy atmosphere, render incomprehensible both the product name and what is being said about it?

In situations such as these a tachistoscope test can be useful. Suppose there are two alternative 4 by 4ft pole signs for a petrol promotion for a tumbler to be given away with gallons of petrol. Motorists might be further encouraged to patronise the station if they felt sure they would be getting their quadruple Green Shield stamps as well. On the other hand, the clutter might obscure the nature of the offer and put motorists off.

A test might work in the following way. Two versions of the poster are prepared, one with and one without the Green Shield stamp information (see Figure 6.1.) Matched samples of 100 motorists are exposed to a colour slide of one or the other of the alternative designs by means of a tachistoscope—that is, for very brief time intervals, gradually increased. (See Chapter 7 for further details of method.)

After each exposure, informants are asked what they can see: the following communication pattern might result for the two alternatives, after six exposures ranging from one-hundredth to half a second.

Cumulative % recognising offer		VERSION A	VERSION B
1/100sec	1st exposure	—	—
1/50	2nd exposure	10	—
1/28	3rd exposure	36	4
1/10	4th exposure	76	20
1/5	5th exposure	95	44
1/2	6th exposure	100	72

Figure 6.1 POSTER WITH AND WITHOUT STAMP OFFER
A tachistoscope test was used to assess the effect on
overall communication of adding information on stamps

After six exposures some informants simply could not get the point of the offer being made to them, although there is no exact way of relating these figures to reality (how long do motorists on average look at such signs?). The ability to communicate in a split second is relevant in this field and the doubts about the Green Shield stamp version were confirmed.

Another method of testing for impact was developed by Jack Potter at Alpha (UK) Research Ltd for one of the company's clients. Alternative versions of the test posters are treated photographically so as to appear to be in a street site. This is done quite easily by pasting a colour shot of the art work on a blow up of the hoarding and its immediate surrounding and making a 35mm transparency of the resulting mock-up. (See Figure 6.2.)

Figure 6.2   TEST POSTER FOR UNIFLOW
This was placed in position by special-effect photography

Supposing there are three alternatives, then three matched samples of informants are recruited and each sample is exposed to one of the test slides. Informants are told in general terms that the research is concerned with their impressions of outdoor scenes, forecourt layout, street furniture—anything that obscures the advertising interest but is not a downright lie. In the hall, the test slide is shown with twenty or so other slides held for a few seconds; some contain posters, most don't. When the slides have been shown the informant is asked, incidently, if he noticed any advertisements. Typical results from a list of alternative travel posters are shown below:

	(CLARKSONS VERSION A)	(CLARKSON'S VERSION B)
Recalled	%	%
Clarkson's poster	8	21
Travel poster	18	37
Worthington	21	19
Beer	5	4
Nescafé	7	9
Coffee	3	3
Any other product	4	5
None recalled/DK	34	29

The advantage of the method is that it gets fairly close to simulating the real-life situation in which the attention is distracted. Experimental control is difficult, however. Informants must not know initially exactly what is going on and the whole operation has to be very tightly run.

Impact testing of outdoor material calls for more ingenuity in test design than other forms of advertising research. A great deal of work has been done in the signalisation function of petrol signs and forecourt layout. Films simulating the drive past stations have been made for test purposes and eye movement techniques have been employed.

An example of this kind of approach is provided by work carried out for National Benzole on their mast-head pole sign. In depth research on another subject, the feeling was expressed that the National sign was rather less distinctive viewed from the roadside than competitive signs and that motorists might be driving past it. How was this to be proved or disproved?

A mock-up of a street scene was prepared in four versions identical in every respect except that each had in it a different pole sign—National and three competitors. A series of slides including one of the test scenes was then shown to matched samples of motorists who were told to suppose they were driving along low on petrol; would they press a button as soon as they saw the chance to fill up? Their reaction times were compared and it could be seen that there were differences between the signs in their signalisation capabilities. (See Figure 6.3.)

Figure 6.3   NATIONAL BENZOLE PETROL STATION SIGN
RECOGNITION TEST
The time motorists took to recognise competitive signs
against a common background was measured to test
their relative impact

So far we have talked exclusively about impact, as the research for other elements closely follows that of press advertising. To redress the balance and give a truer sense of proportion, here is a questionnaire designed to test the relative merits of two poster designs.

QUESTIONNAIRE

1   Which of these things would you say interested you?
Driving . . . . Travel . . . . Architecture . . . .
IF NO TO DRIVING: Do you in fact drive?
RECRUIT INFORMANT AND TAKE TO TEST LOCATION

We are now going to show you some colour slides of outdoor scenes and we are particularly interested in what you think of some of the buildings you will see.
SHOW INFORMANT TEST SLIDES (TWENTY) FOR FIVE SECONDS EACH

2   Which building appealed to you most?

3   And which least?

4   Did you notice any posters when you were looking at the pictures?

YES	1
NO	2

IF YES: Which?

5   What was the poster saying?

6   Can you describe the picture to me?
IF———NOT RECALLED:

7   Do you recall seeing posters for any of the following products?

Tobacco	1
Beer	2
Coffee	3
———	4

PROBE FOR BRANDS
IF ——— NOW RECALLED BY NAME OR BY DESCRIPTION ASK Qs 8 AND 9. IF ——— NOT RECALLED GO TO Q10

8   What was the poster saying?

9   Can you describe the picture to me?
SHOW ——— ADVERTISEMENT FOR THREE SECONDS
TO ALL:

10   Can you describe the poster to me? PROBE FOR SIZE AND
DETAILS

11   Which of the following words and statements would
you say applied to the poster?

	APPLIES	DOES NOT APPLY
Eye-catching	1	1
Different	2	2
Dull	3	3
Persuasive	4	4
Ordinary	5	5
Humourous	6	6
Appealing	7	7
Striking	8	8
What you would expect from . . .	9	9
Better than most posters for . . .	0	0
Imaginative	1	1
Unmemorable	2	2
Does not stand out	3	3
Unbelievable	4	4

12   Does this poster remind you of any other advertising
you have seen for ——— either in newspapers or magazines or on television?

Newspapers/magazines   1
Television   2
Other   3

IF SIMILAR ADVERTISING SEEN ASK Q13, OTHERWISE GO
TO Q14

13   Can you describe the advertisement/commercial it
resembles?

14   Would you say this poster was directed at somebody
like you or somebody who was different in some way?

SAME   1

DIFFERENT   2

15   In what way the same?

16   In what way different?

17   This poster has already been shown in another part of
      the country. What do you think happened to sales
      of ――――― when the poster was shown?

      Sales:
Increased a lot	1
Increased a little	2
Stayed the same	3
Dropped a little	4
Dropped a lot	5

18   Finally is there anything you particularly like about the
      poster?

19   And is there anything you dislike about it?
      SHOW ALL THREE ――――― POSTERS

20   Which one do you like best?
      A   1
      B   2
      C   3
      Why do you say that?
      SHOW CHOSEN ――――― POSTER FROM Q20 AND ―――――
      POSTER

21   Which of these do you prefer?
      ―――――   1
      ―――――   2
      Why do you say that?

The issue was decided not by impact at all in this instance but
by answers to Q14. Considerable alienation effects were being
produced by one of the designs and it was accordingly eliminated.

6.2 Radio commercials

Radio is a cheap medium from a production point of view. It
costs comparatively little to produce a range of radio commercials. This means, on the one hand, that for research to raise
doubts about one commercial in the range need not be so agon-
ising as in the case, for example, of a finished television commercial. But against this, there is less motivation to investigate
the virtues and defects of material that has been cheaply executed. Consequently, there is much less pre-testing of radio
commercials than for advertisements in other media. What

tends to happen in cases where they *are* pre-tested, is for the ad to be pick-a-backed on to the end of a couple of groups, which were themselves conceived for a different purpose.

But there are other reasons, too, for little money being spent in this area. The first is that there are no firmly established techniques in Britain which command respect. (Nor, for that matter, do there seem to be many elsewhere that we could borrow, if 24 hour recall is discounted, which is a post-testing device.) Secondly, the nature of the medium is disconcerting to anyone whose pre-testing philosophy is to approach a problem by frontal attack.

Some people *listen* to radio. Others *hear* it. There are all kinds of jobs which can be occupying their attention. Most advertising is probably picked up casually or incidentally. But nowhere is this more obvious than with radio. This makes it seem almost perverse to contrive a situation in which someone is required to pay full attention to a test advertisement and then talk about it. If someone in real life, as opposed to this test situation, registers a message from a radio commercial, it may often be by dint of repetition, rather than because of a successful once-off communication.

A test situation that replicated something like real experience would involve a protracted series of exposures to a test commercial, within its natural context. It would span several days, rather than one day. It would almost certainly be post-testing, rather than pre-testing. It would take time and money. Then—when the communication recall and image questions are answered and analysed—how do you interpret the results? There are all kinds of reasons why recall may be low—possibly because the radio programmes were not switched on as often as they would normally be, possibly because of the strength of the competition that week. If they are high, there is no telling what other messages may have been picked up from other media, or from point of sale during the period of test.

But, however unpractical and profitless this exercise might be, the principle of *casual pick-up* in radio commercials needs to be borne in mind in pre-testing. The following are two methods which can be used—one qualitative, the other quantitative:

1 *QUALITATIVE RESEARCH*—A group discussion is

convened, preferably in an interviewer's home. As informants arrive they are asked to sit down, have some coffee, look at a magazine and wait until everything is ready. It is important that all should be in the target market for the brand commercial, and that all should be regular radio listeners. But this has had to be established without alerting them to the fact that the research is about a radio commercial or revealing the brand.

During the ten minutes or so while "we are waiting for everything to be ready," a prepared tape is playing. This tape incorporates programme and commercial material; including of course the test commercial. The tape recorder should be hidden but with the sound output connected to a radio, which is on view, so that the informants think that what they are hearing is a normal broadcast. The tape should not be too loud, or too soft. The test commercial can appear twice on the tape. Normal discussion should be allowed during this period; most informants are rather quiet at such times, almost as if in a doctor's waiting room.

The tape is switched off and the group discussion starts. This can begin with talking about the use of the product or the product field. Gradually attention is focused onto different brands and the claims that are made for them. Careful note is taken of any spontaneous discussion of the claims made for the client's brand in the test commercial. At this point, the convener may decide that as different people in the group have different levels of awareness of the test commercial, the issue of who has registered what should be settled individually. Each informant is then asked to write down, separately, what they can remember being told about brand X in radio advertising. Some will be unable to reply. Others will have more or less elaborate recollections, often combining material from other advertising—which is more often found with radio commercials than most other media. What is written down needs to be probed later in the discussion, because some informants become "tongue-tied" when they put pen to paper, and may in fact know much more than they show at first. The value of the written section lies in allowing a chance for some evidence to be free from prompting within the group.

Informants then talk about the commercial, and the interviewer can direct this discussion on to those aspects of the test advertisement that are relevant to his brief. His interest may be primarily in finding out what has been communicated about the product; what impressions it gave about using the product—or about the users; anything that will reflect the way that the advertising is contributing to the desired strategy. If necessary, he may even play the tape again and focus attention on certain aspects of it.

What has been gained by *not* putting the commercial on a slab, as it were, right at the outset?

Divorced from their context, catchy and apparently successful radio commercials can sometimes sound naive and embarrassing, instead of childlike and fun. The message that they deliver may, on the other hand, seem crystal clear when played specially, whereas in context it may be overshadowed by its entertainment value or by the sexiness in the presenter's voice.

2   *QUANTITATIVE RESEARCH*—A friendly supermarket manufacturer may transmit a test commercial among the canned music and the store's own announcements in the course of an afternoon.

If the brand concerned is a fast-moving product stocked by the supermarket, a behavioural measure of throughput is possible: consumer off-take of the brand that afternoon can be compared with off-take on other afternoons. For this to work, rigorous maintenance of facings for the advertised brand is crucial, with checks on competitive facings and competitive activity. This kind of measure is going to be too insensitive for brands with a slow repeat-purchase cycle.

Other measures that are possible involve personal interviews conducted with shoppers who appear to be in the target market, as they come away from the checkout point. They can be asked about communication, their knowledge of the brand and their reactions to the commercial in whole or in part. They can be asked brand image questions, too, comparing the results of these questions with comparable figures gathered on control afternoons. Those shoppers who are observed to buy the advertised brand can be approached to talk about their purchase and the factors leading up to it.

These methods described so far manage to conceal the researcher's purpose during the course of exposure to the test commercials. But there are some cases where *comparative* research on new ideas for commercials is required. In such cases, a research situation can be arranged in which a series of ideas is tried out on tape, and informants' reactions can be examined to help decide:

1 Which are the best ideas to progress?
2 Are there any ideas which should be dropped? Why?
3 Are there any suggestions in the research on how these ideas should be improved?
4 Are there any new ideas?

One such exercise was conducted by the Leo Burnett Creative Workshop for Iron Jelloids. Group discussions were organised in which women who were more than averagely disposed to self-medication were recruited. This helped establish that they were in the right target market without alerting them to the specific product and brand that was being advertised.

Four test commercials had been prepared for Iron Jelloids, each consisting of a kind of "playlet," which introduced common stories and problem situations, for which Iron Jelloids offered some relief. At each group, the first playlet appeared inside a commercial break of four different sorts of radio commercial. These were discussed in general. Their attention was directed towards the Iron Jelloids playlet. The other three test commercials were then played, and reactions to them were compared.

It is important to note that, except in the case of extreme results, this kind of test can tell little about the overall effectiveness of the commercials or the campaign. It is essentially research that is diagnosing how consumers are likely to react so that radio advertising can be improved.

In this test, the psychologist arrived at these interpretations (among others) set out as guidelines for the creative team:

1 The playlet form had to be kept *brief*, so as not to disappoint and antagonise housewives who might think they were listening to the start of a real play or soap opera.
2 The male voice-over was best if was deep, dark, authoritative and symphathetic—rather like a doctor with a good bedside manner.
3 Children could play an important part in setting up the problem situations—implied criticism of a housewife

and mother's performance of her role was acceptable from children but not from husbands or other adults.

4   Big drama situations would be less effective than everyday problems because of the lesser likelihood that they would arouse feelings of personal relevance.

7

Mechanical Aids
in Advertising Research

Buyers of market research are often invited by market research companies soliciting new business to come to their offices and have a look around. As a spectacle, looking round a market research company's office ranks second to a guided tour of Neasden Public Library. In order to inject a little interest into the proceedings potential customers are often taken to a perception laboratory where they can peer into boxes, have electrodes stuck to them, twiddle dials, press knobs and generally enjoy themselves. Often the machines do not work or are in some state of development but this does not detract from their entertainment value. How useful are these machines?

7.1 The two principal
divisions in perception research

Most of the equipment used in advertising research falls into two principal categories. It is important to understand this basic differentiation because the two fields of study involve quite different objectives and they stand at different levels of development and usefulness.

1 *VISUAL PERCEPTION*—Typically advertising material is displayed in a highly competitive environment. Magazines and newspapers are flipped through casually with only a few seconds' attention being paid to each of the many advertisements. Posters remain in the field of vision for only a short time as they are passed by. In the supermarket, a pack is in danger of being swamped visually in a sea of similar packs,

hastily scanned by the shopper. Consequently the ability to attract attention and to communicate quickly is at a premium. The measurement of visual impact in this sense has led to the adoption of equipment and techniques used in the psychological laboratory. Although this is not the only kind of visual research carried out commercially, it is the most common and most useful. Initial impact and communication are only limited variables in the complex of advertising objectives but they are vital ones and we can measure them fairly accurately at a technical level.

2 *PHYSIOLOGICAL MEASUREMENTS*—Physiological measures, such as heart beat and rate of sweating—to name but two among many—can provide an indication of mental state. The object in taking these measures is to find out what people feel—intrinsically a much more difficult proposition than discovering what they can see. Dissatisfaction with conventional interviewing techniques is the impetus for this kind of research. Essentially the principle is to assess emotional and intellectual response directly by measuring the physical correlates of mental activity, thus hopefully cutting through the barriers of rationalisation and inability to communicate. Clearly the prizes to be won in this attempt are glittering. However, whereas tests of visual perception are well tried tested and accepted, assessing emotional response by physiological measures still requires the solution of some pretty complicated problems.

7.2   Equipment and
techniques used in visual perception

TACHISTOSCOPE—Of all equipment used in advertising research, the tachistoscope has given the most valuable service. A tachistoscope is a machine which can show a test item for brief controlled periods of time—usually fractions of a second. It thus simulates the brief exposure which most advertising material initially receives.

There are several kinds of tachistoscope. Perhaps the simplest is a slide projector fitted with a camera shutter over the lens. A colour slide of the test item can then be projected at normal photographic speeds.

Another kind consists of a viewing chamber which an informant looks into, to see the actual test item. The simplest kind again uses camera shutters over the peep holes which expose and cut off the field of vision.

More sophisticated machines have the optical arrangements so designed that when the informant looks into the box he sees the test item appear in the field of vision in which his eyes are already focused. This avoids the disturbance of a sudden flash of light and the need to change focus. Such machines have electronic timing devices which are superior to camera shutter mechanisms.

More rarely, stereoscopic or binocular tachistoscopes are used. These can expose two test items simultaneously, one to each eye.

Tachistoscopes can be used to test the relative legibility of different elements in advertising material. Alternative type faces, type arrangements, presentations of brand name and product name, layout of illustration, etc, can be assessed in terms of their efficiency in getting attention and communicating quickly. It must be made clear at the outset that the concern here is technical efficiency in communication; whether these various elements are aesthetically pleasing to the consumer and whether they are consistent with the brand image the advertising is projecting are quite different matters and must be assessed separately.

Whatever the subject of the test poster, pack, or press advertisement, the basic methodology is the same. Each test item is exposed to a separate sample of informants. At first the informant sees the stimulus very briefly (say one-hundredth of a second) and he is asked to describe what he has seen. Further exposures of increasing duration are given and after each he recalls all he observes. Thus one can see which elements—illustration, slogan, brand name, etc—take most and least time to make themselves known. Separate samples are used because of the considerable learning effect which would be encountered when testing basically similar items. Matching is normally carried out on age and any other variables which might be relevant (such as brand usage) and a process of screening eliminates informants with abnormal vision. For each matched sample one can then see the relative length of exposure which on average a particular visual element needed before recognition. A coupon offer on a presss ad for example might be noted by half the informants at second exposure in one sample but require twice that time with an alternative layout in the other sample. It can be concluded that the former advertisement would be at an advantage compared with the latter in gaining attention for the coupon.

PRESS ADVERTISING—The tachistoscope can be used to test the ability to communicate quickly of any element in the advertisement. Differences in layout can produce quite marked variations in communication with the basic content of the ads being the same. The relative legibility of type faces is also a factor which lends itself to this kind of testing. Recently we were asked to advise on the use of serif against sans serif type in an advertisement. A simple tachistoscope test readily settled this issue.

Clearly a tachistoscope test is in no sense a substitute for a normal copy test but is a means of solving problems which lie beyond the reach of conventional interviewing.

POSTERS—In some respects posters are more suitable for study with the tachistoscope than press advertisements. A press ad often is trying to convey a relatively complex message and its success is dependent on the skill which goes into putting the message in a persuasive form within the framework of an attractive presentation. Posters are usually conveying a simple message in conditions where they are often seen briefly when impact and rapid communication really count.

Quite often one has to strike a balance between a device which captures attention and any actual message conveyed. An example of a tachistoscope test is given in Chapter 6.

PACK TESTING—Assessing the relative value of alternative pack designs can legitimately be regarded as a function of advertising research. A pack performs many of the principal functions of an advertisement and pack design is very much the concern of advertisers.

The tachistoscope is probably used more in pack testing than in any other research field. In modern marketing conditions the need for fast-moving consumer goods to proclaim their identity quickly and efficiently has never been greater.

Tachistoscope testing is often useful in seeing that they do.

A tachistoscope test can determine on a comparative basis how well the pack identifies the product; in other words, does a bottle of lemon squash look like a bottle of lemon squash. More important perhaps, it can, again on a comparative basis, determine which elements of the graphic design are strong and which weak. Usually the most important element is the brand name and the tachistoscope will reliably establish which pack can communicate this most effectively. In modern shopping conditions this is clearly important and when literally millions of packs of a product can be sold even marginal advantages are worth having. Certainly the cost of any research should be well covered.

Brand communication is not the only factor which can be tested. One might want to know from a number of alternative designs which was the most successful in proclaiming a special offer, trade mark, house symbol, the purposes for which the product can be used, and so on.

Packs can be shown singly as described previously or in a display of competitive brands. Testing single packs will provide a detailed account of the communication content of each pack separately. A mass display test will demonstrate how well the pack establishes its brand identity in relation to its competition. Exposure periods are normally rather longer than is the case with single displays and brand familiarity as well as perception pure and simple will determine the results. However, this is a feature of the real life situation and it does not invalidate the findings; it just makes interpretation more difficult.

INTERPRETING TACHISTOSCOPE FINDINGS—How much weight should be given to visual impact?

In general terms the relative importance of impact will be determined by the circumstances in which the advertising material is displayed. A poster intended for roadside display will be more dependent on its visual impact than, say, an Underground train card. Similarly a pack for a competitive fast-moving consumer line will rely more on its impact value than a pack for cosmetic items in which attractiveness is much more important and the display conditions are quite different.

Visual impact is just one variable in the total advertising situation and many others must be taken into account. The danger is that because this element can be measured accurately and reliably at a technical level it assumes a disproportionate importance in decision making. To take pack design as an example, in addition to attracting attention and identifying itself a pack must make some favourable contribution to the brand image and also be pleasing to purchasers. By printing the brand name in large black letters on a white background anyone can command speedy brand recognition. The trick is to achieve communication within the constraints imposed by the other functions the pack has to fulfill. With posters and press advertisements the same line of reasoning holds; the aim is to achieve impact within limitations of the total advertising objectives.

A common problem, and a nasty one, is that a new pack often compares unfavourably on impact with the one it is intended to replace because of the familiarity factor. Here one has to balance what, it is to be hoped, is a temporary disadvantage against permanent gains—usually in brand image modernisation. The calculation can never be an exact one. Impact as measured by a tachistoscope has never been converted exactly into sales terms, nor for that matter has brand image. In this situation the best safeguards are the experience of the researcher who, from previous experience, can tell whether a particular shortcoming is abnormally large and the soundness of the manufacturer's judgement in considering a pack change to be necessary.

VARIOMETER/SHADOW BOX—A variometer also measures visual impact but is used more rarely. Instead of the period of exposure being controlled as it is in a tachistoscope, the amount of light available to view the test object is varied. At first the test item cannot be seen but gradually as illumination increases more elements in the test item become visible and these are described by the informant. Elements which are recognisable at low levels of illumination are assumed to have greater legibility than those which need a higher legel of illumination before recognition occurs.

One popular machine consists of a viewing chamber with a silk screen placed in the centre thus creating two separate compartments. Each compartment is illuminated by a light source which can be dimmed or brightened at will. Initially the light in the compartment nearest the informant is bright and the rear compartment which contains the test item is dark. Very gradually the light in the front compartment is dimmed and that in the rear compartment increased. The test item then slowly becomes visible with the visually dominant elements appearing first.

A similar effect can be achieved by polarising filters or by removing a succession of neutral-density filters one at a time.

Compared with the tachistoscope the variometer has the disadvantage of not providing such a realistic test of overall communication as the total stimulus appears only at the end of the test. However, it is used for many purposes for which a tachistoscope is used.

One advantage of the variometer is that intersubject variations are not great so that small samples can be used. Additionally two items can be placed in the apparatus at the same time and it can be seen which one achieves its visual objectives first on the basis of a straight comparison. Although one can tell only that one item has more impact than another in a certain respect without knowing the extent of the difference, very often this is all that is required. Moreover, the need for matched samples is eliminated with resulting economies.

APPARENT-SIZE METER—Apparent-size meters are used exclusively in pack research. The design on the surface of a pack can create optical illusions about its size. Packs of exactly the same dimensions can appear to hold different amounts of the product. If a pack appears to contain less than in fact it does it is at a clear disadvantage in any value-for-money judgement. This factor can be assessed quite easily by means of an apparent-size meter, which is an adaption of the depth-perception apparatus used in psychological laboratories.

The apparent-size meter consists of a viewing chamber in which the pack is placed on a movable platform under the control of the informant. There is a vertical light strip in the chamber and the informant must move the platform until he considers the pack to be in the same plane as the light strip. The nearer he places the pack to himself, relative to the light strip, the smaller it appears to him. Conversely, informants who place the pack farther away are under the impression that it is larger than its actual size.

Tests of apparent size are fairly infrequent mainly because designers are alive to this problem and seldom fall into obvious traps. Intersubject variations in judgement are small and any suspicions can be allayed or confirmed on the basis of quite small samples. Usually a man who thinks he has an apparent size problem, has.

EYE-MOVEMENT CAMERAS—One can, in theory, deduce a good deal from knowing in what order a person looks at the elements in a visual field and the length of time devoted to scrutinising each element. With a press advertisement it would be interesting to know whether the headline or illustration first attracts attention and whether the body copy is read. Similar information for posters and pack displays would enable one to draw conclusions about the contribution each visual element makes towards the overall capture of attention.

Unfortunately studies which provide such useful information are extremely rare. The employment of eye movement measures in advertising research presents a tantalising spectacle. It is known that eye movement data is useful and that it can be obtained in the pychological laboratories of the universities but it has not proved an easy measure to use commercially. Few research organisations carry out eye movement studies in the course of their day-to-day operations.

The stumbling block is that eye movement is a complex combination of the movement of body, head and eye and accurate recordings are very difficult to make. Various systems have been tried.

CORNEAL REFLECTION—Light from a small source is shone onto the cornea (surface) of the eye and its reflection photographed simultaneously with the objects the eye is looking at. The optical design is such that the developed film shows the reflected light as a small white ball which traces out the path of vision over the display. A television rather than cine camera can be used and in both cases a very accurate account of eye movement is obtained, although occasionally the result looks like a table tennis match played in the fog.

Despite the theoretical accuracy which can be achieved, the apparatus is mounted to an extremely heavy crash helmet and the light source with its attendent prism system is quite close to the eye. Strong men have been reduced to an abject mass of quivering jelly taking part in experiments; taking weight off the informant by suspending the apparatus from a supporting bracket creates a gallows effect and does nothing to calm the victim.

However, by making some sacrifice in accuracy and realism one market research organisation, BCR, has produced a system which some have found useful. The forehead of the informant rests against a padded bar and he sees the advertisement projected by colour slide larger than life at a distance of 2 or 3ft. Accuracy is not, therefore, pin-point as it is not entirely certain how much the informant takes in by peripheral vision and there is some movement of the head possible in relation to the display. However, eye movement patterns have been tracked which (and this is important) in the context of a depth interview have proved meaningful and of diagnostic value.

ELECTRICAL ACTIVITY OF THE EYE—Two electrodes are fitted to the eye, one above and one below. Electrical activity resulting from movement of the eye can then be picked up, amplified and recorded in the form of wave patterns. The patterns can then be converted into eye movement by means of a wave analyser and computer. Sophisticated machines used in the US space programme actually provide an ink trace of the eye movement instantaneously.

Unfortunately the investment required in equipment would make no economic sense to any research agency or department.

DIRECT EYE RECORDING IN A VIEWING CHAMBER—In systems of this kind the informant's head is held very still by means of straps, clamps or a bite bar and his eyes photographed looking at a display. A frame-by-frame analysis of the film can be carried out to deduce eye-movement patterns.

Here the problems are that the situation is unrealistic, the results are not very accurate and analysis is tedious in the extreme.

Several other methods have been tried but most have drawbacks which make them ill suited to consumer research—for example, the informant must wear special lenses.

Another technique was developed at the Institute for Market Psychology, Mannheim, and taken up by BMRB in this country where it is known as DEMOS. Informants are invited, ostensibly, to take part in a group discussion but they are required to stay in a waiting-room until the discussion is ready to start. Lecterns of the kind seen in public libraries surround the walls of the waiting-room and, hopefully, the informant looks at the newspapers and magazines on them. Hidden cameras then record both his eyes and the reading material at the same time. A committee of psychologists decide from the record the exact pattern of eye movement.

After a certain flurry of excitement initally, DEMOS seems to be another method which has failed to be taken up in the mainstream of advertising research. The inconvenience of operating the system does not really seem justified in terms of the accuracy of the results. An intelligent observer with a stopwatch could probably do as well simply watching somebody read in an entirely normal situation.

MEMO-MOTION CAMERAS—Certain problems encountered in marketing research can be resolved simply by watching consumers and seeing what they do. Do housewives surreptitiously open jars of baby food on the supermarket shelves and sniff at the contents? As they are unlikely to admit the fact if they do, a hidden observer in a supermarket will supply the answer. In situations where observation by an investigator is difficult, a cine or television camera taking shots continuously or intermittently can do the job. Cameras used in this way are called memo-motion cameras.

In advertising research, memo-motion cameras have been mainly used in the study of outdoor advertising, a notoriously difficult medium to research. The size and characteristics of the audience reached by posters can be assessed by placing hidden cameras on the hoarding and taking shots of the scene in front of it at predetermined intervals. From the developed film one can see how many people were exposed to the poster and of those how many appeared to be looking at it. This procedure is known as the "Stop-Motion Sample" technique and is associated with Alfred Politz Research Inc.

Memo-motion cameras can be used as substitutes for observers in other kinds of advertising research. Cameras timed to take shots at fixed intervals will, on the same principle as the poster research method, establish the nature of the audience looking at the set when it is actually switched on in normal use. Clearly both practical and ethical problems are involved in all kinds of observational work.

7.3 Equipment and techniques
used in physiological measurement

We mentioned earlier that measuring physiological variables which are known to correlate with mental activity can overcome some of the problems associated with normal interviewing. Another aspect of the interest in physiological measurements is that established techniques of motivation research using individual or group interviews are probably very close to the limit of their development. There has been no significant change in the methods of conducting motivation research in the past twenty years and I doubt whether the next twenty will see any radical innovations. At present each established research agency is generally speaking as well equipped as any other to carry out the necessary data-collection functions in the form of group discussions and depth interviews. Differentiation is based principally on the skill and creativity of the man directing the research; his flair is frequently more important than both the raw material at his disposal and the research technique he employs.

The position in the study of emotion by non-verbal physiological means is quite different. In this case we are at a relatively early state in development and investment in technique has nowhere near reached the point of diminishing returns —or any returns at all, the cynical might observe.

EMOTION AND BODILY CHANGES—On a common-sense level, the fact that certain physiological changes can indicate what a person is thinking or feeling is a matter of everyday observation. People blush with shame, squirm with embarrassment, are flushed with happiness; the very fact that these phrases are clichés testifies to the generality of the phenomena they describe.

Apart from these obvious correlates of emotion, other more subtle manifestations are to be found. Over twenty bodily changes will accompany, in a more or less sensitive way, activity occurring in the mind. Rates of pulse, sweating, salivation and blinking will vary; muscular activity around the stomach undergoes continuous changes—there are many others.

All these activities are controlled by the autonomic nervous system which has the task of adapting the body to changes in the physical or mental environment. One part of it (the sympathetic system) acts rather like an accelerator and produces increased activity in the face of a stimulus; the other part of it (the parasympathetic system) acts like a brake and has the job of bringing the body back to normal after a period of increased activity. The constant interplay of the two leads to a kind of equilibrium.

Of the many variables which will indicate the degree of activation in the autonomic nervous system which is the best one to take? This question has many theoretical ramifications but the practical limitations in obtaining measurements largely determine the choice of indicator in advertising research. By far the most widely used measures in tests of advertising have been the rate of sweating and fluctuations in the size of the pupil of the eye.

PSYCHO GALVANIC SKIN REACTION (PGSR)—Sweating particularly on the palms of the hand is a sensitive indicator of the state of activation or arousal in the body. Only minute secretions are involved and normally they cannot be observed. Palmar sweating is not dependent on temperature changes, being controlled by emotion only. Nobody quite knows why this should be so, but it is.

The study of this skin reaction (PGSR) has a comparatively long history and it is probably the most used and best documented physiological measure.

Measurements are obtained by passing a small current, undetectable by the informant, through the skin on the palms of the hand by means of two electrodes. Resistance to this charge varies according to the amount of sweat present and as the voltage is constant it can be readily calculated. A simple meter can be used to take observations or the output can be transformed into a continuous record either as a sound signal on a magnetic tape or a moving line produced by a motor-driven pen. Devices of this kind are sometimes known as lie detectors and have a limited use in criminal investigation.

Most forms of advertising can be subjected to PGSR tests. The informant has the electrodes attached to the palm of the hand and looks at the test material—pack, poster, press advertisement or television commercial. Tape recorded concepts can also be used as a stimulus. Experimental conditions can significantly influence the results and care is needed (as it is in all perception research) to ensure that the informant is not overanxious or otherwise disturbed by the research procedure.

Principally the test is aimed at discovering the magnitude of the informant's reaction to the various items tested. Over the period of exposure this is obtained by summing the fluctuations produced by means of a metering device. An advertisement which produces a greater amount of activation than another is presumed to have an advantage, other things being equal. As well as providing a record of total response it is also possible, if a continuous recording device is used, to see at what points activation is occurring.

Some care is needed in the interpretation of results because elements in the advertising which are found to be unpleasant or very difficult to understand will produce high readings. Although theoretically this is a serious disadvantage in practice it is fairly easy to sort out positive from negative associations on the basis of a conventional interview which accompanies the test.

PUPIL RESPONSE—The fact that the pupil of the eye is an indicator of mental activity has been known and studied for a long time. Recent interest in the phenomenon has been aroused by Dr Eckhard Hess of the University of Chicago. Most of the work in adapting pupil response to the problems of advertising research has been carried out by Marplan with Dr Hess as adviser.

Compared with PGSR, pupil response has advantages and disadvantages. All test material has to be carefully treated to eliminate brightness variations which could affect pupil size quite independently of any emotional factors; occasionally this means the advertisement or commercial is not tested in exactly the same form as it would appear in real life and it adds to the cost of the research. Measurements are easier to obtain from the informant's point of view than with PGSR, as no electrodes need be attached but the subsequent data analysis is more laborious and costly. Pupil response is not so well documented in the psychological literature as PGSR; on the other hand, serious attempts have been made to validate its predictions in sales terms. Greater sensitivity and freedom from conditioning in the test situation is also claimed for pupil response.

Data is obtained normally by having the informant look into a peep box at a screen on which the test material (slide or ciné film) is back-projected. The left eye is photographed throughout the test period by a camera using infra-red film. After the film is developed the pupil is measured frame by frame and the differences in pupil size are expressed in relation to a neutral control stimulus also observed by the informant. Other systems of recording are possible but they are not widely used at present.

Activation or arousal is indicated by the degree of pupilliary change—the greater the increase in pupil size the greater the reaction produced by the advertising. A normal interview is necessary to aid the interpretation of the pupil-response scores and to assess the ability of an advertisement to convey its sales message.

Some validation of the technique has been undertaken in the study of press advertisements. Encyclopaedia Britannica advertisements, which carried a coupon for readers to send off for further information, were tested by pupil response. The advertisements were subsequently split run, so one could see from a pair of advertisements which had the stronger pulling power in terms of coupon return. Over a series of tests, pupil scores were found to correlate with sales performance—at least in the view of the experimenters.

Arousal resulting from alternative pack designs can also be measured. When social or cultural factors might distort choice in a normal interview situation, a non-verbal measure is useful. In an American study of alternative beer can designs it was found that both Negroes and Whites responded better to designs prepared for Whites than to designs perpared for Negroes.

Pupil response can also be used for pre-testing television commercials. Continuous records of the pupil reaction produced in a sample of informants are summed and shown in the form of a graph. Some measure of total arousal is given by the area contained by the graph (or interest track) and is of great diagnostic value because it indicates where involvement is growing or diminishing. It is thus possible to locate and remedy weak sequences in the commercial.

POLYGRAPH—A recent development in the application of physiological measurement to the problems of advertising research is the introduction of the Polygraph. At present its use is experimental only.

A polygraph in this context is a machine which measures several physiological variables at the same time. Any number can be taken in whatever combination suits the experimenter. Usually four or five are recorded—for example, muscular movement around the stomach (stomach motility), rate of respiration, pulse rate, PGSR, pupil size and blink rate.

Records take the form of a series of wavy lines on a moving roll of paper produced by a number of pens each reacting to one of the variables being measured. One machine used is an adapted electro-encephalograph (designed for measuring electrical activity in the brain) although specially built recorders are available.

Taking several variables at the same time has a number of theoretical advantages. First, the chances of picking up a sensitive measure for any individual are increased. Some people, for example, will show little reaction on PGSR, but will react sensitively on heart beat. (This incidentally has a bearing on psychosomatic diseases: "stomach reactors" are more likely to go down with ulcers than say "heart reactors" who will suffer with cardiac trouble.) Second, the pattern of response as indicated by the various lines is helpful in detecting artefact (changes not directly attributable to the stimulus) and sometimes in refining the emotion being observed. As the record is instantaneous it is also possible to question the informant about particular increases in activation which have occurred during the presentation of the test material.

7.4   Value of mechanical devices

What, realistically, is the value of all this hardware? To answer this we must return to our original distinction between those devices primarily aimed at visual impact/perception and those designed to assess emotional reaction.

Visual perception tests properly used in the context of a total research operation can be extremely useful. The main thing to watch is that the "tail," in the form of the perception test, doesn't wag the "dog."

Pyscho-physiological tests of reaction to advertising material are quite a different matter. We have both ploughed unrewarding furrows in this particular field and are unimpressed by any techniques currently on offer. *Caveat emptor!*

Part Two

During and
After the Campaign

8

Campaign Evaluation
Studies:Some General Rules

8.1 Why conduct them?

People conduct this kind of work for very different reasons. Some of them are anxious to justify expenditure on advertising and want to arm themselves with as much material relevant to their cause as they can muster. At one extreme in this group are the men who understand that a sophisticated marketing company requires an evaluation of its campaign as a matter of course; it is therefore ordered automatically without a second thought, like mayonnaise to go with the cold salmon. At the other extreme are people who are not really concerned with the optimisation of the profitability of the advertiser's business. Their purpose in undertaking campaign evaluation is to increase their personal understanding of advertising theory and they will seize on what looks like a promising case history with a vague feeling that it might pad out a future thesis.

Somewhere in between these extremes there are people who are anxious to conduct advertising research in order to perform the following functions:

1   To get a better understanding of what has been happening in the field, in particular what part was played by the advertising campaign.

2   To find out how the campaign may be improved while it is still running or likely to be repeated.

3   To make a closer investigation of how advertising variables interact with each other, in a particular campaign, media, creative content and the different

reactions shown by different segments so as to improve strategy planning for further campaigns.

Psychologists have found it useful to categorise people according to whether they are primarily motivated by *desire to win* or by *fear of failure*. For the latter group, a campaign evaluation study has an essentially defensive role.

Put very bluntly it offers a chance to see that one has not been fooled. Other people will be trying to get a better campaign, to fulfil its task more efficently and to get more money. It is important to note that one finds these opposing personality characteristics among advertisers, in advertising agencies and in executives in research companies. When you are about to engage in planning campaign evaluation it is well worthwhile considering all the people who are involved, working out the kind of operation they really want and deciding how far their tolerance can be stretched.

Within this overall picture, it is also important to remember that a campaign evaluation study can be produced largely for strategy or largely for tactical ends. One such study might be geared to answering questions such as "Is advertising an effective way of reaching both our primary and our secondary targets, be comparison with promotions and PR?" An exercise may be planned to throw up conclusions such as "The research shows that the money spent in medium X has worked much harder than the money spend in medium Y" or "Those who were exposed to copy A were more likely to consider trying a product than those who saw copy B" or "They seem to have got the idea of quality from the advertising, but missed the point that it is a convenience product." All these, obviously, have tactical implications.

In many of the following pages we are going to be stressing problems encountered in campaign evaluation. Before doing that, we want to emphasise that there is something about reactions of consumers to advertising that has appeared in its media and marketing context that is very different from pretesting work. You cannot work in a laboratory all your life. Finding out about whether and how a few people were affected by a campaign in its early stages—for example, very simply trawling for evidence of spontaneous awareness among a couple of hundred housewives—can be of immense aid in helping the account and brand team to get a sense of reality, while there is still time to influence future policy and tactics. Sometimes they may find that their supposedly impactful campaign has sunk without trace; sometimes there is confusion about a brand; sometimes the right message is rung out very clearly, but when the consumers have looked for the product in the store, they cannot find it; and very often there are indications that the people who are most expected to be affected by the advertising are not quite the same as those delineated in the original plan. All such data are important. Even if it is decided that large-scale sophisticated evaluation studies are ruled out of court for reasons of cost, we do urge that in any event some small-scale operation like the one suggested above should be mounted.

8.2 What are the effects of advertising?

Figure 8.1 shows what looks to be a kind of battlefield. The point of it is that it demonstrates how difficult it is to tease out the influence of advertising on sales from all the other factors which enter into the situation. On the left side, advertising is seen as one of the four main influences which are, or can be, in the control of the advertiser, at least within budget limits. He can spend more on improving distribution; he can pay more attention to advertising; he may put money into or out of promotions; and he can adapt all three of these factors to the circumstances of his market and his strategy aims.

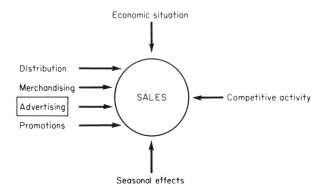

Figure 8.1 INFLUENCES ON SALES

As far as advertising goes, he can spend more or he can spend less; he can change the content or the media; he can link his campaign with the advertising for other brands or a corporate campaign; he may use it specifically to help build distribution or to help push a particular promotion.

It must be obvious that the influence of any of these factors on sales must be greater when all of them are working together, in a way that is consistent with each other. Similarly each of them can, as it were, let the side down in a way that means the rest will also suffer.

We have now reached the half-way stage in the classic argument explaining why sales do not provide a satisfactory measure of advertising effectiveness.

There are other factors which are completely outside the advertisers' influence. The economic situation can influence sales in a way that makes claims on the part of advertising campaigns look ridiculous. In Britain in 1974, rumours of a shortage of paper forced lavatory paper off the supermarket shelves at a faster rate than any lavatory paper campaign has ever achieved or could ever hope to achieve.

It is the same with seasonal effects. A hot Saturday can make an enormous difference to the work-load of a man in the ice-cream van and sales of beer or cider. These are acts of God, not of advertising.

But advertising can be used to capitalise on economic influences—for example, for persuading people to buy a television set before the Budget; or, more strategically, for investing a particular brand with such a degree of desirability in terms of food value, that that brand withstands the effects of inflation and recession better than others. Similarly, advertising can be used to anticipate the balmier days of summer in such a way that there is an automatic link between a rise in temperature and the idea that Woodpecker Cider would be nice to drink. But the degree to which one can claim afterwards that advertising has helped is entirely a matter of judgement—it cannot be measured precisely.

However good an advertising campaign might be, it may seem totally insignificant in circumstances where a competitive brand is suddenly relaunched with a new formula that represents a genuine technical advance, desired by the consumer.

Markets are always changing, or are liable to change. "Competitive activity" may include good or bad advertising as well as factors such as product improvement or range extension. The message of this for the design of campaign evaluation studies is to make certain that:

1　There is an opportunity to check on competitive activity and its apparent effectiveness in terms that are similar to those of the advertiser's own brand.

2　In the course of campaigns, part of the task of evaluation must be to pick up and if necessary investigate and measure any new factors that are changing the terms of competition—for example, reformulations, change in weight of expenditure, etc.

8.3　Recommendations

1　*CONCENTRATE ON CRITERIA RELEVANT TO ADVERTISING AIMS, RATHER THAN MARKETING AIMS*—Whereas at some stage something like awareness of a brand has to be related to purchase and repurchase of a brand, the focus of attention in a campaign evaluation study should be primarily directed to those types of measurement which reflect the work of advertising. This means using intermediate criteria rather than sales, except in cases where—for example, coupon response—the relationship is more direct.

2　*ANALYSE COMPETITIVE ADVERTISING AS WELL*—It is, however, a mistake to assume that the competitive advertising may necessarily be as successful or unsuccessful as your evaluations indicate, given that the advertising strategy may be different. On the other hand, it seems like a denial of responsibility to say "Because we don't know what their strategy was we can't start evaluating what they are doing." This is too glib an excuse for saving money or simplifying everything.

If you have established that in your particular market it is beneficial for advertising to be given a brand distinctiveness, for example, or a very clear personality, and you have information that your competitors are succeeding in these areas—this must be relevant.

3   *USE BASE-LINE DATA*—Very simply, it is the easiest thing in the world to find out three months after a new campaign breaks that there is awareness of your advertising at a level of 50%, and to feel encouraged by this. But what was the level of awareness of your advertising before the campaign?

For many established brands it is very difficult to be quite sure that someone claiming recall of recent advertising is not referring to something that he saw a long time ago. There is also the problem of automatic claims of advertising recall especially in answer to prompted awareness questions. Then, base-line studies for new brands are particularly valuable because they give a chance of showing how the whole market may be affected by the new brand's entry. They are also valuable in adding reality to claimed awareness of the new brand, when informants purport to recognise it from a prompt list. (There always seem to be *some* who claim knowledge of brands that have not yet appeared; this does not mean that the interviewers are cheating.)

4   *ANALYSE PURCHASE DECISION MAKING*—This is particularly important where new product launches are concerned. But there is also a case for paying special attention to buyers, as opposed to non-buyers, when examining the effects of a campaign that might be stressing new features or extending the usage of a well-established brand.

Unfortunately a lot of people have not really got a clear idea why they made a particular purchase. This varies greatly according to the kind of product concerned and the degree of interest that the product holds. People do not go about the streets busily introspecting about what they are going to buy or why—unless something really important such as a house or a car is concerned. However, it is often helpful to know the extent to which purchasers think more about a particular advantage when discussing their last purchase of a product; a change in emphasis may reflect the focus of attention that advertising has shifted from one product attribute to another. Similarly, with advertising which has been extending the target market to new people in the family (husbands, children) who can *influence* a decision rather than do the actual buying, analysis of the decision makes good sense. Inevitably, where new products are concerned, word of mouth, or recommendation of a shop assistant will loom large. This may seem at one remove from advertising, but when these answers are probed carefully in, for example, a semi-structured interview, the terms of the recommendation may show advertising is working at a secondary as well as a primary level.

This kind of work shows that advertising is working, but also that it may be influencing people in a way which had not been planned and which may need careful reassessment. This could be crucial in a situation such as when a proprietary medicine may be promoted for the relief of a symptom but may be bought in the expectation of a cure for something similar but not identical.

5 *ANALYSE USER PROFILE AGAINST TARGET* —Here again the more obvious application is when a new product has been launched. The target is such and such; you then find that the users may be just that bit different. Sometimes, they may even be entirely different. A full understanding of whether the campaign is working is only possible when you know whether you are reaching the people you intended to reach, whether you are influencing them particularly, whether there are other people who are responsible for apparent success and why this should be so. Obviously, further planning is absurd if it is not based on reality.

With established brands, advertising is sometimes targeted in such a way as to try to *change the user profile.* The importance of a brand to its traditional market may be such that any change is a slow business. Where this is the case, periodic checks on the user profile are made; including questions on how long it is since the person concerned started buying such and such a brand.

In many markets, buyers are "promiscuous." They buy several brands over a period of time. The profile is often a question of "Who are those who buy our brand more frequently than the others?" This is more difficult to determine, and is obviously easier to measure by means of panels rather than once-off consumer surveys. This allows the sequence of brand purchases to be studied and compared through the sample, and categories of informants to be drawn up accordingly.

6 *COMMUNICATION IS SHORT-TERM; IMAGE CHANGE IS LONG TERM*—This is a general rule, and as such there are bound to be exceptions.

What is important is not to make the same demands for both communication and image change when setting targets and planning to assess whether you have reached them within a given time period. A realistic target might be to find out the extent to which the target market has been informed about a product characteristic, and to note tendencies towards image change, while investigating by qualitative means whether the reactions to advertising are consistent with the belief that image change will eventually happen.

Just as it is unrealistic to set image change targets, where established brands are concerned, that imply a complete difference of outlook both of the advertised brand and for its competition, within a short space of time, so it is also self-deception to find that a communication point does not seem to have registered after the target has had several opportunities to see the advertising, yet hope that dint of repetition will get the message home satisfactorily.

Advertising should communicate clearly and rapidly in the early stages of the campaign unless there are very special factors involved. Teaser campaigns spring to mind as an exception.

Where new products are concerned, the first indications of the kind of brand image it may be going to have are also relevant to an understanding of what the advertising has achieved on its behalf.

7 *THINK, BEFORE YOU CATCH THE OMNIBUS* —There is an obvious attraction in making use of syndicated omnibus studies for campaign evaluation checks: they are cheap, require less executive time spent in organising the survey and generally offer a broad representative sample and a fast turn-round. You can buy questions on an omnibus just before the campaign breaks, and as most of these services run to a regular timetable, you can position second and subsequent checks at appropriate moments. Some omnibus specialists offer specific samples—for example, motorists, mothers of young children, and the like—which can be economically

tempting, as motorists are more expensive to buy than house-wives.

But there are pitfalls. Not all omnibus surveys stand compar-ison with each other for the sampling methods used, for the briefing of interviewers or for the professionalism of their interviewers. Omnibus work is often boring for an inter-viewer: no sooner does one section start to interest the respond-ent when his attention has to be diverted to the next product field. The danger is that, where a research firm is fully occup-ied, this kind of job may get passed down the line. In the past some interviewers used not only to be contacted by telephone and by post for omnibus studies, but trained for them that way, too. That era is doubtless ended, but differences in stand-ards persist in this form of research probably more than in any other.

It is almost always a mistake to expect to get anything *com-plicated* into an omnibus slot. Do you want the informants to be shown some prompt cards, some stills to remind them of commercials, and a set of semantic differential scales on sheets attached to a ring, to be administered in rotated order? Forget it. Try to imagine the circumstances of the interview. The inter-viewer has to find and cajole informants who fit her quota. She has to ask introductory questions that establish whether the informants are on quota, and to persuade them that they have the time to spare. "It doesn't take long, really." Mean-while, it is probably raining, and a suspicious householder may allow the interviewer no further than the doorstep or the hallway. She has four or five, or possibly more, subjects to cover within the interview. If one of those subjects has more complications than the others, the incentive to simplify it is enormous. Make sure it isn't *your* subject.

For similar reasons, it is unrealistic to expect lengthy prob-ing of open-ended questions, such as you would get as of right in a semi-structured interview, in an omnibus.

But *do* use an omnibus for getting a numerical fix on certain simple easily standardised and measured points, such as spon-taneous awareness, or a brand image check, or slogan recall. Keep these figures in the background of your mind when con-sidering the results of qualitative research among a small sam-ple of consumers who have seen the advertising and bought the product: "This is impressive, because the advertising seems to be making the kind of impression we wanted," you may then conclude "But it still hasn't made any impact on 25% of the target."

Also some omnibus services allow you to build up a bank of people with such and such characteristics for reinterview. This can be very useful when you are advertising a minority product, and only a few people in every hundred will be relevant to your needs: boat owners, or potential boat owners, shareholders, hunters, or mothers of anaemic children, could, for example, be trawled for in this way. The reinterview can then be arranged to probe reactions to advertising in depth.

8   *RECALL BY ITSELF MAY BE MEANINGLESS*—The value of recall data has already been discussed in relation to pre-testing. Chapter 9 deals with specific ways of getting recall data for individual advertisements by way of post-testing.

A recall figure is a statistic. As such, it has *some* meaning. But this is rarely sufficient as an indication of how good or bad a campaign has been. The *overtone* of recall is important, as is the *nature* of the recall. The following is an example.

A recall score may include "I remember the La Bonne Vie commercial. It had two monks in it." So far so good—but the advertiser was not selling monks or monastery holidays.

The *nature* of the recall may include "There were two monks sitting down, and eating bread and cheese. At least, one of them was—the other missed out on it. They were saying how good their butter and cheese were, and wondering if they had enough to send to England." This is more to the point, but it is still factual reportage.

The *overtone* of the recall may include "I felt for the younger monk, who wasn't quick enough on the camembert. The older monk was enjoying it so much, it really made the other one's mouth water. It made *my* mouth water, too." Here there is both evidence of communication and a sense of personal relevance. As well as signalling brand and product availability, the commercial has been stirring or regenerating a desire for it too.

The methodology for getting at the blunt recall score is not exactly right for more subtle investigations of overtone, or even of the nature of the recall. The recall score is a quantitative matter, the other is often best approached by qualitative means and may rely more on interpretation than on a count of the answers.

This is one reason why we recommend that both quantitative and qualitative approaches are considered for campaign evaluation work.

9 *MISTRUST CONSCIOUS APPROVAL OF ADVERTISING*—The best test of advertising is finding that people are starting to talk about the product or service advertised in the way that the advertiser wants. The way that people talk about the advertising comes a poor second—although this can supply clues about why the campaign is working well or badly and how it might be improved.

The public is no better than an advertising agency when it comes to making judgements on whether a campaign is good, bad or indifferent. It is probably worse, because people are tied, as a rule, to what they *like* when they indicate approval or criticism. Agencies recognise—at least sometimes—that a campaign they dislike personally may be successful.

Questions such as "Did you feel this was an effective way of advertising the benefits of drinking mandragora?" are usually completely useless, we have found, as a gauge of effectiveness. They may suggest the level of sympathy with the advertisement, but there are other ways of getting at that if you want them.

10 *CONSUMER BENEFIT AND PERSONAL RELEVANCE*—At some level, this is what most advertising is really about. Any evidence that a consumer benefit is more widely or more correctly understood and associated with the brand, and any evidence that this has some kind of meaningfulness to the individual consumer, are always worth the effort of collecting data. Similarly, evidence that either of these are conspicuously absent is also significant, nine times out of ten, of the possibility that very little more than reminding people of the brand is being achieved.

Some corporate campaigns, arguably, are outside this principle. When the objective seems to be to make people say "Gosh, how big EMX is! How powerful are its mandarins! How inscrutible are its ways! How terrible must be its wrath!" —then it is hard to see consumer benefit or personal relevance spelt out clearly, although the supposed advertising task may have been fulfilled. But even corporate campaigns, nowadays, tend to see it as part of the advertising task to get people to note some advantage that EMX has for society, for the economy, or simply for the well-being of the people it employs. Likewise the increasingly common corporate advertising message "We at EMX cherish the environment and abhor pollution" may be said to have personal relevance, at least to strong environmentalists.

The evidence from post-campaign work on how people talked about the brand, and its advertising, may be thin on consumer benefit. "Whatever," the agency and the advertiser may ask, "happened to it? We thought we made it crystal clear!" The answer often lies in the *other* comments about the advertising—the "vampire" that seized attention, dominated imagination and elbowed out the point that somebody's nasal drops alleviate catarrh. It follows that:

a   Post-campaign study questionnaires should allow for the informant to talk about those aspects of the advertising that made the most impression on him, irrespective of the sales message.

b   This needs to be analysed and interpreted to see whether there is too much concentration on what is entirely irrelevant to communication of benefit, and whether any of this other detail *locks into* the case being made for the brand. For example, if humour is used, is the joke seen as relevant to the brand and what it does or not?

9

Evaluation of Advertisements by Standard Methods

There is a problem of naming here. We describe reading-and-noting studies, and 24 hour recall rests as "post-testing" because they are *usually* tests of the advertising after they have been exposed to the target market. Reference was made under pre-testing to the fact that it is possible to use both methods on a limited scale, provided special arrangements are made, so that they then become pre-tests in the sense that only very limited numbers of people in the target market have seen the advertising.

Here are two examples of the use of these methods as pre-tests would be. First, arranging through the Gallup Poll for special copies of an IPC magazine or a Beaverbrook newspaper to be run off, which are normal for the day or the week except that they contain the test ad. These are delivered to a selected sample and the research procedure continues as below. Two or more ads can be pre-tested in this way with matched panels. The degree of sophistication possible in defining the sample is obviously small, in that housewives cannot be screened for complicated product usage data beforehand. But if an advertiser had access to a panel large enough for the purpose, this problem could, in theory, be overcome. The costs of this work are expensive, and whether it is considered value for money depends on the premium put on the importance of having the sample see the ads in the intended medium. Second, arranging for a television commercial to be screened in a small area—for example Border TV—or from one transmitter, so that only those living in that region can see it, and mounting a 24-hour recall test there.

Similar work can be done to pre-test radio commercials, or the use of poster sites, by restricting exposure on an area basis. Checks can then be made on awareness and communication within the appropriate area.

9.1   Reading and noting

This technique has a long history. Its roots lie in Daniel Starch's work in the USA, starting in the mid-1930s. His procedure was to conduct research among a sample of readers of a magazine, and make measurements of the numbers of that sample who remembered each advertisement in a specific issue. Both spontaneous and prompted awareness would be picked up. Average scores could be calculated for colour ads, for black and white ads, for half-page ads, etc, and eventually similar calculations were made for product fields. This supplied norms, against which an ad's performance could be compared. Ads could also be compared with others in the same issue.

In Britain, the Social Surveys (Gallup) Poll has been running reading-and-notting studies for a long time. A lot of this work has been done for newspapers and magazines because it offers a chance to observe awareness and reported reading of editorial matter. This is of interest to the press in its own right, and it has implications for the comparative value of ads facing particular matter as well. Some ad agencies have tended to treat reading-and-noting as media research rather than copy testing—for example, it gives a view of the comparative value of black and white versus colour, in terms of average scores, which can be considered against comparative costs. Others have considered it more as an ad testing device.

It is important to remember that both "reading" and "noting" are technical terms. The following are the definitions as used by Gallup:

Noting—Looking at or reading an advertisement (or other material), or part of the advertisement, according to the informant's claim made subsequently to the interviewer.

Reading—Reading at least two sentences of the copy of an advertisement, or the rough equivalent in words and phrases, again according to the claim made to the interviewer.

Clearly, neither of these is quite the same as *awareness* of an advertisement. Realising the problem that you are not necessarily limited to what you claim to have seen to be aware of something, in more recent times the procedure has included getting the informant to talk about the way she read the issue concerned, so that a picture can be built up of why certain pages and certain advertisements were not looked at. Occasionally the comments imply rejection, rather than missing out the advertisement for other reasons that have nothing to do with it. An example of the former would be "I'm never interested in that sort of advertisement." An "awareness" score can be constructed by adding those who "noted" the ad to those who gave this kind of comment as a reason for *not* looking at it. For some advertisements this could be important.

But it is still some distance away from spontaneous recall of an ad as most people understand it, for example:

> "Are there any advertisements you remember seeing in this issue of *The Times?*"

> "Yes, I remember there was one for General Accident."

This is another type of measure altogether. But if you organise or commission your own reading-and-noting study, you can of course preface the interview procedure with a spontaneous awareness question, and a prompted awareness question, too, for that matter. "Noting" is then used to "mop up" some undeclared prompted awareness of the ad; "reading" is part of the diagnosis of how closely the informant was involved.

One feature that is difficult to describe is the very specialised way in which the interviewers are trained to take the informant through the issue, marking those pages she has "looked at," after any spontaneous awareness questions are over. It is an attempt to be very thorough, without driving the informant to distraction.

Anyone who claims to have read an ad that is tested in this way is nowadays asked to say what they can about the thoughts or feelings that went through their minds when they first saw the advertisement. This is very close to a form of question used by a number of pre-test specialists, notably E J Clucas. The intention here is to supplement the formalised reading-and-noting data with a more diagnostic tool. There is no doubt that this gives more precise leads for an advertiser or his agency to work on than raw reading-and-noting figures.

However, one main objection to evaluating advertising in this way has always been the nature of the sample. It is not satisfactory, for many researchers, to be limited to a sample of 150 representative readers of a magazine if they are working on advertising which has been developed to do a particular job among, say, canned corn eaters—for example, getting those who know and like canned corn to use it in new ways and buy it more often. If they do not even know the number of canned corn eaters in the sample they can make little of the findings. If they are comparing two canned corn ads, designed to do the same job, from one such test to another, they are in the quandary of not knowing whether a difference in scores is to be ascribed to the advertising, or to the presence of more canned corn eaters. Improvements in this technique have involved analysis of the results by, for example, users *v* non-users. The value of this obviously depends on the size of your market.

It *is* possible to organise your own reading-and-noting research but, given that this involves (or should involve) some very careful training of the interviewers, it seems better to go to a research company with specific experience of it. Should you do so, our advice is to arrange for it to be tailored to suit your problem, not to fit into a convenient slot for comparison with *their norms*. Ask to get spontaneous awareness questions; try to find out what kind of message has been communicated; use a subsample of those who have both noted and read the advertisement, for a semi-structured interview after the basic test itself, to get more diagnostic information; and insist on a sample which is representative of your market, of a magazine's readership. First, pick up purchase behaviour data.

9.2 Twenty-four-hour recall

This form of research is the television counterpart to reading-and-noting. Some will object that one is more valuable or defensible than the other, but the principle is very similar. In a 24-hour recall study, interviewers are required to contact a sample of informants of a particular kind—for example, women aged sixteen to forty-four in the C1C2 social class bracket

—who can show in answer to filter questions that they were watching television during a particular time segment the previous evening.

The households approached to provide these contacts may be selected by a "random walk" sampling method; but for more precise and therefore more "difficult" samples, quota methods may be substituted. The test consists of finding out how many of the *effective* sample—that is, those eligible on demographic and TV exposure grounds—recall having seen the TV commercial that is being investigated during the time segment. After establishing this figure the test proceeds to determine how many recall particular features of the commercial and what playback there is of the commercial's message.

Thorough readers of this book will remember that mention was made earlier (see page 33) that recall figures were the subject of a special investigation and were found *not* to correlate well with sales figures in test areas. Why, then, say much about this test?

Certain respected companies have made their own investigations into 24-hour recall, and have ended up with a profound suspicion of other intermediary measures—like/dislike, persuasion, and the rest. They feel—we believe wrongly—that there is something more tangible, reproducable, relevant and therefore desirable in recall scores, particulary if they are established in a standardised way, every time, for every commercial that they put on air.

In answer to the complaint that it provides arid figures, which may be subject to a large sampling error (on samples of 200 or so), they will reply that the test alerts them to the possibility that they may have an exceptionally intrusive commercial, if the recall score is very high, or, alternatively, a "turkey" if the score is remarkably low. In the former case, they will screen it more often; in the latter it may be withdrawn and examined by means of qualitative work to determine precisely why it does not seem to have succeeded.

The test also has a value in offering a chance for a quantified check (assuming sufficient people notice the commercial) on certain points of communication that may have been in doubt—for example, queries raised by qualitative work at concept or rough treatment stage. But that is not the primary aim.

A 24-hour recall test usually follows this procedure:

1   It is established whether the informant watched television the previous evening or not; if so, which programmes she remembers seeing; careful prompts are given to make sure that the informant has a chance to dredge her memory for unmemorable programmes—for example, "Last night on the ———— show, there was a custard pie throwing sequence in an aeroplane. Was that the programme you saw?"

2   If the informant saw the programme or programmes that make her eligible, she is asked whether she saw all or just part of the programme and whether she left the room at any time. She is asked her opinions on the programme—which may be important, if it can be shown later that a very popular or a very unpopular programme is having an influence on recall or interviewing or following commercials. The questionnaire proceeds by use of a "pinpoint prompt" to establish whether the informant was watching at a point in the programme immediately before and immediately after the crucial commercial break. The answers are checked by questions asking for further details of the programme after the commercial break.

3   Because there are numerous possibilities here—for example, an informant may have switched off during the commercial break and turned the set on again later, or left the room, etc—a further series of questions has to be used to establish whether the informant remained watching during the break itself. Some will be doubtful cases and this is taken into account when the final recall score is summed and judged.

4   Everyone is asked whether they remember seeing any particular advertisement during the programme, for the product field; if so, which brand did they see advertised? The brand name is prompted, to check prompted awareness, if there is no spontaneous awareness. Awareness of the other commercials in the break is checked.

5   Now concentration is focused entirely on what the informant can remember about the test commercial. Apart from story line details, these questions also probe for comment that will reveal whether certain sales messages have got through —for example, "What reasons were given in the advertisement for buying ———— ?"

6   As there is a possibility that those with *prompted* awareness of the test commercial may have said yes because they were thinking of a similar but different commercial screened some time previously for that brand, more questions have now to be asked to determine whether it was the test commercial itself that was being recalled.

7   Finally, questions have to be asked which put the sample of informants in perspective. These concentrate on those points which might artificially raise or lower a recall score, in the event of a sampling freak. For example, informants are asked about whether they were watching television at home or elsewhere, whether it was a colour or black and white, whether they have ever bought the brand—and so on.

Some researchers have suggested that position in the commercial break may have an influence on recall of a particular commercial. There are two reasons why this should be so: those determined to take the opportunity to make coffee in the commercial break may not be quick enough to miss the first commercial in the break, and the expectation of something new and interesting to watch may mean more attentive informants at the beginning or the end. Similarly, when a commercial break appears *during* a programme, as opposed to at the end, it has been argued that there is greater hostility but more attentiveness among those who have been watching with great interest or enjoyment. Such artificial influences on recall have to be considered and taken into account when looking at scores. Certain product fields get better scores on average than others. Norms, therefore, need to be product-specified.

Media planning can create better recall, too. Showing the same commercial, or one of several, at the same time every week, to coincide with a particular programme, can lead to expectation that a brand is going to be featured at that time. Buying several spots in the same evening, for the same commercial, invariably puts up recall—even if only because some viewers are saying "Oh my God! Here it comes again. . . ." Another artifact that should be grouped with these is usually avoided, scrupulously, by the TV contractors. This is the case of the commercial appearing next to a programme or next to another commercial that is unexpectedly complementary to it or in such a strong contrast that it is striking, funny, or both. Several years ago there were protests from a frozen-food advertiser that his commercial for a convenience meat product had been shown in the same break as a dog food. Fortuitously, the eating attitude of the husband corresponded closely to that of a dalmatian, with paws on table. It was no good telling the advertiser that he must have got good recall (comment even reached some local newspapers)—it was the wrong *kind* of recall.

This last consideration is what worries most researchers about recall. It is the quality, not the quantity of recall that is really important. Recall can be bought—with a nude model, with a bobsleigh rushing at the camera or simply with flashing lights and a catchy tune. Recall may be widespread and thin —for example 85% remember it was for X's cakes, which always taste nice and "They said we ought to buy some." Recall may be narrow, but very detailed, and expressed in terms which imply conviction and personal relevance—for example, 45% remember it was for Lyons Hostess Swiss Roll, which is actually rolled up by hand, rare for nowadays, but meaning that they can ensure personally that each product has got plenty of jam and cream, evenly spread, the way that the whole family likes it. Once more, the choice between these results depends on the strategy, but *we* know we would be more encouraged by the latter every time.

To sum up—what do we *believe* about reading-and-noting and 24-hour recall? Both are examples of measurements which are attractive because they have superficial relevance to all situations. But both are simplifications of processes that are very complex and which vary because campaigns are so different and which *should* vary because strategies are so different.

Used as indicators that there may be something unusual about an advertisement which warrants investigation, these measurements probably do little harm and may help. The harm is caused when they are taken as sensitive indices that override other information. For example, ("Oh-oh. Only 63% noting. That's bad. We've got to get back to the seventies. Forget the shrink who told us it's generating belief because it's on a genuine peer-group wave-length.") The harm is compounded when the message is filtered down to the creative team that these scores are magic and that what they must aim at is high recall rather than execution of a brief which is on strategy. Creative teams are always encouraged to be original and distinctive, but the personality of a brand may only develop in a distinctive way if there is a kind of consistency in planning and execution. This can be at odds with a compulsion to stagger the consumers with every insertion. It is also inconsistent with a compulsion to make $x\%$ at all costs play back a feature of a brand, even if they only do it parrot-fashion. This is the road to conformity, towards little notes to creative teams explaining that the best-recalled press ads include squared-up halftones occupying no more than three-fifths of the total area, that headlines must be nine words long—and so forth.

Recall scores are often used on the wrong timescale. A campaign works *over time*, and may not give evidence of delivering what is required of it all at once.

If you want to know what the weather is like, of course it is useful to know the temperature. That is your recall score. But before you plan the day, why not find out whether it is hot and steamy, or hot and dry, or cold and sunny? Why not be brave and take into account those forms of assessment which are less easy to grasp, which rely on more understanding and more interpretation, which may be less easily reproducible and which might alarm the chairman because they are presented in words, not in figures?

9.3 Coupon response

This is relatively clear water. Some campaigns are intended to generate sales *by themselves*, or to stimulate the target market to apply for brochures, or salesmen's visits, which offer the chance for a sale to be made. An ad, the primary purpose of which is to get the included coupon filled in, can be assessed for its effectiveness in a straightforward way. Test ads can be run in national or limited editions of print media, with the coupon suitably coded. Coupon returns are analysed, and the relative efficiency of advertisements can be directly compared.

But it is rather more complicated than this. For instance, one advertisement may be excellent at producing a high coupon response. The numbers of conversions from that ad, however, may be small. Another ad performs less well at attracting coupon clipping, but rates as well or better when conversions are compared. It may take longer, therefore, if there has to be a salesman's follow-up before the true value of a test ad can be known. Naturally, if payment has to be sent with the coupon, the coupons themselves represent the final criterion.

Product: Camping equipment, sold to households
             via couponned ads in the
             national and local press

Size of   Seven-inch doubles
insertions:

Copy style: *Two main versions:*
             A   Mainly illustrative,
                 with several pictures
                 of different kinds of equipment
             B   Only one illustration,
                 with body copy stressing
                 the advantage of the
                 company's products

Coupons: *Two types:*
             X   With a space for the applicant to
                 indicate the kind of equipment
                 wanted
             Y   Simply asking for a brochure
                 to be sent to the name and
                 address to be filled in

Both time and the medium can influence the results. Therefore, ads were inserted in two pairs of local evening papers
over a period of four weeks, one insertion every Friday,
according to the following scheme:

MEDIA

	P	Q
Week 1	AX (90)	BY (55)
2	BY (70)	AX (70)
3	AY (70)	BX (65)
4	BX (80)	AY (60)

Each possible combination of copy style and coupon was tried
out; each in *two* areas; each at different periods of time. This
allowed for a change in the market over time, as well as for
area and media differences.

   The figures for coupon conversions are given in brackets,
on an index basis, next to each code letter. The effect of having

coupon X stands out as particularly important. The difference between the copy styles, in favour of A, is not significant. Keep coupon X and continue experimenting with copy styles while running copy A.

There are side-effects to couponned advertising which are sometimes ignored. In a market where sales depend partly on coupon response, partly on purchase at a retail outlet, or on personal application, this can be important. The most successful ad at bringing in postal sales may be dissuading others in the market, by reason of its brashness and vulgarity in *their* eyes, to credit the manufacturer with the quality hitherto associated with his goods. This means that investigating couponned ads qualitatively can also help.

Qualitative work will also suggest *why* a coupon works or does not work well. Otherwise one is watching the results coming out of a black box, with nothing to suggest to the creative team about *how* they should improve their targeting.

10

Suggestions for
Campaign Evaluation Studies

At the outset we must stress that the choice of measurements to be made must really depend on what is considered to reflect the aims of the *particular* campaign. For example, if your campaign is for a political party, you might well ignore many of the suggestions that follow and concentrate on:

1   Voting intentions.

2   Awareness of issues stressed in the advertising.

3   The image of the party leader (if portrayed in a particular way in the ads).

—and you might usefully cross-analyse the results of these questions by the amount of exposure to the media used in the campaign that subgroups of the sample have had, and by detailed recall of the principal advertisements. But the two examples given below are expected to provide at least a guide in many advertising situations. They each have a basis in fact, but have had to be heavily disguised.

10.1   Deodorant campaign

This example concerns the deodorant market. Brand Q has been on this market a long time. More recently it has suffered from competitive activity at both ends: from other premium-priced brands and from own-label deodorants. A new campaign is designed to restore interest in Q; to attact past users back to it and encourage the current users not to drift away by reminding them of the quality of the brand as an effective product, while drawing attention to ways in which it has been adapted to have more appeal. The advertising platform for the new campaign is "Take a new look at Q, a brand you know and respect as one which does its job well, and is now available in three exciting new perfumes." The new campaign is being tested for four months in Anglia, an "average" Q area. A combination of television and press is used, with local editions of two women's magazines. The press medium is also being used nationally, while television is being used selectively in certain areas. The expenditure in Anglia is matched in the other areas where TV is being used. There are no promotions being tested, although the new fragrances are being strongly merchandised with point-of-sale material in Anglia.

PROCEDURE—A before and after test is organised in Anglia and, as a control, in a combination of three other areas in which the old TV campaign is still running. The same sample size is intended for Anglia as in this combination control area. Using more than one area as a control decreases the chances of comparisons being made useless by a major competitive change in one area.

The purpose of this quantified study is to measure the impact of the new campaign, to find out whether it makes the primary and secondary targets more aware of brand Q at the top of their mind, and more curious about it; to see how the image of Q is affected by the campaign and, in particular, how its standing *vis-à-vis* other brands is affected in terms of consumer preference. The research also has to suggest how far the campaign, as opposed to the new fragrances, is responsible for any improvements, how far the advertising has been received in a way that generates more attention for the brand, and more sympathy with it, and whether there are any ways in which the advertising has not been fulfilling the promise it showed in pre-testing, so that improvements could be made before it is used nationally.

The action to be taken on the results would be to use them to interpret comparative area sales data and, after considering both these sets of information, to kill, adapt or immediately extend the campaign.

A subsample of those demonstrating spontaneous awareness of the campaign are to be given separate semi-structured interviews, immediately afterwards, to get a deeper understanding of their reactions to the television and press advertising, separately and jointly. (Only for the test area.)

The advertising is spread evenly across the four months. The post campaign study is mounted in the week following the end of the advertising. Five hundred women interviewed by matched quota sample, each area, each check.

QUESTIONNAIRE

Classification

Name, address	Place of interview
Age	Personality scales (if
Social class	life style, or similar data
Marital status	has established that some
Area type	are linked with brand
Test area *v* Control	choice or frequency of use)

Media
Exposure to ITV
Frequency of ITV exposure
Reading habits
(women's magazines)
—including regular readership

Product use and purchase behaviour:
Do you ever use any of these products *yourself?*
Which have you got at home *now?*
(EXCLUDE ALL WHO DO NOT PICK DEODORANT BOTH TIMES FROM LIST)
Which brand of deodorant are you using at the moment? . . . Any other? . . . Which *type?* . . . Any particular *perfume?* . . .
Is this different from the brand of deodorant you *usually* have? . . . Which is *that?* . . . (DETAILS AS ABOVE)

1   What other brands of deodorant can you think of? . . . Any more? . . .

    FIRST TWO MENTIONS   OTHERS

2   Are there any brands of deodorants for which you can

remember seeing any advertisements recently—say, in the past three or four months? . . . Any other brands you have seen advertised? . . .

3a   Here is a list of brands of deodorants. Are there any here that you know of but haven't mentioned so far? . . . Any others? . . .

b   Are there any others here that you can remember seeing any advertising for? . . . Any others? . . .

c   Please tell me which of these brands you yourself have ever tried—I mean at *any* time.

(POST-CHECK ONLY)

4   I am now going to read out the names of four brands. (Note—THREE ARE CONTROLS, SELECTED BY ROTATION) Please tell me anything you have seen or heard about them that is *new*—I mean, any way in which they have been changed recently.

P ———— Q ———— R ———— S ————

(POST-CHECK ONLY)

5a   One brand has brought out new perfumes recently. Do you know which this might be? . . . IF YES

b   Which brand? . . . What are the perfumes' names? . . .

c   Has any other brand brought out new perfumes recently? . . .
IF YES

d   Which brand? . . . What perfumes? . . .

(BOTH CHECKS)

6   I am going to read out a number of descriptions of various brands. Please tell me which brands on this list *you* feel are best suited by each description. You may mention as many brands as you like, or you may say none of them.

a   Better quality
b   Unreliable
c   New perfumes
AND SO ON, SOME POSITIVE, SOME NEGATIVE

7a   Again using this list, try to imagine you are going into a shop *tomorrow* to buy a new deodorant. Which do you feel you would prefer to buy? (Assume that each would be at the price that you *usually* find it.)

b   Supposing you couldn't try that one, which would you choose?
CONTINUE THROUGH THE LIST

c   Are there any here you feel are so boring and old-fashioned that you wouldn't want to buy them?
Which? . . . Any others? . . .

PRE-CHECK CLOSE INTERVIEW
POST-CHECK ONLY CONTINUES
IF Q ADVERTISING SEEN

8a   You mentioned that you have seen some advertising for Q. Please tell me all you can remember about it. RECORD VERBATIM

b   Where did you see this advertising? . . . Did you see any advertising for Q anywhere else? . . . Where? . . .
IF SEEN BOTH ON TV AND IN MAGAZINES

c   May I just check what exactly you can tell me about the television commercial?

PROBE: More than one commercial? . . . What did you see? . . . What was said? . . .

And now about the magazine advertisements . . . .
PROBE: More than one ad? . . . Was there a picture? . . . What did it say? . . .

IF Q ADVERTISING NOT SEEN

9   When I asked about recent advertising you had seen, you did not mention Q. Can you think about that again and tell me if you can remember any recent advertising for Q?

IF NO, GO TO 11

IF YES, PROBE DETAILS AS IN 8 a–c

10a   What kind of thing do you feel that the Q advertisements were trying to tell you about Q?

b   What do you think that most women felt when they saw these advertisements for Q? PROBE REASONS

ANY WHO HAVE MENTIONED NEW PERFUMES FOR Q

11a   Have you yourself seen any of these new Q perfumes in the shops?

IF NO, PROBE WHETHER LOOKED FOR THEM
IF YES

b   Have you yourself bought any? . . . Which? . . .

c   Do you feel you might like to try any of these new perfumes?

         PROBE: Which? . . . Why? . . . Why not? . . .

NOTES

1   All the data is cross-analysed by:

a   The classification

b   Brand in use

c   Ever tried Q

d   Q preferred 1st, 2nd or 3rd

e   Q rejected (7c)

f   Media exposure categories

         (High TV, medium TV, light/no TV, high press, low/no press; and by combinations between TV and press according to numbers)

2   Brand image, awareness of perfumes, brand preference (in terms of Constant Sum Technique), immediate spontaneous awareness, and total spontaneous awareness, to be analysed by detailed recall of any advertising of TV and press advertising separately, and by sight of perfumes in the shops.

3   Exactly the same questionnaire must be used in both test and control areas. Some misclaims of seeing perfumes can then be discounted from the test results.

4   User profiles and profiles of 1st, 2nd and 3rd preference (combined) need to be compared, pre and post, test and control, and then checked against the primary market.

5   Do not expect big changes in brand image for an established brand after a four-month campaign—even given the new perfumes. Brand image research should be a matter of periodic checks, to note trends, especially persistent trends.

6   Q 8b asks for information about the medium in which the advertising was seen. This is useful, primarily because it allows the interviewer, and later the data processors, to understand which advertisements are being referred to and separate them out if possible. Sometimes, they remain a jumble in the informant's comments, but this procedure gives a chance to itemise if the informant can actually do so.

Inevitably, television is overclaimed. Sometimes television is claimed even when it has not been used for five years or more. This is not necessarily a question of "stirring the dregs" of the memory of past campaigns, although sometimes press or outdoor work seems to do precisely that. Many people think automatically of television when advertising is mentioned, and some even transpose detail in their minds from another medium into the cathode-ray tube. When a support medium comes over as the dominant one in the recall of when advertising was seen, this can mean that it has transcended the main material; the possibility of redeploying advertising money must be considered. To "transcend in this kind of situation can mean "come near to" or "equal," when the main medium is television and the support is, for example, local press—for the reason outlined above.

10.2   New product campaign

A new food product is being launched, nationally. It is a pack of breakfast rissoles (Mortimers), which are sold from a cool cabinet, are kept in the refrigerator and are placed under the grill to heat them and bring out their flavour of eggs, tomato and bacon at breakfast time. The target is the young ABC1 housewife. The advertising consists of television, with posters being used as a supplementary medium in selected areas. Couponning, to encourage product trial, is used in London.

The launch is national, to pre-empt anticipated retaliation from other food manufacturers. The TV commercials feature a well-known theatrical and television couple (Ben and Philomena Hamme), continuing their popular comedy series on busy mornings. They are demonstrating the desirability of grilling a quick Mortimer for breakfast, when they need a tasty, substantial dish, but lack the time for conventional grills or fry-ups.

The posters act as reminders, showing the inimitable Hammes offering each other a Mortimer over the breakfast table with the slogan "Pack muscle into your breakfast with a Mortimer."

The amount spent on the launch varies from £1½M national equivalent to £300K by area, according to whether posters are being used there or not.

PROCEDURE—A consumer survey split into two equal waves, one in the fifth week of the launch and the second in the twelfth week. The sample consists of two sections, at each wave:

Subsamples	Wave 1		Wave 2	
	A	B	A	B
	1000	(200)	1000	(300)

In each wave A comes first. It consists of a quota sample of housewives with controls for social class and having a job, overweighted towards ABC1s and the under 35s. Some sampling points are poster areas; some are coupon areas.

In each wave B is a *derived* sample. It is derived by trawling for users of Mortimer—which means calling on housewives at home, on a random-route basis, with interviewing extended into the evenings, in order to get some working housewives, and using a filter question designed to determine purchase of Mortimer without showing that this is the criterion. Interviewers are paid for contacts as well as for completed interviews —this is most important. The number of contacts required is calculated from the penetration figures for Mortimer in A. This has to be counted rapidly by hand from the first A returns.

In the second wave, B could be planned to yield 150 first time users and 150 repurchasers—depending on calculation of whether this is economically possible.

Once it is back-weighted A is a normal sample. B is a special sample, which will enable the nature of the purchaser to be studied in more detail—how she has or has not been affected by advertising.

Note—Panels and omnibus services can also be used to produce a B sample, but not in the time allowed here.

QUESTIONNAIRE

A   *Classification*

Name	Age
Address	Social class
Area	Marital status
Area type	Household
Area with TV only	composition
Area with TV and coupon	Working or not
Area with TV and posters	Personality scales

Media
Exposure to ITV
Frequency of ITV exposure

1   Please tell me:

a   What you and your family had for breakfast this morning?

b   Is this different from what you normally have for breakfast? . . . Let's take your husband first: what does *he* usually have for breakfast?
CONTINUE FOR REST OF HOUSEHOLD

c   Is this different from what you eat at weekends?
CONTINUE AS 1b

2a   Have you heard of any special breakfast foods that have come on the market recently? . . . Any others?
IF MORTIMER DESCRIBED BUT NOT NAMED

b   Please tell me everything you can about that one . . .
PROBE FOR REAL NAME
IF MORTIMER NEITHER DESCRIBED NOR NAMED

c   Recently a product has come on the market that you heat up under the grill for breakfast. Have you heard of anything like that?
IF YES, PROBE AS ABOVE
IF NO

d   Does the name Mortimer mean anything to you?
IF YES, PROBE
FOR THOSE WHO HAVE NO RECALL OF MORTIMER
WHATEVER, TAKE CLASSIFICATION AND CLOSE INTERVIEW
OTHERS CONTINUE

3 Here is a list of products (SHOW LIST CONTAINING NAMES OF BREAKFAST PRODUCTS)

Could you please tell me which of them you have-

a Ever bought?

b Bought in the last two weeks?

c Got in the house now? (IF YES, ASK TO SEE IT)

IF MORTIMER NEVER BOUGHT, GO TO Q6
OTHERS CONTINUE

4a Can you tell me roughly how many packs of Mortimer you have ever bought, altogether?

b Have you always paid the full price for a Mortimer pack or have you ever used a coupon to get it at a reduced price?

c The very first time you bought some Mortimer, can you remember what you said to yourself when you decided to get some?

5a Who in your family likes Mortimer best for breakfast?

b Who else has ever tried it?

c For each one who has ever tried it, could you please tell me what they have told you they feel about it?

PROMPT: What do you think they feel about it?
Housewife
Husband
Children aged 12 to 15
Others

d Do you think you are likely or unlikely to buy Mortimer again? PROBE: Very much, or just a little?

e Please comment on your reasons for saying that.
PROBE FULLY

6 Can you remember how you first noticed or came to hear about Mortimer? . . Please tell me all about that.
PROBE FULLY

7a Have you seen any advertising for Mortimer? IF NO, GO TO Q10

b Where? . . . Anywhere else?
IF TV MENTIONED

c   How many commercials can you remember seeing on TV?

FOR EACH

d   Tell me all you can remember about that one.

PROBE FULLY

IF POSTERS MENTIONED

e   How many different posters have you seen?

FOR EACH

f   Tell me all you can remember about that one.

PROBE FULLY

IF OTHER MEDIA MENTIONED

g   Tell me all about these advertisements you saw in . . . .

8   Thinking about (all) the advertising you have seen for Mortimer—what would you say were the main things that the advertising was trying to say about the product? PROBE FULLY

9   What kind of people do you think the advertising was most likely to persuade to try a pack of Mortimer? PROBE FULLY

10a   Have you ever received through your door a coupon for Mortimer offering you the chance to buy it at a reduced rate?

IF YES

b   Did you use it?

IF NO

c   Is there any particular reason why you didn't use it?

PROBE

11   Have you ever found yourself in a shop looking for a pack of Mortimer or asking for it and not being able to find any?

B   *Contact interview*

Please tell me which of these products you have ever bought. SHOW LIST OF NEW PRODUCTS

IF MORTIMER NOT MENTIONED TAKE CLASSIFICATION, CLOSE INTERVIEW

IF MORTIMER MENTIONED CONTINUE AS IN A: Q1; 3b and
c; 4 to 10

CLASSIFICATION AND PERSONALITY SCALES

Notes

1 Personality scales here would include attitudes towards
feeding the family, cooked breakfasts, innovation and tradition, plus any others which are imagined to have a possible
relevance to the kind of person who accepts or rejects the idea
of Mortimer. Comparison of B with (part of) A will show
whether and how far Mortimer buyers are in fact different.
This could have implications for whether the advertising platform and the tone of the executions are right and how to
improve them next time.
2 Buyers and repurchasers of Mortimer are to be analysed to
see how far their profile is consistent with the target market for
the advertising. They must also be compared with others in the
sample for what they have got out of the advertising, both altogether and by each medium.
3 Media exposure groups are to be calculated in terms of frequency of watching ITV. Awareness of Mortimer, and recall
of the TV and poster campaigns, is to be analysed by media
exposure.
4 Q1 can be analysed by purchase of Mortimer to judge the
extent to which it has made itself part of a *regular* diet as
opposed to remaining an occasional choice. Regular Mortimer eaters can then be analysed. Which members of the family
become regular Mortimer eaters, has implications for future
eating situations in advertising.
5 Q3 includes a "pantry check." Most informants are happy
about this. It helps establish the *minimum* proportion who
have the product in use at home; and it cuts out mistaken
claims to intimate knowledge of Mortimer at an early stage, as
well as false claims based on the hope of winning a free product or a prize.
6 Q5 can be studied to see how far *users* demonstrate enthusiasm for the same points that are made in the advertising.

This could lead to adjustments in future advertising. Complaints, on the other hand, may reflect dissatisfaction that some of the advertising has been misleading or overselling. This gives a quantitative fix on the areas that are to be probed in the qualitative research.

7   Q6: often only a minority will be able to say what first attracted their attention to a new product. *But*, if a particular point has been specially instrumental, this will be reflected in the answers. A very high figure for word-of-mouth—for example, "My cousin told me it was worth a try"—should *not* be taken as indicating that the advertising was weak. Getting people to talk about a new product is arguably an important function of new product advertising.

8   The figures for awareness, penetration, repurchase, etc, are analysed by area, to give this kind of picture:

		ALL HOUSEWIVES	TV AND POSTERS	TV AND COUPONS	TV ONLY
CHECK I	Base	1000	350	350	300
Proportion who were		%	%	%	%
Spontaneously aware of Mortimer		20	27	20	11
Able to recognise and describe Mortimer after prompting		55	57	54	53
Purchasers of Mortimer (ever bought)		5	7	7	1
Who used a coupon		DNA†	DNA	4	DNA
Repurchasers of Mortimer (2 + times)		2	3	2	*
CHECK II					
Spontaneously aware		54	60	50	49
Able to recognise		76	79	74	74
Purchasers		11	15	10	5
Used a coupon		DNA	DNA	5	DNA
Repurchasers		5	7	5	2

† = does not apply
* = less than 0.5%

Bases shown are unweighted: weighting would have been needed to balance the sample.

This particular table suggests several things. Notably:

1 The combination of television and posters seems to keep the product more vividly in mind—namely, the big difference between the areas in spontaneous awareness. But the difference flattens out on recognition or prompted awareness; the advertising and promotion tactics seem to perform at a similar level in terms of getting a basic knowledge of the product across. Whether the greater "share of mind" gained through television with outdoor advertising is more a function of the combination *or* of the merit of the posters themselves will come out of analysis of the way in which the informants talk about the advertising in each area.

2 The value of couponning at gaining awareness and encouraging trial in the first weeks can be computed. The costs of couponning then need to be considered in relation to this value.

3 The combination of television and poster advertising seems to have stimulated sales, and to be encouraging repurchase more than the other approaches. But before hard-and-fast conclusions are drawn about purchase and repurchase rates, Q11 (about difficulty of obtaining Mortimer) must be analysed by area, as also should distribution and stock levels from retail audit sources. Distribution variations *could* be influencing the picture.

4 After three months of heavy advertising, there are still a lot of housewives (about 1 in 4) who are unaware of Mortimer. Other breakdowns will show how many of the *target* are still unaware. If the campaign is shown to have been more successful at getting the ABC1 under 35s to know about and try Mortimer, well and good—although there may still be a job to do. This can be measured. But if cross-analysis shows that relatively more C2s have been influenced, then the fault may lie with media selection or the tone and appeal of the advertising, or both. Media exposure breakdowns can throw light on the first possibility (see next chapter), and the qualitative research can do the same for the second.

11

Special Analyses on Campaign Evaluation Work

Sometimes it is not sufficient to take the results of questions on a consumer survey and analyse them in simple tabular form in order to understand how the advertising is working. At a simple level just asking for the data to be broken down by this or that variable can serve to increase understanding. Breaking down advertising awareness by social class may tell you that you have had your message registered more clearly by C2DE housewives, and breaking the data down by readership of the *Sunday People* may tell you that readers of that newspaper are also more likely to have got what you wanted to tell them. There is an open area of question, however: which of the two variables, social class or readership of the *Sunday People*, has *explanatory* as opposed to *descriptive* value?

It is quite possible for either of these analyses to throw up a correlation that is entirely incidental. That is to say, it may be purely and simply by virtue of *Sunday People* readers including more C2DE housewives, that you have got a particularly large proportion of the latter registering the advertising. In other words, readership of the *Sunday People* may be crucial to awareness of advertising, while any idea that the advertising has particular attraction to C2DE housewives may be totally erroneous. In another instance, readership may be incidental —as in the case where advertising simply did not appear in the newspaper, but because on television it appealed to C2DEs, their higher readership of the newspaper produces the artefact that there is something between it and advertising effectiveness.

How do you tell whether the correlation between two variables is meaningful or purely a matter of chance? Again at a simple level, you can obviously ask for analyses within analyses; in the example above, you could break down advertising awareness by four groups: ABC1 readers, ABC1 non-readers, C2DE readers, and C2DE non-readers. This is less practical where you have a small sample or where, in order to get a full understanding of what is involved, you may need breaks within breaks within breaks.

In some cases, common sense can help. For example, knowing that a newspaper was or was not on a schedule gives you an obvious lead, but not all such problems will yield to simple deduction or intuition. The qualitative work which we have consistently proposed as an important concomitant of large scale campaign evaluation studies can help here by virtue of showing, in much greater detail, the kind of feelings people had when exposed to the advertising or when buying a new brand for the first time. Nothing that we suggest in this chapter should be taken as denigrating the importance of qualitative work. But here we wish to discuss analysis aids to sorting out the figures which may *explain* from the figures which may simply *describe*.

11.1   Tree analysis

Most data processing or computer companies nowadays make use of programs which allow categories of informants in a survey to be analysed in the form of a tree. The procedure that is perhaps most commonly used is called AID (Automatic Indicator of Difference). The purpose of the tree analysis is to get better understanding of the category of people in terms of the variables which you have available for analysis which when ordered in hierarchical form give you successive splits like a diagram of the Binomial Theory, or an upside-down tree.

This is best explained in the form of an example. Some time ago at Leo Burnett, advertising was prepared for a government department which was tested out in one area of the country, to see whether its use in conjunction with distribution of leaflets and mailing to personnel officers would result in increased awareness of the importance of keeping a particular form for social security purposes. The effectiveness of advertising was monitored by the use of a before-and-after study in the test area (Birmingham) and control area (Manchester). Local press was the advertising medium used. The dependent variables used for checking the results were awareness of the form, its nature and the level of importance placed on it by informants. The results were not as easy to interpret as one hoped from a first look at the computer printouts. Awareness of the form and its purpose seemed to have increased satisfactorily in both areas, and we were able to calculate the advantage in using the local press medium at a particular weight in terms of the extra people in Birmingham who demonstrated awareness. But there was a peculiarity about the level of importance attached after the test in two areas. Put bluntly, the superficial suggestion of the results was that if you did *not* advertise the form in the local press the increase in the number of people attaching a high importance to keeping the form would be greater. This paradox was investigated by using an AID run on the people who were aware of the purpose of the form and thought it important and those who were aware and thought it less important in Birmingham and Manchester separately.

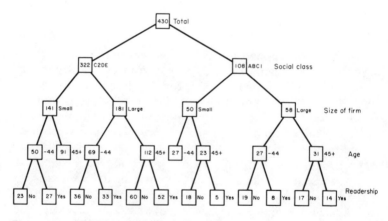

Figure II.I   SECTION OF AID ANALYSIS:

AWARE/NOT IMPORTANT IN BIRMINGHAM

The computer was programmed to split each of these categories successively, on a number of variables which might have had a bearing on the issues. The order of the splitting depends on the degree to which there is a sharp division on each variable. It obviously makes more sense for the first split to be nearer the 50:50 level than 90:10, because the latter instance is simply a confirmation of a high correlation. Figure 11.1 shows a section of the "tree" that emerged for those in the "aware / not important" category in Birmingham.

What does it all show? For one thing it shows that there are large cells of elderly lower-class people among the category of those in the test area who were aware of the form but denied that it had great importance; these people could be in large or small firms, so that one theory that there might be a problem of elderly workers being overlooked in large companies when it came to explaining benefits was not supported. Neither was the theory that failure to register importance was linked with less exposure to the advertising, at least as far as this segment was concerned. But there *was* a sign of such a link among the middle-class segment, and this was confirmed by a comparison with the corresponding tree for "aware/important" for Birmingham informants.

There is a point beyond which tree analysis cannot help. Why *exactly* did elderly C2DE workers who had been made aware of the form not believe it was important to them? The open-ended question in the standard survey did not yield much on this, except for some rather equivocal comments- —for example, "I expect if I really need anything I'll get it anyway." The tree analysis cannot explain this either. Qualitative work is necessary among the specific segment. It turned out that many of this group had tended to associate the form primarily with sickness benefit for men with families; many no longer had a whole family to support, and they had long since become accustomed to sickness benefits appearing without the need of a special form.

11.2 Factor analysis and cluster analysis

Researchers often tend to associate these techniques with work conducted before a campaign. The St James Model, for example, will factor-analyse the descriptions of brands that consumers use, so that they appear conveniently grouped as attitude factors; then it calculates "importance weights" for each factor in terms of correlations between brand preference and accrediting a brand with the descriptions concerned; then it calculates the scores achieved on each factor by each brand and by the "ideal brand." The implications for advertising concept development are the distances between the advertiser's brand and the ideal brand, on important factor dimensions. Our view is that this is a somewhat naive application of St James Model data, as it tends to exaggerate the importance of intrinsic variables between brands, and it seems to deny the virtue of a brand being different, and going after a distinct segment of the market.

But factor analysis can be used after the event, too. A crude examination of the relative degree to which a new brand has gained certain brand image characteristics after its launch campaign gives a rough idea of what image the advertising has been contributing towards—especially if non-users are compared with users, to allow for the influence of product trial. But which image characteristics go with which? Many may be consistent with each other; some may be inconsistent. Sometimes it's hard to tell: "Does the impression of quality tend to go hand-in-hand with 'more expensive than the others'? Or is 'expensive,' an implicit denial of value for money, and therefore of quality?"

A simple correlation matrix can answer some of this. This is very easy and cheap, to add to any analysis programme. It can be used for brand image data, either in yes/no form or in scalar form. A section of the matrix might look like this:

BRAND IMAGE DIMENSION

		A GOOD QUALITY	B GOOD VALUE	C NOURISH-ING	D FREELY AVAILABLE	E etc
A	*Good quality*	1.00	0.83	0.63	- 0.12	
B	*Good value*	0.75	1.00	0.82	0.01	
C	*Nourishing*	0.49	0.72	1.00	0.10	
D	*Freely available*	-0.23	0.14	0.15	1.00	
E	. . . and so on					

This would show several things of interest, whether the correlations have been worked out from attitude measurements for all the brands in a field or for one single brand. Taking the case of one brand, it is clear that those who believe it to be good quality tend to hold a similar opinion about its value. Both these dimensions correlate highly, although to a lesser degree, with attitudes towards its nourishing properties. But none of these points have anything to do with a sense that it is freely available in all shops. In fact, there is some evidence, though slight, that being thought freely available is regarded as incompatible—that is, negatively correlated—with good quality and value. This is a point which will need to be remembered in future advertising.

But how are all these dimensions organised? Is there some hierarchy, whereby certain attitudes tend to hang together, forming a factor that may be more predictive of likelihood of buying the brand than others? Factor analysis can be used to organise the data in this way. Researchers argue about some of the interpretations to be put on the results—particularly with the assumption that *all* the important imagery is sorted out by these means. (For instance, attitudes towards using a brand may be independent of having a high opinion of it; and there is no factor analytic system that cannot be shaken up by a totally new approach.) But the factor analysis does what mathematics allow it to do—to produce objectively determined groupings. In the instance above, it might show that there was, or was not, a factor of "exclusivity," composed of the negative of "freely available," and the positives of "good quality" and "good value." This could not be assumed from the correlation matrix.

CLUSTER ANALYSIS is used to group people rather than data. The principle is similar to factor analysis in that it performs this grouping objectively, according to connections between individuals that the human eye could not observe, weigh up, retain and compare without computer help. All kinds of variables can normally be used for cluster analysis. That is to say, a sample or subsample of informants can be clustered in terms of demographics, advertising awareness, or attitudes to brands—or by some combination of these. Personality or general interest data is often used for this, to find out more about, say, light users of a product to learn how best to approach them next time. Where scalar data is concerned, the procedure is often three-stage: first, to work out factors for the attitudinal data, then to score each respondent on each factor, then to cluster the respondents according to their factor scores. An account of this process is given in section 12.4 in the BEA case history, although it was used there in pre-campaign work.

Continuing the hypothetical example given above, cluster analysis might have revealed that new users of the brand concerned divided into three main categories:

1   Informants fitting precisely into the primary target market, with high exposure to advertising, who rate the brand fairly high on the "exclusivity" factor and very high on a "goodness" factor, which includes "nourishing."

2   Informants fitting half in and half out of the target, with medium exposure to the TV campaign, but very high awareness of the supporting press campaign, and who rate the brand very high on "exclusivity."

3   Informants who are mostly outside the target, with low exposure to the advertising, who like the brand because it tastes good and "makes a change" but have little regard for its "exclusivity" or "goodness."

Information like this tells you much more about *who* has been affected by the advertising, and what they feel is reflected in the product, and who have become purchasers for reasons other than those suggested by the advertising and what they have found in the product. The relative size of the three groups, and their relative interest in *re*purchasing, will suggest how important it is to keep or adapt the primary market definition and what kind of balance of claims makes sense in future advertising in which media.

Similarly, cluster analysis can be used to get more detail about informants who are aware of the brand but have not bought it. This can help by pin-pointing resistances and allocating them across the subsample, tying them in with demographics and media exposure. One important contribution of cluster analysis is to show precisely how homogeneous, or otherwise, a certain subsample really is. The divisions between clusters may prove to be very tenuous or very sharply defined. As for how many clusters one should expect to find in a given situation, too many technical papers are delivered on this subject to be discussed in the space available here.

11.3   Media-exposure analyses

At its simplest, a media-exposure analysis may consist of comparing those who did against those who did not have a chance of seeing a particular campaign. How do these two subgroups, you ask the computer, compare in terms of brand awareness, purchase, or attitudes to the brand? (Comparing them for advertising awareness is interesting, too, but from a methodological point of view of testing the accuracy of certain question-and-answer approaches.) Knowledge of a brand among those who have *not* been exposed can be presumed to come from other sources—word-of-mouth, point-of-sale material or an impulse purchase, etc.

But media-exposure analysis is usually more complicated: first, in terms of measurement; second, in terms of the interpretation to be put on the findings of cross-analysis.

Take a mixed-media schedule, in which television and press are being used. A campaign for a car might be expected to feature on television, national press, local press and magazines of special interest to motorists. *Some* portions of the target market will be exposed to *all* the advertising in all media—they will be heavy ITV viewers, who are also regular readers of all the press media on the schedule. At the other extreme, there may be some (not necessarily all hermits—some people never watch television advertising and a good many have cancelled or cut their newspaper order since recent price increases) who are exposed to none of this advertising. In between, are all grades of exposure level. The problem is to organise them into groups that represent both volume of exposure, and *type*. For example, the breakdown groups might be as follows:

ITV EXPOSURE

All
Motorists

HEAVY			MEDIUM			LIGHT		
Nat	Nat	Other	Nat	Nat	Other	Nat	Nat	Other
and	press	press	and	press	press	and	press	press
other	only	only	other	only	only	other	only	only

This gives you nine cells. The size of your sample may be too small to make it practicable. If standard National Readership

Survey questions are used (including standard ITV viewing frequency questions), then—except with very specialised samples—it should be possible to calculate in advance how many you are likely to get in each cell. Even if the cell sizes are likely to be small, it is often worth getting the preliminary computer printouts in this degree of detail before deciding to amalgamate certain cells for further analysis or presentation.

In the above examples it was calculated that very few informants indeed would see no press advertising at all least among motorists), therefore there is no provision for them in the breakdown groups. Similar judgements have to be made in most media exposure analysis.

Some people read three newspapers, while others read one or two—or none. Their frequency of reading each will vary. Complex press schedules need to be studied in order to provide weights to be given to individual newspapers, according to the number of insertions each one gets. This affects exposure quite as much as regularity of readership. The computer instructions, therefore, must be to allocate informants to each of the high-, medium- or low-exposure categories according to all three of the following:

1   How many publications they read.

2   How often they read particular publications.

3   How many insertions were in the publications read with different degrees of regularity by the informant.

It is not easy, but it can be planned in advance, and the practicality of the breakdown criteria can be checked by hand when the first questionnaires are returned from the field.

Poster exposure has been studied and researched in order to find out how to categorise people by frequency of exposure to outdoor media. We are not convinced that any system is sensitive or reliable enough, except in the special case of outdoor being restricted to Underground train cards or railway stations. Then, it is a simple matter to calculate exposure according to regularity of travelling by these means. But calculations involving shopping trips, etc, seem very suspect to us.

What about interpretation? Consider the table given in

Figure 11.2. The easiest line to start with is the straight one
(— . — . —). This means that of the whole sample 60% were
aware of the brand advantage of product X, and that this
proportion held for those who watched ITV a lot, a moderate
amount or not at all. If this is found to be the case *before* a
campaign, so much the easier for analysis afterwards. If there
were differences, these would have to be taken into account
before pronouncing a verdict on the meaning of
measurements taken *after* the campaign; moreover it would be
important to check whether some other variable were not
responsible for this state of affairs—for example, more users
among the high-exposure group. It is not just a matter of
weighting appropriately at the second stage; it is important to
check whether that other variable was affecting the issue again.

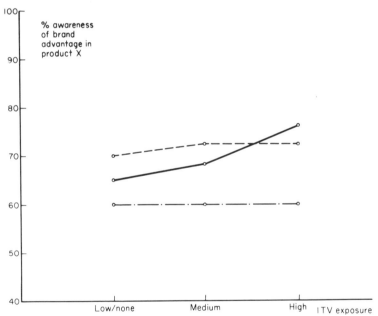

Figure II.2 AWARENESS OF BRAND ADVANTAGE ANALYSED
           BY MEDIA EXPOSURE

What if the straight line persists, again at 60%, *after* the campaign? Superficially, it would seem that the campaign had no
effect whatever. But the composition of the sample in terms of
users, and anything else liable to influence awareness of the

brand advantage, would need to be compared with the pre-campaign sample before one could be clear about that.

If, however, the post-campaign line proves to be —— in Figure 11.2, compared with the straight line, then there seems to be an indication of the effectiveness of demonstrating the brand advantage on television. The more likely somebody is to watch the commercial, the more likely he is to get the point. *But*, a similar point to that made above applies: this group may now include more users. Indeed, one would hope that greater usage of product X would follow from the spread of understanding of its brand advantage. Is it by virtue of trying the product (possibly by promotions?) that the brand advantage is known, or from the commercial. Further analysis should throw light on that. So should an examination of other data—for example, *how long* have the high-exposure group users been using product X? How many of these recall the details of the advertising that tie in with the brand advantage? How many bought because of a promotional offer? This point has been laboured somewhat, to show that media exposure analysis, like all other advertising research data, needs to be regarded *in conjunction with other findings* before it is really meaningful. No figures, or computers, will do the interpretation for you.

What of the third line on Figure 11.2 (– – –)? While the second line suggested that the more television advertising that is used, the more awareness of the brand advantage might spread, this third line implies that moderate exposure alone might be sufficient to squeeze as much of the effect as one can out of the medium. The previous reservations about comparability of the subsamples still apply. But assuming they are comparable, it might be supposed that there is a proportion of the target population (30% according to Figure 11.2) who are either resistant to the idea of product X having a brand advantage, *or* so loyal to or attracted by a competitor that they take no notice, *or* are completely uninterested in the product field anyway. One or more of these possibilities may apply, with the possibility that television (or the television treatment) is unsuitable for communicating this point to some of the target. If another medium were involved—and the increase in awareness of the low/none group in the third line on Figure 11.2 suggests that some source other than television was communicating to them—then the third line *could* mean that the combination of that medium with television was very effective. Again, you have to dig deeper to be sure: is it the magazine advertisements or the television commercials that are being played back by those who have registered the brand advantage?

The scale of the increases, of course, are important for interpretation, too. For example, the closer that the high-exposure group get towards 100% awareness, the more expensive the medium becomes to achieve this particular effect among the rest of the target population, but the more satisfactory the past campaign is shown to have been.

Media-exposure analyses are seldom self-explicit, but they add a great deal to the richness of the material of campaign evaluation, particularly where the implications for future media choice are concerned.

11.4 Disaggregated data

There is an easy way of explaining the principle of disaggregation. Take 100 housewives: twenty were found to be using Macleans toothpaste after an advertising campaign. Of those 20, twelve claimed to have bought Macleans on the previous occasion. Four of the others had done so, too. The net gain appears to be 4%. Of the twenty current buyers, fifteen showed awareness of the campaign; of the non-buyers, another fifteen showed awareness. All these figures tell us something about the campaign. But so far, they have all been treated in a conventional way: by looking for proportions out of the total and for sub-proportions of those proportions.

Thinking about it suggests that it might be a useful aid to understanding of how seeing the advertising might be linked to propensity to buy Macleans, if we could follow through the experience of individuals. This would show, for instance, what kinds of purchasing pattern are most frequent, or "modal," and how these are affected by the intrusion of advertising. One modal pattern might be:

PRE-CAMPAIGN RATIO OF LIKELIHOOD OF PURCHASE OF		RATIO OF LIKELY ADVERTISING EXPOSURE		FINAL PURCHASE RATIOS	
Macleans	2)	Macleans	2)	Macleans	3
Colgate	1)	Colgate	1)	Colgate	1
SR	1)	SR	1)	SR	1

Then, naturally, it is a question of determining how frequently each pattern appears, and how much of the target it describes. To get this kind of information, one must be able to record and analyse the sequence that applies to each individual. This means dealing with "disaggregated data."

It can be done by hand. But, mercifully, computers can now take away the slavery, leaving us with the choice of input, and the interpretation.

Panel data lends itself to a disaggregated approach. If somebody's purchases and media exposures are checked on a weekly basis, you can be that much more certain that reported changes of brand will not be smudged by memory problems. If you know all about the times at which television spots or press ad insertions have been occurring, you can superimpose this information on each individual's record.

Two interesting papers have been written on pilot work of this kind by Colin McDonald of BMRB and by Bryant and others in the USA. They both demonstrate a clear short-term effect of advertising on the likelihood of brand choice.

The task of undertaking this kind of operation for an individual advertiser is considerable, although if he has access to consumer panels anyway, and can cover several fast-moving brands at once, it should not be uneconomic. Measurement of long-term effects, involving long chains of disaggregated data, does require commitment to strategy that may seem too restrictive to some advertisers, less so to others. In the future it may be considered an industry task to get this kind of information and establish more precisely what can be expected from advertising.

11.5   Models using disaggregated data

For some years now, advertising researchers have been showing increasing interest in simulation models. Typically, such a model might involve collecting data over a period during which advertising of different kinds and at different levels has been used for various brands in a product field.

Purchase data is picked up, with media exposure, and individuals' records might be represented in terms of varying degrees of likelihood of maintaining loyalty to a brand or increasing use of this brand. Once the data is "banked," a computer may be instructed to inform you what the effects would be of making this or that change in advertising—for example, doubling expenditure or adopting a competitor's copy platform.

Arguments against this kind of procedure tend to be based on the observation that markets are always changing, and that they are dynamic. The difference between these two concepts is between overall change, such as a gradual tendency to use less and less of a product and substitute something else, and retaliatory competitive action aroused by one's own tactics for a particular brand. But for many markets the major changes and the likely kinds of retaliation can be built into the model on the basis of experience.

Traditionally, the data bank has been filled with "hard" data. This has been a disincentive to many who believe that advertising input is more subtle than just the expression of a broad theme like "nourishment" at such-and-such a volume of expenditure.

Scimitar, a model used in Britain by Peter Sampson of Interscan, makes use of qualitative data as well as hard figures such as rates of purchase. Some of this is an exhaustive analysis of purchase decision making and feelings about using the product. When this is loaded into the bank, calculations can be made of the likely effects of, say, adopting this or that new advertising theme or splitting the advertising thrust between husband and wife instead of just concentrating on one of them.

Much of this work is still exploratory. People are still learning how to use simulation models—especially where advertising is concerned—in the best way. But those who find a good use for models, for their particular market, earlier than the rest, stand to save and gain a great deal of money. If market simulation *works*, it is far less costly than setting up experiments to try out new advertising strategy and tactics; and it will put a temptingly high value on the idea that stands the best chance of winning sales.

11.6   Experimental situations

We do not propose to spend a great deal of space on area tests and time tests.

We believe they can be and sometimes are informative. But, in the very nature of things, they are usually fraught with problems. In a large number of cases, advertising tests are not subjected to exactly the kind of evaluation that was intended in the first instance. The reasons are legion: the competition may have changed; the marketing strategy may have changed; the market itself may have changed. A new product introduction in the test area may have vitiated the basic test. This does not necessarily mean that holding the test in the first place was wrong. There *are* ways of approximating to area test situations, but they are never quite the same. An area test gives the chance of changing an advertising variable in real life, using most media in the way you would use them nationally, in order to see the results in sales and in intermediate measurements.

It is perhaps the most positive way of helping one answer that most intricate of advertising problems—how much should be spent?

The past should always be feeding the future. This does not mean slavishly reproducing past formulas to get the same balance between above- and below-the-line that you had before, on the principle that "It seemed to work out all right, really." It means scrutinising what actually happened to measurements like immediate brand awareness when the budget was halved (or doubled) last year, and how long the effect lasted. It also means taking the trouble to find out exactly what is happening, in communication terms, to the brand of a competitor who has suddenly upped his spending to the point where he dominates on television. This can tell you whether he is likely to repeat this exercise as well as whether you should not be thinking in terms of something similar. (The creative *content* is obviously an intervening variable—but we must assume here that information on this would be sought at the same time, so that the argument can be reduced to *pressure*.) Other advertisers produce their own experiments, which you can evaluate too.

Campaign evaluation work has been outlined in the previous chapter. Here it is worth mentioning that sales data can be a useful addition, but cannot be the sole criterion for deciding what will happen when you vary advertising expenditure by such and such an amount. Two very simple factual examples can help indicate why this should be so.

Fast-moving consumer product for housewife purchase. Launched in two test areas with heavyweight (£¾M national equivalent) and middleweight (£350K national equivalent) support respectively. Here are some indices for the two areas:

	HEAVYWEIGHT AREA	MIDDLEWEIGHT AREA
Second week after launch		
Consumer sales (rate)	100 (index figure)	105
Brand awareness (spontaneous)	20%	15%
Brand awareness (prompted)	38%	35%
Penetration (ever bought)	3%	4%
Repurchase (bought 2 + times)	—	—
Sixth week after launch		
Consumer sales	120	122
Brand awareness (spontaneous)	41%	36%
Brand awareness (prompted)	82%	50%
Penetration	6%	7%
Repurchase	1%	1%
Twelfth week after launch		
Consumer sales (rate)	130	130
Brand awareness (spontaneous)	75%	45%
Brand awareness (prompted)	91%	66%
Penetration	12%	15%
Repurchase	3%	1%

An intriguing picture. The result in terms of consumer sales offtake suggests that spending at a rate of more than the middleweight level is sheer waste. But the other indices suggest something quite different. Distribution, in fact, did not keep pace with the consumer interest in the product that the advertising had aroused. Moreover, the heavyweight area had attained (whether by accident or design) more intensive competitive activity in the form of promotions and advertising. The critical effect of these was to keep the sales of the new brand down to the level reached in the middleweight area.

Decision, therefore, about the appropriate advertising weight to be applied actually had to rest *partly* on research data, and *partly* on a reasonable assessment of the degree to which distribution could be relied on to capitalise on what advertising would achieve, over what period of time. Competitive activity, too, had to be judged—by experience and by whisper. Almost invariably, budget-setting exercises that go beyond a shot in the dark, or the inertia principle of repeating last year's dose plus *x*% for inflation, involve a joint consideration of objective research data and impressions of what a company can achieve in terms of production and general marketing, in the face of competition. It is unnatural to expect anything more from research by itself.

The situation on assessing the relationship between sales data and advertising pressure has not changed since 1962, when Wolfe, Brown and Thompson presented these conclusions for the National Industrial Conference Board:

> Generally, it is not considered reasonable to use sales results as a basis of measuring advertising effectiveness, except where advertising is the dominant sales force, where the effects of advertising are quickly reflected in shipments and billings.

But the point is that other research data does not provide as complete a picture as would allow a precise calculation to be made of how much has been spent to what purpose, let alone how much should be spent next year. Other research *helps*, as we shall show, but it can never tell the whole story. This is one reason why we believe that budget setting by models is an interesting game rather than a practical exercise (although we do respect the value of constructing a model of how one believes advertising works in a particular market, which is another matter altogether).

Here are three examples of the kind of figures from the past that can and should have an influence on these questions. To any advertiser who has not got these kinds of data, it is perhaps less than helpful to point out what might have been useful—except that he can at least plan what to get hold of the next time round. To an advertiser who *has* access to it, this may prompt him to wonder why he has not been shown it being used before.

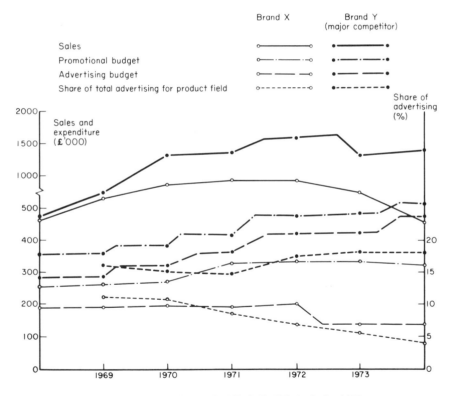

Figure 11.3 SALES AD EXPENDITURE AND SHARE

Figure 11.3 shows a comparison between consumer sales, promotional and advertising expenditure, and share of advertising, for two brands, X and Y, in a fast-moving consumer goods market.

The difference in strategy adopted in 1970, and again in 1972 shows up clearly. For brand X, promotional expenditure was held steady, to enhance its profitability. Brand Y has pursued a more consistent growth policy. In 1971, the proportion of money spent below-the-line for brand X increased considerably, while expenditure on main media was cut back. This mix seems to have held sales more or less steady for about two years, but the brand was then more vulnerable to the difficulties of the crisis in late 1973 and early 1974. It is worth noting the decline in share of advertising for brand X, which is out of proportion to the decline in the amount being spent. At a particular point, we might assume, the identity of brand X became less clearly defined, less competitive than brand Y. There is enough evidence to suggest that brand X's advertising required heavier expenditure.

Of course, certain other assumptions could be made too, from this date—for example, that the promotional tactics used for brand X turned sour, or even that the brand X sales force progressively deteriorated. The data needs to be reviewed against all other information about the marketing variables concerned.

Broadbent and Peach, on the basis of a large number of Leo Burnett case histories, have suggested three kinds of chart that are generally useful in this area:

1   Plotting sales and expenditure (both absolutely and as shares) for major brands, with other influential factors such as price changes, promotional activities and external factors such as temperature change or sickness benefit returns, if these are relevant to sales.

2   Plotting the current ratio of advertising share to sales share against the percentage change in sales on the previous period.

3   "Dynamic difference" plots, such as changes in market share against the difference between advertising and market share, either for complete years or shorter periods.

An example of 3 is given in Figure 11.4.

This is only a scrap from a whole market, to give an idea of what the data actually look like. When figures for other major brands are plotted as well, a more sensitive indicator of how advertising pressure may be related to sales within a given market begins to become apparent.

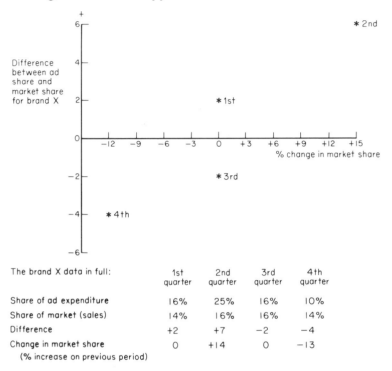

The brand X data in full:	1st quarter	2nd quarter	3rd quarter	4th quarter
Share of ad expenditure	16%	25%	16%	10%
Share of market (sales)	14%	16%	16%	14%
Difference	+2	+7	−2	−4
Change in market share (% increase on previous period)	0	+14	0	−13

Figure 11.4   ADVERTISING SHARE v MARKET SHARE

Selection of the time period for study needs care, and trial and error. In some markets, pressure relates more to *future* change.

But none of these methods will solve budgeting problems by themselves. In conjunction, they can give a better understanding of what greater or less advertising expenditure is likely to lead to, on the basis of historical evidence and in relation to other market influences.

Response functions are an important concept. Figure 11.5 shows the shape of the response function curve that is normally found in research. But it must not be expected that it will be closely similar for every brand in every competitive situation. "Response" means an advertising effect—any which makes sense in a given market. It could be applications for a brochure; it could be the proportion made aware of a product characteristic. The graph shows the extent to which research has established that the response increases, relative to advertising expenditure, which is usually expressed in terms of spots or insertions.

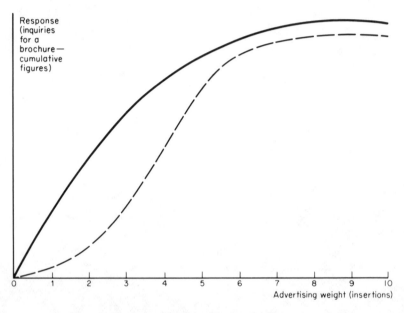

Figure II.5   RESPONSE FUNCTIONS

In this example, the advantage of advertising the brochures beyond the fifth insertion is questionable. The law of diminishing returns is applied. But in some cases advertising will be meant to achieve *more* than simply inquiries for a brochure. This makes the concept of "response" difficult to apply sometimes, although it can be useful to plot *several* curves, so that, for example, sales and image change can be contrasted.

The *dotted line* shows what a response function for the use of television or radio might be in a campaign where a long-term effect is envisaged in the strategy. One or two exposures may not achieve much—hense an S-curve rather than an F-curve. Few S-curves have actually been reported in the literature, but this may be because response functions tend to be worked out more often for situations where the "response" is simple to measure and short-term advertising effects are expected.

A response curve *can*, in fact, offer some help towards the question posed earlier about how low a budget could be allowed to fall before it is cut altogether. In the example given, it might be concluded that fewer exposures would get rid of a tidy lot of brochures, even if one cannot afford five—which would be the most effective rate of expenditure. However, it is still only looking from one angle at the question. The best answer might be: "Rather than spending £*x* to get a lower estimated number of brochure inquiries, try direct mail so as to keep the number up, or offer incentives to agents to give away *our* brochure."

Part Three

Special Problems

12

International

Advertising Research

The principles remain the same. Only the problems get bigger. This chapter will follow the pattern of the book by considering the pre-testing problems first, followed by those which beset international campaign evaluation. Then there will be case histories, illustrating each in turn.

12.1 Pre-testing

First try to be clear in your mind whether what is being developed is an international or a multi-national campaign. The former needs only a basic set of ads produced in one country which—it is hoped—will also be suitable, once they are translated, for other markets. A multi-national campaign allows for more elasticity in the expression of the advertising strategy in each country, while retaining the overall look of a consistent campaign. This distinction is important, because it affects the kind of pre-campaign research that makes most sense for creative development.

INTERNATIONAL CAMPAIGNS—Concept research might as well be confined to one major market, as no concessions are being made to local differences in outlook or motivation. Often we get the feeling that with such campaigns greater importance is put by the advertiser on *visitors* from the major market getting a reminder and a warm feeling from seeing a familiar layout in a foreign country, than on hitting an appropriate wavelength to the consumer in each foreign country, to maximise the marketing potential. This *Anschauung* has been described by Jack Potter in an *Admap* article as "There shall be One Sign, One Sound, One Sell. . . ."

Put like this, it sounds naive. Why *shouldn't* foreigners be different? But the philosophy is prevalent, being refuelled by the desirability of lower costs, greater administrative convenience and avoidance of small local agents becoming either inadequate of "uppity" in their attempts to get their advertising right.

Meeting this situation, pre-testing has to fit itself into the pattern. Adequacy of translation, in message communication and in overtone, will be important points to check. Whether or not the message is discerned as relevant, or whether the illustrative material is suitable may not be regarded as actionable—although, logically, these could be crucial, and the researcher must point out such conclusions, however unwelcome, when they obtrude.

MULTI-NATIONAL CAMPAIGNS—Research is used to determine to what extent a common advertising platform is viable in several countries, and then how best to express this in each country—*primarily* to optimise the campaign locally and *secondarily* to have a consistent look and stance that is recognisable across borders.

Here there are several basic marketing points to be considered before advertising research is called in:

1   Is the brand identical in each market in terms of its
       awareness, franchise, availability, formulation
       packaging, and the stage reached in its life cycle?
2   Is the target consumer identical in each market in terms
       of his interest in the product field, his profile, his experi-
       ence of competitors, his attitudes to the country of ori-
       gin?
3   Are the media comparable, in terms of availability, the
       kind of message and situation that they can show, their
       coverage of the target market?

If this marketing homework has been done, the advertising researcher can be properly briefed and told the constraints within which exploration of a common advertising theme has to be conducted; it can also save a lot of time—by making it clear, before anyone has worked too hard on an impossible brief, when the circumstances clearly favour entirely separate campaigns.

When both the product and the target are up-market, sophisticated and well-travelled, the chances of a campaign having a style that commends itself to the sum target in different countries are obviously enhanced. But a product that is closer to the basic needs of ordinary people may require distinctly different presentation, having regard to local customs and expectations. A similar antithesis can be drawn between products that rely on or are frank about their foreign origin in all countries but one—for example, Coca-Cola—and products which are more cautiously fitted into the traditions of local marketing and perhaps manufacturing—for example, many brands of coffee, confectionery, toothpaste, patent medicines, etc.

The early stages of multi-national creative development cry out for qualitative work. In addition to the basic questions of what aspects of the brand have appeal for the target market and for what reasons, there are a number of other topics that have to be sensitively probed and interpreted. They include the way in which people talk about (or keep silent about) the functions of the product, according to local custom or taboo; any ritual associated with the product, or the occasions of use; any aspect of product function that is regarded as beneficial or poetic, and may allow a brand to have a product plus; the presence or absence of social class overtones in the use of particular brands or products.

All this may vary considerably from country to country. It is not sufficient to know that they like the taste of your biscuits in different parts of Africa. For advertising effectiveness (and to avoid local outrage) you must learn which hand may be shown raising the biscuit appreciatively in the air. The left hand may be all right in Johannesburg; in Lagos it is reserved for a radically different operation.

This example is but the tip of a whole iceberg of differences in custom. It takes a psychologist, we believe, to conduct and interpret this qualitative work well, and to discuss the differences in findings from country to country afterwards. Moreover, the psychologist needs either to be of the country he is researching in, or to work very closely with a native.

This brings us to the first big problems. Qualitative research is more expensive in most other countries than it is in Britain. There are good experts to be found in most European and

American markets, and in many of the Asian and Australian markets. South African research is well developed, too. But to get really good people in each country, you have to *pay*. Next, customs vary in qualitative research, as in other things. An interview guide prepared for Swedish depth interviews generally gets to the main subject matter very quickly. The same document might seem brusquely curt in Spain or Portugal, where a more gradual unfolding of the business, allowing the respondent to tell some favourite stories about his experience —possibly only distantly related to the subject matter—seems to lay a more acceptable foundation to the interview. Some latitude must be allowed to individual local expertise to cover the brief the way *they* believe best.

Presentation of material, whether in concept or rough treatment form, needs to be carefully prepared in each country. It is not enough to say "Warn them that they are only seeing possible claims used in advertising, not advertising itself," and trust that this will be interpreted in the same way. One psychologist we know in Paris goes through a five-minute "lecturette" on the nature of the advertising process before revealing concepts; a certain Milanese likes to announce, with appropriate gestures, "This is no advertisement, this is a fundamental claim!" and unveil the concept as if it were a biblical text; a Spaniard apologises for the absence of pictures. Obviously, these variations will affect informants' frame of mind very considerably, when being shown material, and this must be expected to reflect itself in their reactions.

International pre-tests are undoubtedly easier when the objective is to find out whether the advertising can communicate commonsense information about a product, on a logical, rational plane. Tests for impact, and to some extent for involvement, are fairly easy to replicate. Problems arise when humour or the establishment of a mood is involved. When the object of the advertising is to make use of either of these means for gaining consumer attention and sympathy, or investing a brand or a corporation with a particular aura, the premium put on having a good psychologist involved in qualitative work is even higher. He has to sift the evidence, when such a campaign meets different reactions in different countries, to see which of the following may apply:

1   In country A, this humour is less-well appreciated than in country B.
2   The translation has failed to capture the lightness of the humour.
3   The mood of luxury/importance (or whatever) runs up against consumerist objections in country A. Not so in country B.
4   The visual cues do not have the same image associations in each country.

A hard job, but not impossible—given good people and thorough content analysis.

Does humour travel anyway? Jack Potter says it does. He organised research on Esso's famous Tiger campaign in several countries. Even the Save-the-Tiger follow-up campaign, which was conceived in England, managed to put a big question mark against the myth that humour cannot be international. Pre-testing was begun with pessimistic doubts about whether this English whimsical humour could possibly fire on all cylinders on the Continent. In fact, he found that French, Italians and even Germans appreciated it as much as the English, who reacted very well. Possibly the fact that these markets had already been introduced to the Esso Tiger had a lot to do with this; it gave them a common preparation for the mood and tone of the follow-up campaign. Individual interviews were used here to make sure that informants' *own* reactions were coming through, not simply group-contrived humour.

But translation with the right "feel" to it can make an enormous difference to the way humour is received. Mark Lovell's experience suggests that only banana skins and similar universal vehicles are really international. He once pre-tested advertisements featuring "spouse fares," whereby a man buying an airline ticket can buy a second for his wife at half-price in England and Germany. The English headline was "Your wife is only half the man you are." This came across as amusing—a light-hearted way of putting it. In German it was at first rendered *Ihre Frau ist nur die Hälfte wert.* This came across as unfunny and slightly offensive. Explained, it still seemed heavy-handed. The joke in English *defies* literal translation which retains light humour. The tone is much closer in this completely separate adaptation of the message: *Wir sagen es Ihnen, bevor es Ihre Frau erfährt: British Airways gibt 50% Nachlass für alle Frauen, die ihre Männer nach London begleiten.* Literally—"We're telling you, before it reaches your wife: British Airways is giving a 50% reduction for all wives who accompany their husbands to London."

This goes to show how important it is to pre-test before assuming that humour and mood will travel; and to involve the copywriters in the analysis of the primary data, especially informants' initial reactions and comments, if they are saddled with the task of translating rather than transposing into a foreign idiom.

Group discussions are difficult in certain countries at certain times, because they might be felt to constitute a political meeting. Interviewers are usually released from prison fairly quickly, but good fieldwork time is wasted. If in doubt about this, try individual interviews.

The availability of theatre tests and hall tests for television is very sparse, even in major European markets. This is partly because television is a less important and more restricted advertising medium; partly because there is usually a stronger tradition of qualitative work in advertising, combined with the case of individual interviews for press ad testing. Folder test principles seem to be well understood in most parts of Europe, but we recommend that you attend the briefing, all the same, and ask for test interviews to be done, to make sure that the procedures are observed by all the interviewers.

It was in order to have a system that could be applied in all their offices, for all their clients, that the research directors of several Leo Burnett companies put together a technique called Leotest. There is a press and a television version, intended for use during the early stages of campaign development. The principle is to have a module of thirty semi-structured interviews comprising the test, which are always conducted among the primary target market. The first five questions and the method of exposure of the test treatments are invariable. Thereafter, the system is flexible, allowing for inclusion of specific questions of importance to the particular brand, or the campaign, or the market. Because there are local interviewers in the major markets who are trained to apply Leotest, a request for pre-testing of a sensitive kind can be arranged by telex, with the results of a multi-country study available in a matter of days.

One last warning: it is sometimes tempting to pre-test an idea destined for several countries in "international" areas, such as Earls Court or Golders Green, to save money. Such areas are almost "countries" in their own right. No one is exactly the same abroad as he is at home, and his experience is certainly not the same. The advertising you are used to, and the media in which they appear, condition your reaction to a treatment exposed in a test. Get on a plane and meet the real target.

12.2   Post-testing

There are many ways in which international campaign evaluation work is very similar to that which you organise inside one country. Here we want to concentrate on the differences.

Interviewing standards vary. If you are going to attempt before-and-after checks on consumer awareness, try to buy the best fieldwork in each country. It is worth paying over the odds for it. The important thing is to be sure that you are dealing with interviewers who *care* that they do not prompt brand names in spontaneous awareness questions; that they rotate the order in which they send out brand image dimensions; that they probe the extent of advertising recall. It is all too easy to order the same campaign evaluation job, with the same questionnaire, in each country, and find that points like these are introducing undesirable artifacts into your research findings.

Achieving a standardised questionnaire is something of an art. The straightforward questions such as "Where did you see this advertising?" present no problem. But brand image scales and adjective checklists need a great deal of care. Itinerant students are usually suspect. A dictionary can lead you far astray. "What sort of person drinks ——— brandy? Is he (a) like-able? (b) proud? etc" is the kind of question that can help get a feeling for the image that a campaign may be influencing. But you cannot really compare the figures of those choosing the description "proud" in England, with *stolz* in Germany; and how close the parallel is with *fier* in France is arguable, according to context. Interpreters, not translators, are needed.

There are omnibus surveys in many countries, which offer a

chance to cut campaign evaluation costs. But:

1   Their standards vary.
2   Their mode of operation can vary, even when an international research company is running them.
3   They should not be used for anything but the simplest awareness checks.

How is the data to be analysed? Qualitative work must have separate reports, by area, with an overall summary prepared by an independent party who can note similarities and inconsistencies dispassionately. Quantified work, however, really needs tables like the one below. This is taken from a study of a fast-moving consumer product in several countries. Several possible problems hit you in the eye:

1   The two components of spontaneous awareness are spelt *out*. Experience tells that however slavish this seems, it avoids errors. Otherwise somebody, somewhere, is bound to categorise, where the others are accumulating figures.

SPONTANEOUS AWARENESS : POST-CAMPAIGN
(Pre-campaign figures in parentheses)

	ALL COUNTRIES	FRANCE	GERMANY	BRITAIN
Base all informants	900	300	300	300
Proportion mentioning spontaneously	%	%	%	%
Brand X among first 3 brands	12(8)	10(10)	15(8)	12(7)
Brand X *not* in first 3 brands	14(10)	11(4)	15(12)	15(12)
Total spontaneous mentions :	26(18)	20(15)	30(20)	27(19)
Proportion mentioning spontaneously				
Recent advertising :				
for brand X	22(8)	18(19)	29(2)	21(4)
for brand Y	9(5)	4(7)	– –	23(7)
for brand Z	8(7)	4(4)	12(11)	8(9)
for other brands	18(9)	3(4)	40(20)	12(3)

2   Some competing brands require separate consideration in each country. There is an obvious gap of brand Y in Germany: it is not sold there. The "all countries" average for brand Y is therefore meaningless. There *may* or there may not be a leading German brand hidden among "others" (possibly the market is more fragmented). The table needs extending to allow for all mentions above a certain figure—the criteria to be agreed between all parties to the research.

3   The immediate question that springs to mind is whether the *same* interviewers were doing *both* the pre- and post- campaign checks in Germany and in England. The gross rise in recall in the post-campaign check varies considerably from country to country. Before proceeding with interpretation, all possible differences attributable to interview bias must be rooted out.

4   What has been happening to brand Y in Britain? The size of its pre-post shift is remarkable. Figures for advertising appropriations for the three months *preceding* the campaign, and for expenditure *during* the campaign, must be worked out for each brand in each country. (It is vital that corporate campaigns are investigated here, too, as these may be local, not international, and can influence awareness just like individual brand advertising.) If expenditure for brand Y did *not* rise in Britain, two nasty possibilities must be squarely faced; perhaps the brand X campaign was insufficiently branded, or the copy for brand Y may be electrifyingly brilliant. A less unpleasant but important possibility is heavy promotional work—apart from advertising—by brand Y.

5   Why did brand awareness and advertising awareness move in different ways in France? Answer: the advertising had less impact, partly because of a strike interrupting magazine production; meanwhile, retail distribution had been improving.

The example on page 234 shows that one is always looking for answers behind the answers, where international research is concerned. As much of the background marketing as possible needs to be established by desk work *before* post-mortems of this kind.

It is always worth considering whether or not a standard coding frame for each country needs to be designed for the open-ended questions. Where the copy varies from market to market, there will obviously be some different answers to cope with. But standardisation does help ávoid situations like the following:

REACTIONS TO THE ADVERTISEMENTS SEEN

	FRANCE	GERMANY	BRITAIN
Proportion seeing the ads for brand X	89	120	100
Proportion saying they:	%	%	%
Liked the picture of the food	15	12	—
Liked the family eating	10	2	—
Liked the family enjoying their food	—	22	40

The above makes it obvious that lumping together code lists from several countries, and putting down the figures from the computer printouts, leaves a lot to be desired. How many double-codings were possible in each country? How many categories were overgenerously amalgamated? How many points under "others" should be added to the categories on the table? All these questions will not appear (or will at least be controllable) if the coding frame is agreed internationally *before* the computer tapes are prepared and the runs are ordered. This applies to questions of multiple coding just as much as to coding categories.

If you are anxious to perform more complex analyses of the data—for example, an AID run on those most in favour of the product in each country, versus non-enthusiasts, to see how far there are links with media exposure and awareness groups—it is important to ask for your own computer tape from each research company involved. Our experience is that this is best ordered *before* the research begins. You cannot assume that each company in each country will have a common procedure for dealing with complex runs. Better to do it all in one centre in the same way.

12.3 Pre-testing case history

This is an example of work done for a brand that is truly multi-national.

The form that the pre-testing took was a broad exploration, by means of group discussions and depth interviews, of the way in which the target market in each country talked about minor ailments. Positioning concepts could then be tried out on them, also by qualitative means.

Product X performs the same function for Europeans, irrespective of their nationality. It is a product which soothes stomach pain as well as headache.

The preliminary work showed how very considerably European countries vary in the language they use to describe minor ailments. Underlying these variations there are differences about the kind of problems which they will admit to meeting with any frequency. The way that they see themselves, as well as the way that they enjoy life, has a lot to do with this. The results showed that it was possible to distinguish three broad categories of country, in terms of the differences between users of product X and its competitors:

	COUNTRY TYPE A	COUNTRY TYPE B	COUNTRY TYPE C
Symptomatology	Take pride in the life style that gives them hangovers	Admit to occas-ional hangover (self, or fam-ily)	Deny cate-gorically that they could suffer a hangover
Brand positioning	For "the morning after"	For *head-aches* and upset stomachs	For *upset* stomachs, and head-aches

The brand positioning must also take into account, in each case, the degree to which competitors put themselves in simi-lar positions and the point that the brand has reached in its life cycle. But any expression of brand positioning—in the form of advertising, packaging or point-of-sales material—has got to be geared to what people *say* they suffer, irrespective of what they actually *do* suffer.

The second-stage work dealt with situations that could be accepted as being right for product X, as well as right for the informant. Criteria for judging that a situation could be right were implied personal relevance, after analysis of spontaneous comment; and credibility *vis-à-vis* product X.

Admittedly, most Europeans, in the middle and upper-middle classes, go to restaurants, parties, weddings. . . . But they differ in the kind of event they will identify as a frequent part of their lives, whether in fact or in fantasy.

It is perfectly possible to investigate advertising ideas in this kind of market by way of structured interviews, to check on impact, communication or product attributes, and the like. But in this kind of multi-country work, especially in so personal an area as proprietary medicines, it seems far more important to the local creative team to understand what nuances may lie underneath superficial acceptance of an advertising theme.

12.4 Post-testing case history

This is an examination of campaign evaluation for BEA, (now the European division of British Airways) in 1971-72. In order to clarify exactly what was to be investigated, and how, it is necessary to start the account earlier, so that the purpose behind the Captain's Campaign for BEA can be understood, and the choice of criteria can make more sense.

The airline business in Europe has grown fastest among those sections of the population in each country that are most likely to respond to a European as opposed to a nationalist approach. They live in major conurbations, belong to higher income brackets, and have enjoyed longer education. They are more concerned with what goes on outside their borders. They may, very likely, have some connection with a company which is developing an international campaign in which there would be a strong sense of identity in the advertising, irrespective of the country and language in which it appeared.

When it is considered that, by definition, the target market of air travellers must have a high probability of exposure to advertising in a language not their own, the umbrella campaign makes a lot of sense.

Pre-campaign, a series of research operations were mounted for BEA to see how far this principle was tenable, once consumer needs and attitudes were examined, and, if it were, what the umbrella theme should be.

The advertising task was seen to be composed of the following elements:

1   To help achieve a better overall image for BEA, as an airline with which it was desirable to fly.
2   To make BEA more obtrusive and give it more character in people's minds.
3   To provide a platform on which to mount specific tactical operations—selling holidays, new routes, etc.

The target market was business air travellers and holiday air travellers, in European countries (excluding Britain), the Near East and the Middle East.

An alternative strategy would have been to encourage each country to prepare an advertising approach for its own market that took local attitudes to flying and to BEA into account, and announced and merchandised particular packages to that market without any reference to broader issues. It is fair to say that at the beginning of the research programme the desirability of an international campaign was clear, but the rationale for developing and enforcing one was still open to question.

The following shows the complete programme of research for BEA starting in autumn 1970.

Autumn 1970
1   Exploratory research into attitudes to air travel, to airlines and to a set of advertising concepts for BEA (in France, Italy, Sweden and West Germany).
December 1970
2   Quantified attitude survey, including attitudes towards a set of positioning treatments for BEA (in France, Italy, Spain, Sweden and West Germany).
January — February 1971
3   Pre-testing a campaign developed from stage 2 (in Italy, Spain and West Germany).

September 1971
4   Pre-campaign awareness and image check (in France, Italy and West Germany).
December 1971
5   First post-campaign awareness and image check (in France, Italy and West Germany).
March 1972
6   Leotest pre-testing six campaign variants in Germany and Italy.
December 1972
7   A campaign-effectiveness study (in France, Germany, Italy and Greece).

The concepts investigated in stage 1 fell flat for various reasons. One of these, for example, showed BEA as "the friendly airline," and featured a cartoon of a friendly aeroplane. In Sweden the idea of a friendly airline seemed to be a luxury the Swedish travellers could do without. To them is was distinctly less important for an airline to be friendly than to be punctual. But the French, although warmer to the idea of friendliness, were unwilling to credit the British character with the sympathy and extroversion that friendliness seems to imply.

This is an example of the kind of overlay of intercountry differences complicating the already difficult problem of sorting out attitudes to a concept as such—the desirability of a friendly airline—from reactions to the likelihood of its being true in relation to the brand (credible *vis-à-vis* the British character).

Stage 2 had the task of quantifying hypotheses from stage 1 in a way that had to indicate:

1   Which was the best concept, or composite of concepts, on which to base advertising—*and*
2   How far would this be released across the target, from country to country—*and*
3   What kinds of requirements from an airline clustered, and which were independent of each other—this supplied the image dimensions on which progress was to be measured.

Here, matched samples of air travellers in five different countries were required to put importance values on a range of fifty advertising claims. These were chosen to cover the range of plausible claims for individual airlines that were either being used by different companies or had at some time been considered possible. While most of them could have been adopted by any airline, for example:

> "This airline has the best and most comprehensive bar service."
> "This airline has an exceptionally thorough maintenance operation."

—there were a small number that could, in fact, apply only to BEA, in the context of European travel, for example:

> "The British airline with British courtesy and good manners."

Two forms of analysis were conducted. First the data was factor analysed. Then a cluster analysis was performed to categorise air travellers according to airline attitude factors.

A thirteen-factor solution yielded attitude groupings that were in nearly all cases both internally consistent and intelligible. The cluster analysis was more complex yet, on inspection, richer. Here is an example of one of the clusters in the six-cluster solution:

Example: "Hard facts will reassure me" (Cluster 2)
Significantly different from the rest of the sample on:

Factor 10   They are not impressed by promise of an efficient organisation.

Factor 13   They are impressed by a solid, verifiable claim of safety.

Factor 7   They want technological details, rather than details about comfort, service, etc.

Factor 6   They value details of thorough maintenance, playing down the question of rapport.

Factor 9   They are not impressed by claims about staff who can anticipate problems and needs.

Some of the correlations that were short of significance backed up the conclusion that this cluster discounted human intervention, was anxiety-prone and needed hard facts.

The task now was to cross-analyse cluster classification by country and by holiday *v* business. This yielded valuable information on several important questions. Was there, for example, a business *v* holiday traveller dichotomy that transcended national differences in judging an airline's acceptability or desirability?

The results showed that there was sufficient common ground in terms of an airline's priorities for a European theme to make marketing sense. There was a complex of features that could be considered as reflecting aspects of reliability that were important throughout the major European markets. But what spelt out desirable reliability in one country was different from what implied it in another. Connected with this was the finding that relatively few informants wanted reassurance about reliability, ignoring other discriminating features. Many, in fact, subscribed to the views of one cluster, which might be expressed thus:

> A big company, with fast planes, won't let me down. And, even if it does, at least I'll go down *in style*, with a good bar service and attentive staff to hand!"

This cluster considered as important the following claims:

> "Provides the best in-flight duty-free service both in price and variety"

> "The food is the best offered on any flights in Europe."

—while relegating these to a lower position:

> "The best safety record in Europe."

> "Has very highly trained ground crews."

The intercountry differences were matters of flavour and emphasis. The concept of reliability, combined with elements of personal service, was relevant to a wide spectrum.

The positioning treatments were shown separately from the simple concept claims. These were much closer to rough treatments, except that they were deliberately angled to feature one way in which BEA might have a strong appeal by virtue of what it could offer as a British airline. One showed an air hostess caring for a child, suggesting that the tradition of the English nanny still thrived in the cabin crew, and was reflected in considerable care for all passengers, young *or* old. It bombed out.

But another of the six positioning treatments, which praised the British pilot as being both a strong and a reliable figure, proved reasonably involving. When shown this treatment the informants discussed it more freely and with more personal relevance than they did the others—for example, "With a British captain, I feel more secure." He was respected for skill and for imperturbability. He was undeniably British. He seemed almost like the natural pilot of an airline. The sense of reliability, combined with concern for personal service and a certain flair, found an expression in him. Not a perfect expression—because the positioning treatment was very rough, and in some executional ways it was wrong. But it was something to build on.

The Captain's Campaign ran in Europe from October 1971 through 1972 and 1973. It consisted mainly of press advertisements both in colour and in black and white. There was some later development into television, in Germany, and into outdoor work extensively. Changes were required in 1973 because of the need to publicise the merging of BEA and BOAC into British Airways. But the captain's presence was still there in renewed form in 1974—a link which the consumer has come to expect. This in itself is a testimony to a strong campaign idea.

The campaign evaluation work began with a base-line study in September 1971, to establish just before the campaign broke:

1   Immediate awareness of BEA.
2   Spontaneous awareness of BEA.
3   Spontaneous awareness of BEA advertising.
4   Image comparisons between BEA and other airlines on dimensions determined from stage 2.
5   Detailed advertising recall and impressions of the main message.

All these were important measures to take *before* the campaign, even 5, where the answer "It's a safe airline" could have conceivably been chosen as an inspired guess, relating to the former campaign in the previous autumn.

Media exposure questions were asked at the base-line as well. This is important because media selection did not change so much as the campaign itself—therefore an effect observed later, showing that awareness correlated strongly with exposure to more newspapers and magazines in the schedule, might logically have been simply a repetition of the status quo. Breakdowns of awareness, etc, by media exposure *before* the campaign might sound an unnecessary luxury, but it is vital if one is to be sure of one's ground afterwards.

Sampling problems are difficult in this area, because of the need to match pre- and post-campaign samples in terms of business and holiday air travel, frequency of air travel, experience of the airline in question and exposure to the media that are in the schedule—as well as simple demographics, such as sex and age. In practice, a quota sample with all these controls interlocking is uneconomic. The sample size has therefore to be large enough to allow for weighting, after the survey is complete, to make sure that the before and after samples are strictly comparable. Restricting the samples to certain towns is a help, as newspapers (especially in Germany) tend to be local.

This is the kind of situation where it is tempting to wonder if one might not save trouble by reinterviewing the first sample at the second stage. The objection that carried the day here is that interviewing about airlines, and asking questions about their advertising and their image, must be an influence on the informant, possibly leading to heightened curiosity about their advertising.

The countries chosen for the campaign evaluation studies were Germany, Italy and France. These were the major markets and attitude differences observed in earlier research were more clear-cut among these than between others. Two hundred were interviewed in each country at each check.

The first check after the base-line study (conducted as an exact replica of the base-line study, apart from specific probes of BEA advertising at the end of the interview) took place after the campaign had been running for three months. The purpose of this was to ensure that any important changes indicated by research, either to copy or to media, or to the rotation of "captain" subjects within a country's schedule, could be made before the next burst in spring.

Qualitative research was conducted among a parallel sample of twenty-four informants in each country, who had *both* medium or heavy exposure to the media used, *and* demonstrated spontaneous awareness of the advertising. This stipulation increased the chances of having informants who had had an opportunity of seeing most or all the press ad subjects; their descriptions of the campaign would therefore indicate which of the subjects were stronger and lingered in the mind. Comparison could also be made between the German use of five subjects and the Italian use of two subjects, in terms of their intrusiveness and influence on the consumer.

Three months is too short a time to measure a *permanent* shift on a big issue in the brand image of a well-known airline. It is also not long enough for a researcher to understand fully whether the campaign is going to be strong or not, and in what way, over a length of time. But it is sufficient to see whether there are any serious drawbacks or opportunities for improvement. At this stage reactions were very positive, as the following suggests:

GERMANY, ITALY AND FRANCE

Spontaneous advertising awareness	Up from 13 to 34%
Associations of BEA with:	
Key characteristic A	Up from 20 to 34%
Key characteristic B	Up from 22 to 28%
"I would rather avoid this airline"	Down from 12 to 5%

It is significant that the findings were consistent in all three countries. But there were important differences in the *degree* of change from one country to another, for example:

	GERMANY	ITALY	FRANCE
Awareness of BEA advertising (spontaneous and prompted)	%	%	%
Check 1 (base-line)	25	37	27
Check 2 (after three months)	58	46	50

The biggest increase, in Germany, went hand-in-hand with the largest amount of detailed recall at check 2 and the most accurate interpretations of what the advertisements were meant to be saying.

Part of the differences could be explained in terms of different levels of advertising pressure, especially competitive advertising pressure. But it proved useful to inspect this more deeply.

Extended interviews among those with high exposure to the media in each country suggested that the *way* the target looked at certain media varied importantly, and this affected the likelihood of stopping to consider identical BEA ads in each country. This is a question of the relationship between a national and the different functions that separate kinds of print medium have to fulfil for him. Newspapers and magazines are never identical across borders and their functions are not identical—even when their readership profiles are very similar.

In brief, the depth research in Italy suggested that media changes and a different balance in the campaign variants on the original advertisement would be more effective there.

There was also a strong suggestion that the Italian mix of two Captain's Campaign subjects needed to be increased. In Germany the impact of the campaign had gained from having more expressions of the captain theme. It was important that informants' discussions of what they had seen (in individual interviews) showed that these variants were giving the Germans *complementary not fragmented* messages, and that these were all consistent with strategy.

A year after the base-line check a further study was conducted. Again, the procedure was identical. It was felt important to do this further work at the same time of year as previously, as attention paid to holidays, and therefore to airlines and to airline advertising, probably varies through the year. This is not an established fact, but it seems plausible.

Check 3 showed that the advances made at check 2 had been held, but that further improvement in awareness and image figures was slow going. In the meantime, the competition had responded and was showing gains in share of mind in BEA markets. Possibly some plateau was being neared, consisting of less interest in going to Britain and therefore less interest in

Your Captain wishes you a pleasant flight.

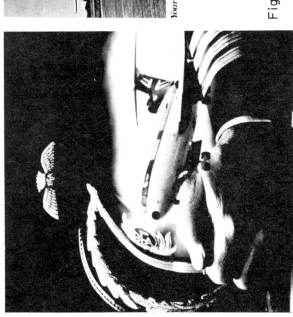

"Ladies and Gentlemen, this is your Captain speaking...."

Figure 12.1   BEA CAPTAIN'S CAMPAIGN
Two examples, one showing a
development into a tactical
selling message

BEA and, partly, perhaps, of antagonism towards Britain-for example, "I don't like the place and I am ignoring their airline." This is speculative. But the impact of the campaign itself, and good reactions to it were still very easy to find. There was no sign of "wear-out," even in one country as opposed to another.

By this time the campaign had been successfully adapted to tactical purposes and some measure of effectiveness was also available in the form of satisfaction in BEA offices about the level of uptake of new offers that had been promoted with the captain forming the frame or background. (See Figure 12.1.)

In 1973 and in 1974 the Captain's Campaign continued, but in new guises. The advertising aims changed, following the merger with BOAC, and the campaign evaluation work had to be restructured accordingly.

13

Difficult Target Markets: Children and Chairmen

The title of this chapter represents a marriage of convenience. There are other kinds of difficult target, of course. But children and chairmen often provide the biggest challenge to the advertising researcher. It may seem a far cry from a campaign for a children's chocolate bar to an appeal to readers of *Fortune* and *Business Management* to reconsider the versatility of a particular merchant bank. But both these targets are very similar in their suspicion of whether an advertisement has been contrived for them by someone who understands and is in sympathy with them or by someone who is off their wavelength. Both are very touchy in their reactions against a patronising offer. Both need a carefully devised and consistent approach from advertisers *and* from research interviewers. Both exert considerably more influence (over housewives or over purchasing departments) than their individual spending power suggests. Both tend to be protected from the harsher realities surrounding them.

13.1 Children

Pre-campaign, it pays handsomely to find out at first hand what children in the presumed target group are like. Children's interests, pastimes and expectations change from decade to decade—sometimes sooner. The kind of home that the average child is used to, the kind of holiday he remembers, or hopes for, the heroes whose pictures he wants—all these are so transient, especially nowadays, that even a young creative department is ill-advised to trust to memory of what kids were like when they were kids. Earlier puberty for girls and the teeny-bopper phenomenon have each affected the scene profoundly. And no one knows when the changes are going to stop.

Some psychologists believe, on the other hand, that despite changes of these kinds, there are certain stages that all children pass through in their intellectual and personality development, when certain fears and desires predominate. The age at which children are most intrigued by magic, for example, is usually agreed to be between seven and nine; this is sometimes explained as coming at a time when a child needs fantasies about controlling or restructuring his environment. When the need passes, his interests change. Later interest in magic is less usual (with the exception of magic tricks, where the child *is* in control) and has an element of regression in it.

Psychologists, even if they disagree about explanations of childhood behaviour, are an important source of information about children in the early stages of campaign development. Teachers, too, are often very fertile sources of information about particular crazes—how they build up, what they are connected with, what wishes and fantasies they satisfy and how they die or are displaced. Both these kinds of informant are worth including in a schedule of depth interviews or a brainstorm session in which they are presented with stimulus material which might include children's groups recorded on videotape.

Specialist informants, among whom youth leaders are often good value where older children are concerned, have the advantage of having seen *a lot* of children at different ages. They can judge how far a sample or a target is different from children on either side of the age bracket or the social class group.

But there is no substitute for watching children themselves. Conventional groups are often too formalised for researchers and the creative teams to observe them talking and behaving naturally. For under twelves, a play-room or a small hall is often a good situation for introducing stimulus materials, such as confectionery, biscuits, ice-cream or toys and games, and then watching what they go for and what they do with it. The researcher can go round from time to time and pick up conversations about the material or start them up. Sometimes it is useful to set up a miniature shop (which in many cases replicates what they are used to in modern classrooms) at which they can spend real or paper money for different items. Later their purchases can be compared and they can be encouraged to talk about what attracted them to this or to that and whether they were satisfied with the results. Obviously, depending on the state of campaign development, it is easy to introduce rough ads or packs or radio commercials from a tape into this scheme.

The mini-shop game is easier to get children than adults to play unselfconsciously. It bypasses any need to get them to "Think back to the last time you bought some ice-cream" as well. A problem with children who have started primary school is that memory tests of this kind are too closely associated with classroom work. They suspect there might be a "right" answer—and panic, or forget.

Adapting conventional interviewing techniques to children from five up to the age of twelve is based on a false premise. This is that they are simply scaled-down adults, so that simplifications of adult questions will do. From twelve onwards, depending on their maturity, their literacy, or the nature of the interview, and if they feel they are being appealed to to behave as adults, they will often rise to the challenge. Their precocity may take the form of wanting to be model informants, and therefore being unnaturally helpful, but they are usually genuine and honest.

Under five, they had better be left alone! Thus there are two main groups:

Aged 5 to 11 Specific research design required.
     12 to 15 Some adult research methodology possible. Complex qualitative work may need specific design.

But this does not mean that all children within these age brackets can be safely combined. Any research that will make demands of an informant's:

Memory	Ability to classify object
Logical deduction	Ability to generalise processes, or behaviour
Imagination	Use of language
Self-revelation	Reading ability

—must be organised in such a way that no one who is too young and inexperienced is recruited and that children of different ages are comparing one another's performance, rather than reacting to the stimuli that the researcher presents. When in doubt, it is best to stick to children in the same 12-month, at most 24-month bracket, if they are to be next to each other (in a group or a mini-group) or if they are to be questioned in exactly the same way, with no allowance given to the interviewers to vary the procedure. When children of different ability confront each other in a group, the less proficient may become inhibited, shy, resentful, bored. A bored child in a group has been known to *bite* an insensitive researcher.

Even where it is merely a matter of different interests, or preferences for a promotion idea, at different ages, it is dangerous to mix the ages, as opposed to examining coeval subsamples separately. Most children have an enormous resistance when it comes to expressing enthusiasm for an advertising presentation, that they may very well appreciate, if they have just seen younger children expressing enthusiasm for it. Similarly, youths of 16, 17 or 18 would often prefer death to being overheard humming music associated with a teeny-bopper idol.

Mixing the sexes is not usually a problem up to the age of eleven. Certainly boys and girls below twelve tend to decry the opposite sex and pretend to disdain them. But, unless they have been educated in a segregated school, they usually adapt to one another's company in a group situation fairly quickly. Above the age of eleven, there is more mutual suspicion, more role consciousness and more posturing in the research situation—until they leave school.

Some regard advertising research with children as a matter to be left to experts on children. Several research agencies have, not unnaturally, pressed home this point. The Child Research Centre in New York is one such specialist. It believes that group work with children should involve these people: a group leader who is likely to be a creative dramatics expert, experienced at playing with children and getting their confidence; a market analyst who is concerned with getting the research task put into operation by the group leader, and who prowls about to ensure that nothing is missed; a "court stenographer" who picks up comments and "non-verbal comments"—for example, a grimace at seeing a particular advertisement—relating them to the precise child who made them. As might be expected, a tape recording of a group where ten children are invited to express themselves freely does not offer an easy ride to the content analyst, without the court stenographer's crib-sheet.

The advantage of the child specialist is that he can pre-empt trouble by warning a researcher of what a child will not be able to answer and by noticing when group dynamics or a personality problem between informant and researcher are proving of greater influence than the advertising stimuli. The specialist can also call on techniques with which to unblock a child's inability to articulate what he feels. Some such techniques include:

1   Urging young children to shout out their answers all at once, and then repeating them individually.

2   Getting them to draw or act out their feelings.

3   To act out advertisements, particularly television commercials, to see what part of them they feel to be important or significant and what parts they misinterpret or avoid.

4   Attending a group with a friend, to whisper and confer with, so that the braver can present their joint view.

5   Using dolls as a projective technique—for example, getting girls to dress and play with dolls in a way that brings in a product they are shown advertised.

These are just a few of the aids to qualitative research a children's specialist can provide. But it should be pointed out that many psychologists in ordinary research companies or in advertising agencies can master the principles—*provided* they have somebody who is good with children. This is probably the major factor that determines success.

John Goodyear, of Market Behaviour, has done a large amount of work with children. His view is that the size of a children's group should be closer to seven than to ten, and that more than two adults in the room is liable to disturb the research. He is anxious that a child should be in an environment that is or becomes familiar easily, and he feels that too many people in the room are disturbing. We agree with him. We also feel that paired interviews for the fives and sixes, rising to about six or seven in a group of ten-year-olds, is a help towards making children feel at home and motivated to contribute. Making the adult get down to floor level, on cushions, is a help in this direction. No one likes craning his neck upwards to an interviewer for very long, least of all a child.

One further way of simplifying an interview situation for children or, for that matter, for any sample of informants who find it difficult to be articulate about their imaginings with regard to the feelings they have about an ad or a product as presented by an ad, is to use the Gallery Technique. Here a wide gallery or pictures of different types of individuals, some recognisable by name, some not, is shown to a child, and he is asked to say:

> "What sort of man do you think it was who said 'Try some Happicola' on the television just then? Can you point out which of these it might have been?... Can you tell me a lot about this one you pointed to—is he a nice sort of person, or not so nice?"—etc.

This makes it a much easier task to understand the impression that a presenter made, than trying to get a child to visualise and then describe somebody in the abstract.

Much of what has been said has concerned qualitative research. This is because it is in most cases unwise to attempt quantification, except of very simple issues—for example, to find out how many children of a certain age can understand a particular slogan or like a particular pop star. Flexibility is crucial in researching advertising, among young children especially. Hence a folder test, or a structured theatre test of a commercial is probably best not attempted. Both demand—if they are to work properly—too rigid a format. At twelve and over, simple folder tests, or tests of advertising within comic magazines previously issued to the informants, can work reasonably well. Even so, careful assessment of reading ability is important, and it cannot be assumed that all children read comics of certain kinds.

CASE HISTORY: CURLY-WURLY—The birth of Curly-Wurly, a top-selling chocolate count line, bought primarily by and for children aged seven to twelve, took place at Leo Burnett in London. A group of children were allowed to wander around a room with all sorts of confectionery on display. Many talked about different kinds and refreshed their memory of them from time to time. Roy Langmaid, who took the group, encouraged them to expand on the kind of sweet they felt they would really like to be able to buy. A composite of the replica suggested Curly-Wurly, a bar which was "like a curly-wurly squiggle," which "went on and on" and had "nice toffee inside that lasted and lasted" and "was covered in chocolate." Prototypes were made and tested among other samples of children. Enthusiasm was regenerated at each research stage.

It is significant that here, children had indicated not just the product characteristics, but the kind of promise that the product had to have as well, and also (very nearly) the name. A lot of the early advertising concept work, therefore, was covered by convening, and interpreting, very informal group discussions. Much of the advertising research work was directed towards making sure that children continued to perceive the basic benefits and promise of the product, rather than working out what they should be told about it. The same applied to the product testing work, too.

Three treatments were developed for launching Curly-Wurly in a test area in the North-East. Each was trying to do the same thing: to tell children within the age group that Curly-Wurly was an exciting chocolate bar, shaped like its name, with a centre of chewy toffee, covered with milk chocolate, and that it lasted a long time, making it very good value at 2½ pence. The treatments each had their own supporters, in the agency and at Cadbury-Schweppes, which makes the bar. They were all for TV:

1   Cartoon treatment, featuring children in a sweet shop in a joke situation.
2   A film using Terry Scott, impersonating a 10-year-old schoolboy.
3   A group of children at a party out of doors, with a jingle that had a strong beat to it.

The decision was taken to pre-test these ideas in the form of rough films. The pre-testing was conducted with groups of children in Newcastle, in the test area, because it was felt that reactions to Terry Scott (a southern comedian) and possibly to the kind of music used in the jingle commercial might be different there than in London. Group discussions were again used, at which small groups of children were exposed to one of the three films first (by rotation), and asked to talk about the product they had just seen. The second film was judged to be the best launch for Curly-Wurly, on these grounds:

1   Communication of product attributes.

2   Consistency of appeal across the age bracket.

3   The strong sense of fun surrounding the product, and the commercial.

Put very briefly, it was a case of Terry Scott being liked, while the joke he was making—about his pals being unable to talk because they were all busy chewing Curly-Wurly—was entirely relevant to what was being communicated. The cartoon treatment did its job, but with less fun and less originality. The jingle appealed musically, but put some children off because it was too age specific in the children shown. (It can be hypothesised, too, that some children rumbled the "party," and were unconvinced.)

When the product was launched, normal plans for campaign evaluation had to be considerably revised. Consumer demand outpaced supply to the extent that advertising had to be withdrawn temporarily.

13.2   Chairmen

Chairman, senior executives, directors and doctors are a rather more difficult proposition for advertising research than children. At a practical level there are fewer of them and they are relatively inaccessible. Being sophisticated about advertising—possibly being responsible for handling advertising themselves—they are not easy meat for the researcher.

Assuming the target market consists of a small number of customers with a large amount of purchasing power, getting a reasonable sample is the first hurdle to be overcome. Here the problems are those facing any industrial researcher. Samples have to be selected from circulation lists, trade directories, telephone directories, files of customers, and so on. Putting together a good sample can be difficult and time consuming. If you want, say, a sample of a 100 men with financial responsibility for medium-sized firms who are not already clients of the financial institution being advertised, the clerical work is immense. Directories are out of date as soon as they are published. City centres are redeveloped and addresses change; firms go into liquidation, merge, change their names. Agglomerations of companies mean that the same individual may turn up in six different concerns.

Having drawn the sample, appointments have to be made for interviewers to see the individuals concerned. Secretaries skilled in the art of protecting their bosses from unsolicited contacts have to be persuaded that the interview is necessary and useful. With the best will in the world, an appointment may not be possible within the fieldwork period.

By comparison, setting up a quota sample of 100 housewives takes about fifteen minutes, and the interviewer would quite probably get an interview with the first person she stopped in the street. Advertising research among executives therefore is extremely expensive and large samples are usually ruled out on cost grounds. Postal and telephone interviews are much cheaper than personal contact and are occasionally useful. Simple advertising awareness checks and straightforward company image studies can be carried out by phone but the inherent limitations of this type of interview render it useless for *comprehending* reaction to advertising.

This fundamental understanding of how the advertising relates to real needs looms larger in the business than in the consumer context. Very often the problem is not to consider subtleties of alternative approaches or the niceties of image projection but to gain some idea of what makes the customer tick. Take cars for example. Any advertising team, without research, would between them have some idea of what consumers wanted and why. As individuals they buy their own cars and discuss car matters, sometimes ad nauseam, with their friends. It would seem unlikely that any advertising they produced would be *totally* ill conceived. Let us suppose that the same team had to create a campaign for a range of vehicles for municipal authorities—refuse disposal lorries, sludge carriers and the like—where would they begin? Intuition would not help a great deal. Quite simple research on the other hand would reveal how the mechanics of purchasing were carried out and what the real role (if any) advertising could play in the process. Research would point to the areas closest to the heart of the transport manager—vehicle unreliability leading to screams from streets of housewives with uncollected rubbish might provide an unexpected point of entry.

With established on-going products, too, situations change and advertising could become irrelevant in a different economic climate—the energy crisis, rising commodity prices and an increasing concern for the environment might be grounds for re-examining approaches. Competitive innovation or advertising might also lead to similar reappraisals.

It makes less economic sense, unless the research is being conducted from some other motive, to check alternative illustrations, layouts, slogans, etc. Very often these can be researched more economically among a general sample of businessmen of the same age and social class. If a question of taste is involved, for example, this would not normally be related to the special business characteristics of the informant.

As far as the interview itself is concerned the situation is much more demanding:

1   The informant's time is valuable—even if it isn't he has to think it is valuable. Interviews should therefore be brief and demonstrably relevant—this isn't always easy.

2   In a normal copy research situation with consumers, the informants are co-operative and in some cases slightly one down. They play a more or less passive role in the interview answering sometimes tiresome or absurd questions with considerable patience- curiosity about the aims of the research or the purpose of particular questions is rare. All this is often reversed in executive interviewing. Informants are extremely interested to know who is doing what and why. If a question seems obscure they want elucidation. As a professional stance they do not want to appear to be suffering fools gladly.

Careful questionnaire design is therefore essential. Many questions from the stock-pot of copy test questionnaire are unsuitable. Questions designed to measure image projected, for example, are vague and informants are asked not to think about them too much. Many top executives find this hard to accept. For example, "Company X has a good reputation" would pass muster as part of an image battery in a consumer brand image check. Informants would agree or disagree quite cheerfully using their response to indicate a general evaluation of the company. A chairman would quite reasonably ask "A good reputation for what? Its products? Stock Exchange performance? Export record? Technical innovation? Labour relations?" Sometimes this kind of response is unreasonable, taken in context, and the chairman has his joke at the expense of the interviewer who with tact and training will talk herself out of this situation and *not* allow herself to say "Don't be so childish" (hence the title to this chapter!).

Better by far to avoid this situation in constructing the interview. Give your man plenty of opportunity to express his feelings, offer suggestions and make criticisms with the minimum of structured content. Even if the information is unnecessary from the research point of view, it is better to listen rather than spoil the interviewing rapport. Semi-structuring the interview helps to cover essential points. A typical study might involve twenty to thirty such interviews.

It goes without saying that interviewers for this kind of work must be of high calibre—at ease socially in the interviewing situation as well as being qualified interviewers. They should be able to answer questions as well as ask them without appearing to be evasive yet avoiding the deep water. These qualities demand a high rate of pay, again meaning expensive research. Informants, too, are often given a gift or money as the price of co-operation.

CASE HISTORY—This is an example of research used to form the basis of an advertising strategy; the results of research conducted among a sample of twenty firms which were customers and potential customers of an organisation producing epoxy resin insulators. The producer wanted to keep existing clients and win more. It was necessary to know how, and why, orders were placed. Three main patterns of answer emerged:

1 Inertia—Old orders were renewed automatically, with the same suppliers unless a major crisis faced the head of the buying department (or equivalent) to reappraise and change suppliers. A continuing pattern and avoidance of trouble were more important here than cost-cutting or perfection of materials, provided supplies were satisfactory.

2 *Time and money watching*—Here the buying departments were under constant pressure to trim costs and to prevent any breaks in production for want of particular materials. Junior buyers were encouraged to rove and find out who could supply "waste" at reduced rates. Contacts made in this way could be preludes to bigger contracts, provided the supplier seemed big enough to fulfil orders on time.

3 *Multiple intervention*—In these firms, a marketing director might submit a name for the chief buyer to consider; a senior chemist might confront the buyer with scientific reasons why such-and-such a standard of material was needed —possibly supplied by only one company; production line heads might apply pressure through the board to try for better deliveries by changing suppliers. Big contract arrangements or changes were usually referred to the board, which discussed rather than just rubber-stamped them.

Readership of technical magazines and advertising awareness was picked up for each informant. It will be apparent that there were, in fact, several informants per firm interviewed. Interviewers who knew they were working for a research company, but no more, were instructed to move on from one department to another when it was clear that another part of the decision chain had to be investigated. Differences in outlook within a firm had to be interpreted carefully.

It was decided to strengthen the client company's position among directors of firms of the type 3, by means of prestige advertising in business rather than trade papers—men at board level tended to have the latter delivered but not to read them. This was to increase the likelihood of recognition that the client's name promised a big scale of operation, and both technical and financial reliability, if and when it was mentioned at this level. Some other senior men would get a similar message, and it was expected that these would be persuaded to include the client's name on lists for consideration. This advertising had to be done on a scale that transcended epoxy resin—it had to be mounted for a group of products to get best value for money. An appeal was made for a corporate advertising budget and was successful.

Money that might have gone on advertising to buyers was directed to the preparation of specific items to be sold indirectly by salesmen to buyers in firms of type 2. This made more sense.

But there was also a case for choosing those trade papers and general scientific interest papers that senior chemists read and respected (by no means all), purely for the purpose of flagging their attention to particular advantages of the client's epoxy resin and the developments that were possible for those using it.

The research indicated the jobs to be done and the ways that the jobs might be tackled. This in turn suggested what kind of advertising budget made sense, in what direction.

14

Pack, Name
and Promotion

Trade unionism in advertising and marketing research is not strong. If it were we would at this point be giving a long justification including the testing of packs, names and promotions in a book on advertising research in order to prevent demarcation disputes. In the absence of unionisation our reasons for including these topics are purely pragmatic and can be simply stated: if you are concerned with mainstream advertising you will be inevitably concerned with these other matters.

14.1 Pack research

Pack research has been touched upon in Chapter 7 where we looked at some mechanical aids to pack testing. There are, however, other ways of evaluating impact that are more involved in pack research than visual impact pure and simple.

IMPACT—One mechanical device not specially covered because it is so familiar to everybody is a stopwatch. To some people's taste, a tachistoscope test is far removed from reality: "Housewives don't go round the supermarket blinking at camera shutter speeds." This misses the point, but tachistoscope testing is a technical business concerned with the nitty gritty of perception. A rather more natural question is "How long will it take to find a product in a display?" On a commonsense basis one can readily see that a pack which takes fifteen seconds to find in a display has less impact than one which can be found in five seconds. It is a relatively easy matter to set up tests where matched samples see alternative prototype packs in identical displays and the average time it takes for a housewife to find them is measured.

The other measure of impact can be obtained by short-term recall of test packs. A supermarket display is set up and altern-ative test packs placed on it. The display is exposed to the infor-mant for a few seconds and then covered over. She is asked what products she can recall having seen. Here the pay off mea-sure is the proportion in each matched sample recalling the prototype packs.

The following data were obtained from showing a display of bath additives:

	PACK A 110 %	PACK B 117 %	PACK C 107 %	PACK D 111 %
Product 1	40	36	35	32
Product 2	68	66	69	60
Product 3	68	67	71	73
Product 4	50	52	54	51
Product 5	60	70	64	59
Product 6	32	15	12	18
Product 7	78	56	64	62
Product 8	15	21	15	23

Version A of the test product appeared therefore to enjoy something of an advantage. All versions of the test pack fared pretty miserably in relation to the opposition, however, which caused some heartsearching. The product was a new one and unfamiliarity was the basic problem. As a large-scale promo-tion was planned for the product it was felt that this shortcom-ing would be remedied by massive TV exposure. On judgement it appeared difficult to give the product greater shelf impact and intrinsically the impact of the competition seemed poor; they, too, had bought recognition. Pack A passed muster on this particular criterion but if a shoestring promotion had been planned the story might have been differ-ent.

Shelf impact, however, is not the only issue to be settled in pack research. Apart from proclaiming its identity a pack has other work to do. Its principal additional tasks are:

1   To be pleasing—Other things being equal it is not unreasonable to assume that the more aesthetically pleasing of two packs will stand more chance of being bought; it always helps to have a pretty face.

2   *To project a suitable brand image*—Basically a brand image is determined by the objective characteristics of the product and the overall advertising content. A pack, however, must be consonant with this image and reinforce it. One should, for example, avoid launching a product for the young in a pack redolent of age and stuffiness.

The basic variables in pack research, therefore, are impact, appeal and image projection. Clearly the relative importance of these factors will vary from product field to product field. With cigarettes, image projection is critically important; it has been said that in cigarette marketing all you are selling is the pack. Impact on display is less important. Expensive cosmetic products usually have to be packaged in a highly attractive manner with impact again being relatively less important. With fast-moving food and cleaning products on supermarket shelves impact must rate high as a design requirement.

Frequently, too, the design mix will vary with the life cycle of a brand. A declining product looking rather long in the tooth may be repackaged as part of a rejuvenation programme. Short-term losses in impact, caused by unfamiliarity, may be acceptable if the modernisation programme seems likely to do the trick. Digressing somewhat, we would, in this context, like to warn enthusiastic brand managers about cleaning up the pack designs of their products to keep them up to date. Many a good pack has been emasculated in this way.

Measuring pack image and appeal presents no particular technical problems and in these respects the pack can be treated exactly like a press advertisement. Methods of assessing brand image projection and attractiveness are the same.

Two examples illustrate rather different ways of achieving the same end product. First data from a test of a new cigarette pack. A new extra mild sector in the market seemed promising and the test pack was developed to hit a competitor recently launched in that market. Was it better in terms of image projection and appeal. Standard statements and semantic differential scales were the chosen measuring instruments.

	TEST PACK %	COMPETITOR %
Liking		
Like pack very much	30	38
Like pack	18	24
Undecided	32	29
Dislike pack	15	7
Dislike pack very much	5	2
Image		
For men/women	3.6	3.7
Good quality/poor quality	4.2	4.2
Attractive/unattractive	5.3	6.0
For me/others	4.5	4.7
All occasions/special occasions	3.5	3.4
Mild/strong	4.8	5.9
Old fashioned/modern	5.6	5.7

The test pack was, therefore, not as successful as the competitor, particularly in creating an image of mildness. As the research was conducted outside the test market, advertising influences in creating this difference could be discounted. From open-ended responses to other questions it was clear that the test pack was the wrong colour for a mild cigarette. Back to the drawing board.

Instead of semantic differential scales, agree/disagree attitude statements were designed to check the image projected by a toiletry product. Here are just a few examples

PROPORTION AGREEING A LOT

	PACK A	PACK B	PACK C	PACK D	COMPET ITOR
It looks as though it would be kind to the skin	56	52	54	54	31
It looks a rather cheap product	6	11	5	13	11
It would give you a feeling of luxury in the bath	34	22	28	29	36
It looks very feminine	39	36	26	31	37

Statements are quite useful because informants find them easier to understand and one can be more specific than with bi-polar scales. The danger is that the elementary trap of asking informants meaningless questions and getting spurious answers is there to trap the unwary. "It would give you a feeling of luxury in the bath" comes dangerously close. If informants liked the pack some would no doubt agree with the proposition "It would have a beneficial effect on your toenails."

When pressures are pushing you into this kind of pit it is as well to remember the availability of depth research techniques. A series of depth interviews will usually provide a sensible basis for constructing meaningful scales. Depth research can be used to good effect as well as an aid to producing the original design brief for the packs, show existing packs to a relevant sample of people and get them talking. Creative feedback in this field is particularly rewarding as, for reasons which are obscure, pack designers find research more interesting and useful than other creative people. (See: James Pilditch, *The Silent Salesman—How to develop packaging that sells*, Business Books, 1973.)

14.2 Name research

Considering how central the name of a product is, remarkably little name research is actually carried out. Two main factors are responsible for this:

1 The practical problems of finding even one vaguely suitable name for a product are often enormous. Competitors are jealous of their names and will take legal action if a new name is too similar to an existing one. Many contenders are found to be registered already or to belong to little known products in related fields. When products are intended for international markets, problems increase geometrically. A name innocuous enough in English can mean something extremely indelicate in Serbo-Croat. Enough of these gaffes have been perpetrated to form the basis of a small anthology. Legal difficulties are formidable. Alpha, Jack Potter's company, could operate in Germany only if he had changed his name to Alpha by deed poll—an ingenius solution, thwarted by family opposition.

For many manufacturers, therefore, the luxury of testing a series of names is denied them.

2   Many would argue, with some justification, that any initial unfavourable associations with the name will in the long run be overcome by advertising and promotion. Harp lager is a case in point. When the name first appeared, Harpic lavatory cleaner was being strongly promoted. Clearly the associations were unfavourable and pundits said the product would die the death. However, Guinness valued the name and were vindicated completely in their decision to use it. Massive promotion ensured that Harp meant lager and lavatorial associations were soon forgotten.

Nevertheless, in a situation in which choice is possible, there is no point in handicapping a product with an unnecessarily bad name. Like all other advertising material, a name must have appeal and project a suitable brand image. These functions are readily measured. The other points needing attention are:

1   Above all, suitability for the product.
2   Memorability.
3   Pronounceability (sometimes).

A fairly simple test of names for a proposed new sweet involved showing the product to a sample of housewives and allowing them to taste it before taking them through a questionnaire.

The names were shown at the outset of the interview and removed during the time the informants were eating the product and answering some questions about it. Questions on recall and suitability were then asked:

NAME	RECALLING %	CONSIDERING SUITABLE %
Pretty Blooms	31	59
Floral Delights	31	52
Rosebuds	36	27
Raspberry Blooms	24	63
Parisiennes	50	11
Floral Surprises	20	46
Hearts of Roses	33	12
Floral Fancies	38	36

A series of statements was then read to informants and they selected the names which suited them.

NAME	GIVES THE IMPRESSION OF GOOD INGREDIENTS %	WOULD APPEAL TO HOUSEWIVES %	ATTRACTIVE %	APPEAL TO CHILDREN %	EXPENSIVE SOUNDING %	UNUSUAL %
Pretty Blooms	3	16	24	62	1	9
Floral Delights	17	24	35	26	12	10
Rosebuds	3	8	24	5	28	63
Raspberry Blooms	18	29	27	25	5	11
Parisiennes	18	13	25	1	70	26
Floral Surprises	14	26	18	39	5	9
Hearts of Roses	32	25	23	9	6	21
Floral Fancies	12	35	6	37	1	1

And as a final question housewives were asked which name they thought best.

	NAME THOUGHT BEST %
Pretty Blooms	17
Floral Delights	17
Rosebuds	7
Raspberry Blooms	21
Parisiennes	6
Floral Surprises	16
Hearts of Roses	7
Floral Fancies	12

In this case there was no really clear winner on preference and image data had to be examined closely in relation to total objectives. Also the potential for creative development was another factor. More can be done with some names than others.

The result might have been clearer had there been fewer names. Where reasonable freedom to choose names is possible, there is a strong tendency to test too many. Everybody thinks they can invent names. Technically it is the easiest of creative tasks and christening a product confers a lasting fame on the inventor. Most of the people involved in a project will want their nomination in the test and traditionally the chairman's wife enters a runner as well. Quite apart from a general loss of sensitivity there is a danger of vote splitting if the types of name are not equally represented—for example, one folksy name on a list of eight could emerge as an apparent winner against seven more formal names of more or less equal merit.

14.3 Promotions

Below-the-line promotion can take many and varied forms: money off, banded offers, money off next purchase, gift vouchers, self-liquidating offers, give-aways, competitions, and so on. To examine each type of offer individually would be wearisome but some general principles need to be observed.

One pleasant feature of promotions is the ease with which the effectiveness of many of them can be assessed. The number of entrants for a competition is known and the demand for butter knives can be readily calculated. A photographic processing firm can with experience calculate fairly accurately its returns from a coupon drop of known cost. If it falls below expectation, dustbins are searched for piles of undelivered coupons. An immediacy of response makes possible a degree assessment usually only associated with mail order.

Advertisers used to spending large sums of money in the media to increase brand awareness and improve brand image will turn to below-the-line activity when times are hard or their nerves begin to crack. There is something comforting in the sight of envelopes stuffed with the labels of your product sent in by intending holiday makers wanting their cut-price beach bags. Somebody out there cares.

The three things to be on the look out for in deciding the likely effectiveness of a promotion are:

1   Appeal—obviously.
2   Communication—some offers stating conditions and explaining, say a competition are intrinsically hard to explain.
3   Sampling—exactly who will collect and redeem the coupons or enter the competition. The answers are not always obvious.

Appeal is most conveniently measured where alternative physical items such as kitchen utensils of approximately the same value are checked. Should the offer be a tea caddy, butter knife, water set, sun glasses or beach bag? Here is what a sample of housewives thought:

	%
Tea caddy	17
Butter knife	42
Water set	23
Sun glasses	3
Beach bag	15

Gratifying straightforward research. Incidently, you have to get up pretty early in the morning to beat a butter knife.

Rather more high-powered research is required when concepts rather than objects are involved. Take this example of a collector item for a petrol promotion.

Everytime you visit a Mogul petrol station and buy 4 gallons of petrol, you will be given a free sachet containing three full colour pictures of wild flowers and herbs.

You can also purchase a unique album for 30p. Each picture has a peel-off sticky back and you can collect the pictures in the album. It contains 112 pages devoted to an account of wild flowers in Western Europe as well as a fold-out map showing areas of special interest to the naturalist.

When completed your album will be a valuable collectors' item displaying the principal wild flowers of Europe.

On presentation of the completed album you will receive a free packet of wild flower seeds and be eligible for a "Pick the Flower" competition. All you have to do is rank ten flowers in the album in order of your preference. If your choice agrees with that of an expert panel, you will win one of the £10 000 worth of prizes available.

Trying to assess say six alternative promotions of this type requires patient, thorough and skilful research, though nothing special in the way of technique. Prototypes of the items to be collected are essential if the concepts are to be adequately presented.

This brings us to the problem of communication. Where the offer being made is complicated it usually is worth checking comprehension. Conveying factual information on proof of purchase, the nature of a competition, method of redemption, dates, etc, is not easy but it is essential for consumers to grasp the details, otherwise they will be detered by apparent difficulties or be frustrated when they get hold of the wrong end of the stick. Trying to summarise the content of the explanatory material under a snappy headline can be peculiarly difficult. One headline we were concerned with—which described a fairly conventional packet of glittering prizes: cash, holidays, expensive meals, luxury cars, and so on—was "Live like a film star for a month." In practice the C2DE housewives at whom the promotion was aimed were turned off completely by the headline, the social implications of which they found horrifying.

Asking informants if there is anything about a promotion they do not understand is not terribly rewarding. Quite apart from a desire not to appear dense, misconceptions rather than blank incomprehension are the main problem. Questions can be phrased in terms of other people having difficulties or taking the respondent through a series of check comprehension questions.

Many promotions are aimed at children and sampling problems have to be faced. What relative weight should we give to the views of the children and parents? There is no easy or final answer to this one—each case must be looked at on its merits. Children are a force to be reckoned with though. We have spoken to many middle-class consumerist mums, steaming with indignation, whose offspring have made them send off their three cereal pack tops for a plastic space-man. The special problems of interviewing children are dealt with in Chapter 13.

When a promotion is running, some monitoring of the operation should be considered as it is easy for a promotion to be counter-productive from a PR point of view if snags occur. If collector items are badly distributed, a complete collection may be impossible to make. Long delays in sending items are annoying, particularly where children are concerned. These matters can be simply and inexpensively checked.

Bibliography

1   V APPEL and M BLUM, "Ad Recognition and
    Respondent Set," *Journal of Advertising Research*, 1, 4
    June 1961.
2   JN AXELROD, "Attitude measures that predict
    purchase," *Journal of Advertising Research*, March
    1968.
3   D BERDY, "Towards an Alternative Advertising
    Theory," *Admap*, 1974.
4   Dr SR BROADBENT, *Spending Advertising Money*,
    Business Books, 1970.
5   DI BUCHANAN, "How Interest in the Product Affects
    Recall," *Journal of Advertising Research*, March 1964.
6   JM CAFFYN and NA BROWN, "The Application of
    Psychological Ironmongery to Commercial
    Problems," ESOMAR Congress, 1964.
7   D CORKINDALE and S KENNEDY, "Setting Advertising
    Objectives," Marketing Communications Research
    Unit, Cranfield School of Management, 1974.
8   ASC ERHENBURG, "Towards an Integrated Theory of
    Consumer Behaviour," *Journal of MRS*, II, 1969.
9   JB HASKINS, "Factual Recall as a Measure of
    Advertising Effectiveness," *Journal of Advertising
    Research*, March 1964.
10 Dr T JOYCE,"What do you know about how Advertising
    Works?" ESOMAR Seminar, Nordwyk, 1967.
11 S KING, "How Useful is Proposition Testing?"
    Advertising Quarterly, winter 1965-66.
12 S KING, "Can Research Evaluate the Creative Content
    of Advertising?" *Admap*, June 1967.
13 G KÖNIG, C LAKASCHUS and MRC LOVELL, "The
    Measurement of Pupil Dilation as a Market Research
    Tool," ESOMAR Congress, 1965.

14   H KRUGMANN, "The Measurement of Advertising Involvement," *Public Opinion Quarterly,* 4, winter 1966-67.

15   G LEVENS and E RODNIGHT, "The Application of Research in the Planning and Evaluation of Road Safety Publicity," ESOMAR Congress, 1973.

16   MRC LOVELL, "The Inter-related Effects of Press and Television Advertising in a Mixed-Media Campaign upon Market Signals Exposed to Both," Thomson Award Paper, 1968.

17   MRC LOVELL, "Consumerism and Communications," ESOMAR Congress, 1973.

18   MRC LOVELL, S JOHNS and B RAMPLEY, "Pre-testing press advertisements," Thomson Award Paper, 1967.

19   MRC LOVELL, and JM LANNON, "Difficulties with Recall," ESOMAR Congress, 1967.

20   MRC LOVELL, R MEADOWS, and B RAMPLEY, "Inter-household Influence on Housewife Purchases," Thomson Award Paper, 1968.

21   CDP McDONALD, "What is the Short-term Effect of Advertising?" ESOMAR Congress, 1970.

22   J POTTER, "Polygraph: A new Research Development," *Admap,* June 1968.

23   J POTTER, "Bridging the gap: Creative Judgement and Copy Research," Market Research Society Conference, 1968.

24   J POTTER, "Packaging Research—is it Adequate?" *Advertisers Weekly*, July 1967.

25   J POTTER, "Commercial Pre-testing," *Admap*, September 1971.

26   S SEGNIT and Dr SR BROADBENT, "Area Tests and Consumer Surveys to Measure Advertising Effectiveness," ESOMAR Congress, Barcelona, November 1970.

27   S SEGNIT and Dr SR BROADBENT, "Life Style Research—A Case History in Two Parts" European Research, Part 1, January 1973 Part 2, March 1973.

28   D STARCH, "Measuring the Effect of Advertising on Sales," (five articles) *Printers Ink*, March-May 1964.

29   WD WELLS, "How Chronic Overclaims Distort Survey Findings," *Journal of Advertising Research*, 3, 2, June 1963.

30   C WINICK, "Price Measures of the Advertising Value of Media Context," *Journal of Advertising Research*, 2, 2, June 1962.

31   JF WOOD, "Pre-testing the Advertising," *Admap*, September 1967.

Index